black market™

Created and Written by............Frank J. Barbiere

Illustrated by.................................Victor Santos

Colors by................................Adam Metcalfe

Letters by..............Ed Dukeshire

Cover by..............Victor Santos

Designer...................................Kelsey Dieterich

Assistant Editor...Chris Rosa

Editor...Eric Harburn

black market™

Frank J. Barbiere   Victor Santos   Adam Metcalfe

BLACK MARKET, August 2015. Published by BOOM!
Studios, a division of Boom Entertainment, Inc., 5670
Wilshire Boulevard, Suite 450, Los Angeles, CA 90036-
5679. Black Market is ™ & © 2015 Frank J. Barbiere.
Originally published in single magazine form as BLACK
MARKET No. 1-4. ™ & © 2014 Frank J. Barbiere. All rights
reserved. BOOM! Studios™ and the BOOM! Studios logo
are trademarks of Boom Entertainment, Inc., registered in
various countries and categories. All characters, events,
and institutions depicted herein are fictional. Any similarity
between any of the names, characters, persons, events,
and/or institutions in this publication to actual names,
characters, and persons, whether living or dead, events,
and/or institutions is unintended and purely coincidental.
BOOM! Studios does not read or accept unsolicited
submissions of ideas, stories, or artwork.

A catalog record of this book is available from OCLC and
from the BOOM! Studios website, www.boom-studios.com,
on the Librarians Page.

BOOM! Studios, 5670 Wilshire Boulevard, Suite 450, Los
Angeles, CA 90036-5679. Printed in China. First Printing.

ISBN: 978-1-60886-723-3, eISBN: 978-1-61398-394-2

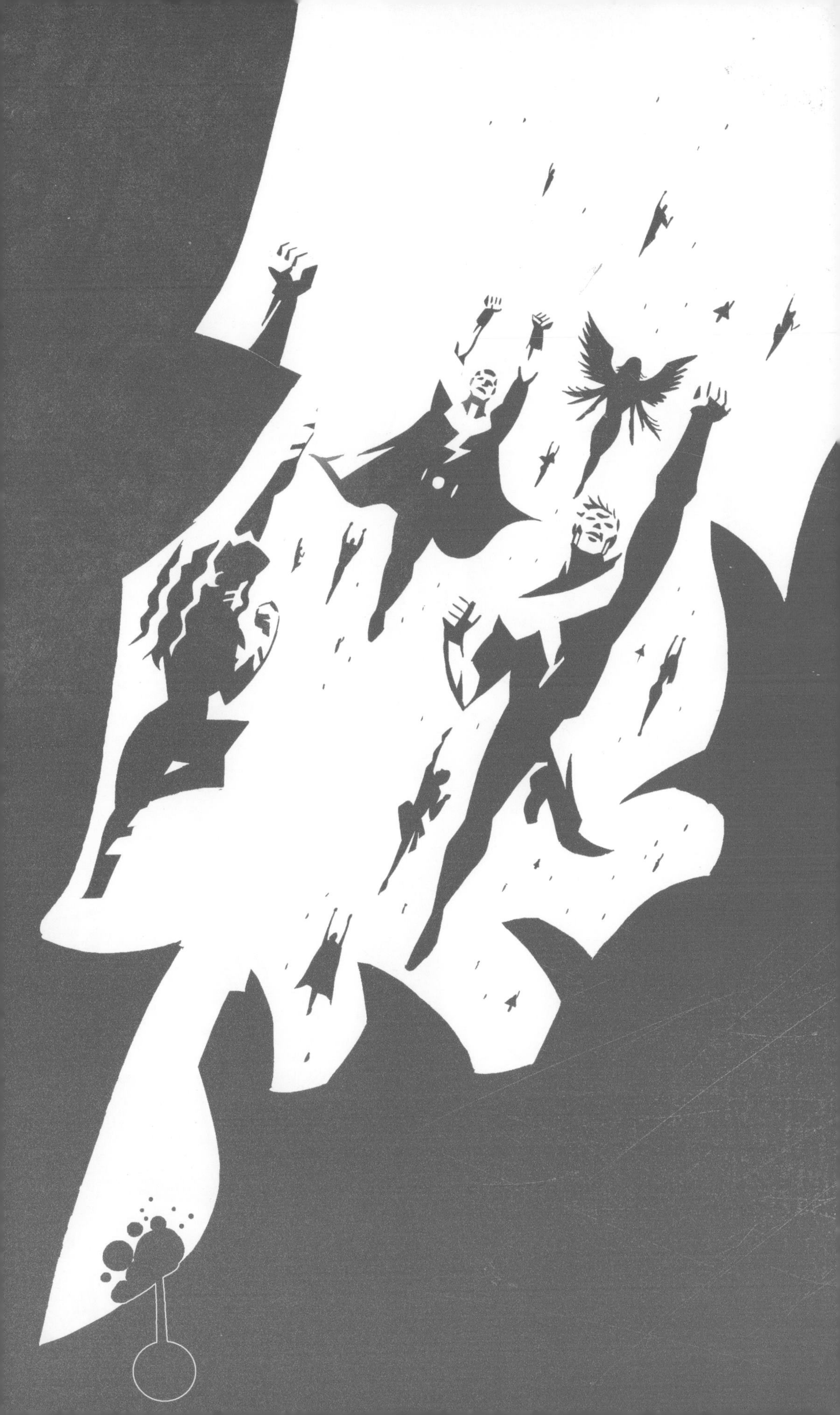

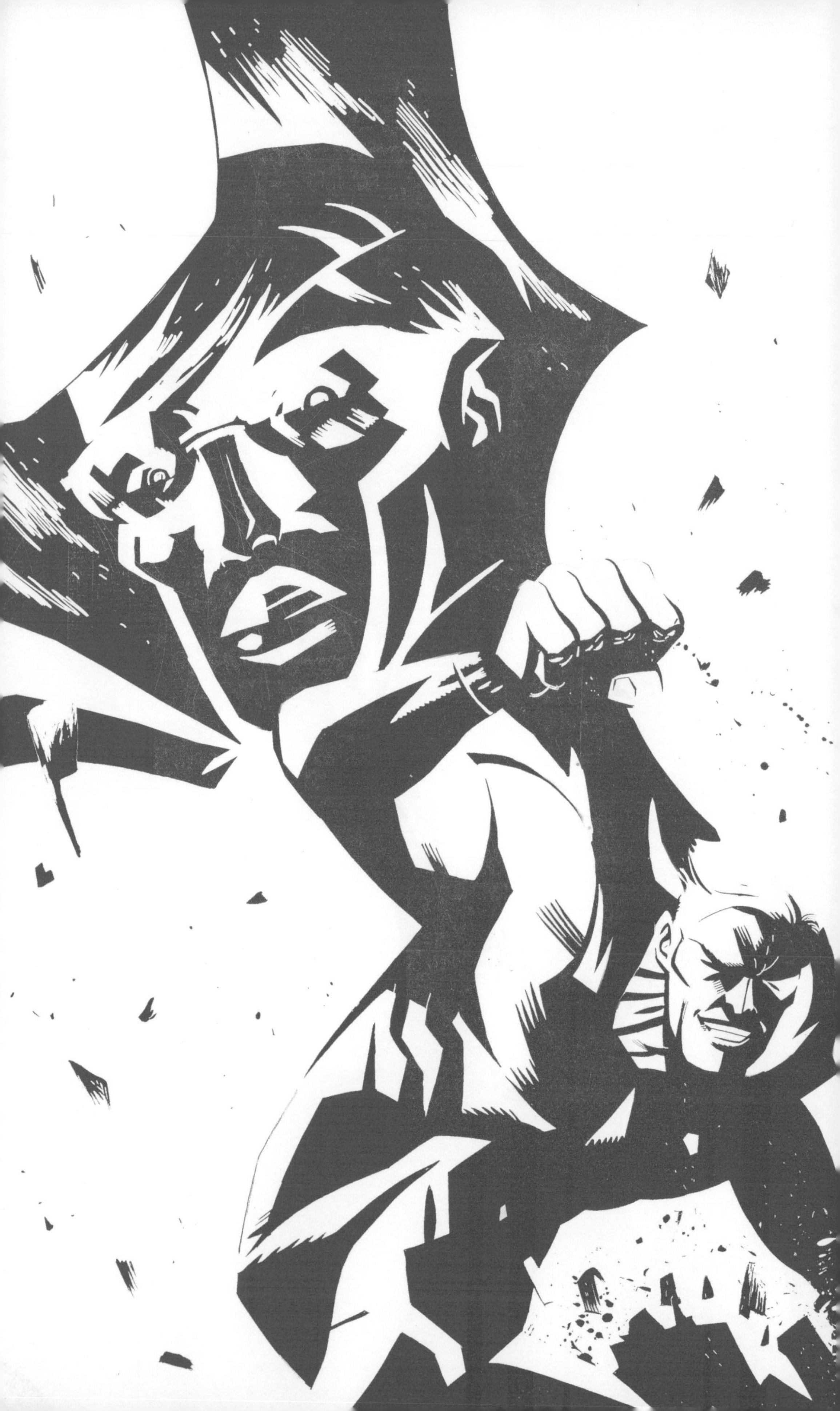

chapter one

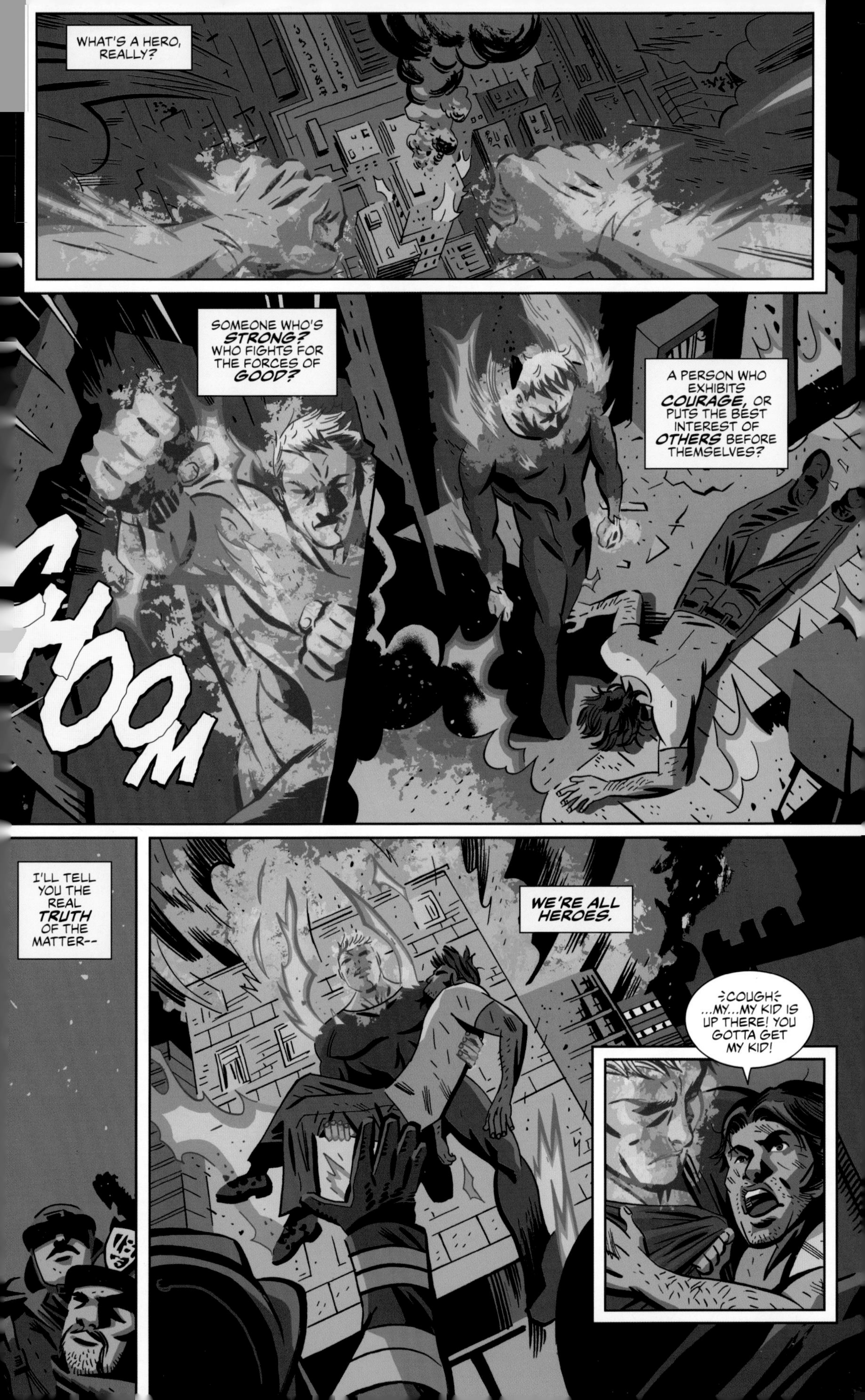
WHAT'S A HERO, REALLY?
SOMEONE WHO'S STRONG? WHO FIGHTS FOR THE FORCES OF GOOD?
CHOOOM
A PERSON WHO EXHIBITS COURAGE, OR PUTS THE BEST INTEREST OF OTHERS BEFORE THEMSELVES?
I'LL TELL YOU THE REAL TRUTH OF THE MATTER--
WE'RE ALL HEROES.
COUGH ...MY...MY KID IS UP THERE! YOU GOTTA GET MY KID!

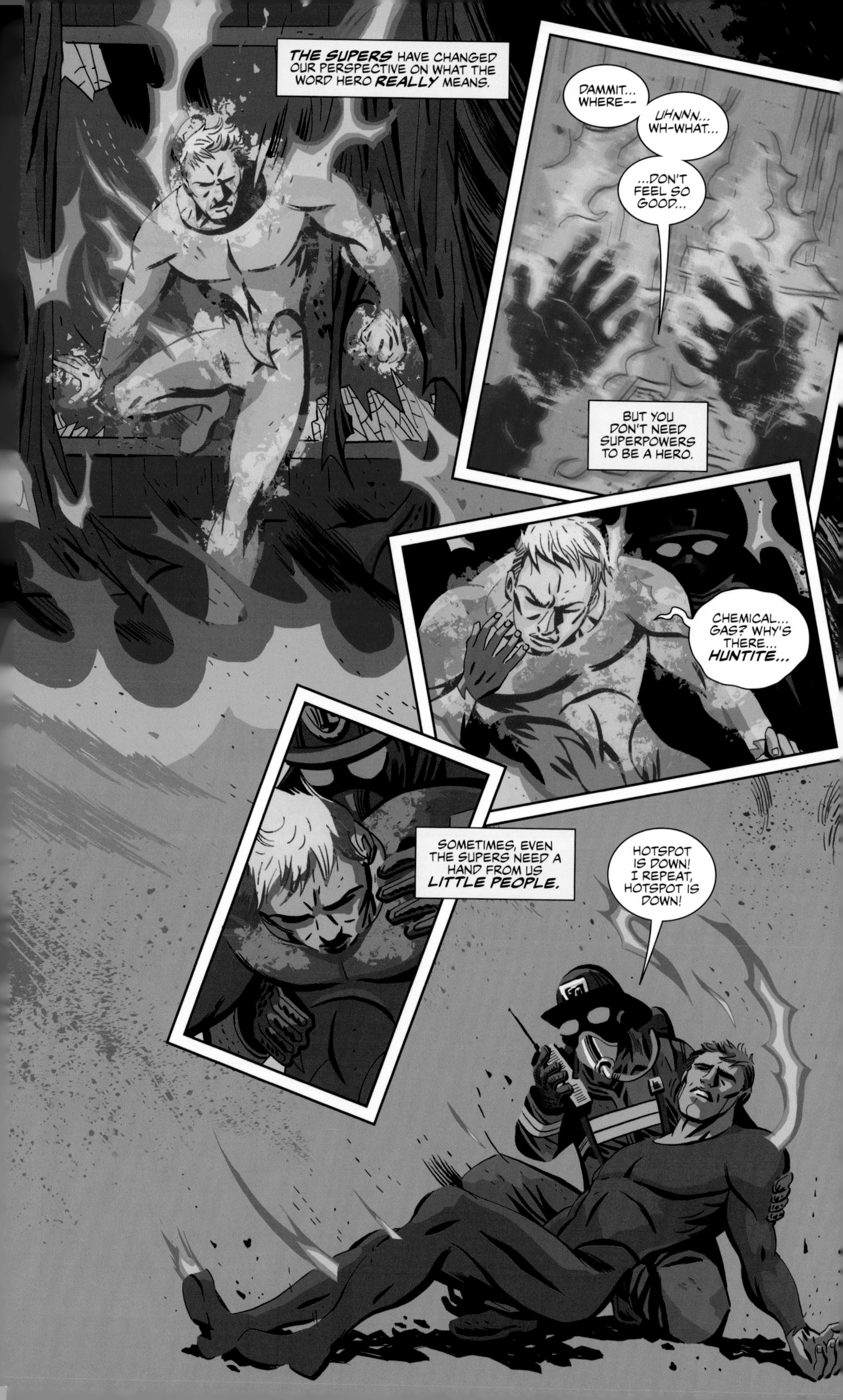
THE SUPERS HAVE CHANGED OUR PERSPECTIVE ON WHAT THE WORD HERO REALLY MEANS.
DAMMIT... WHERE--
UHNNN... WH-WHAT...
...DON'T FEEL SO GOOD...
BUT YOU DON'T NEED SUPERPOWERS TO BE A HERO.
CHEMICAL... GAS? WHY'S THERE... HUNTITE...
SOMETIMES, EVEN THE SUPERS NEED A HAND FROM US LITTLE PEOPLE.
HOTSPOT IS DOWN! I REPEAT, HOTSPOT IS DOWN!

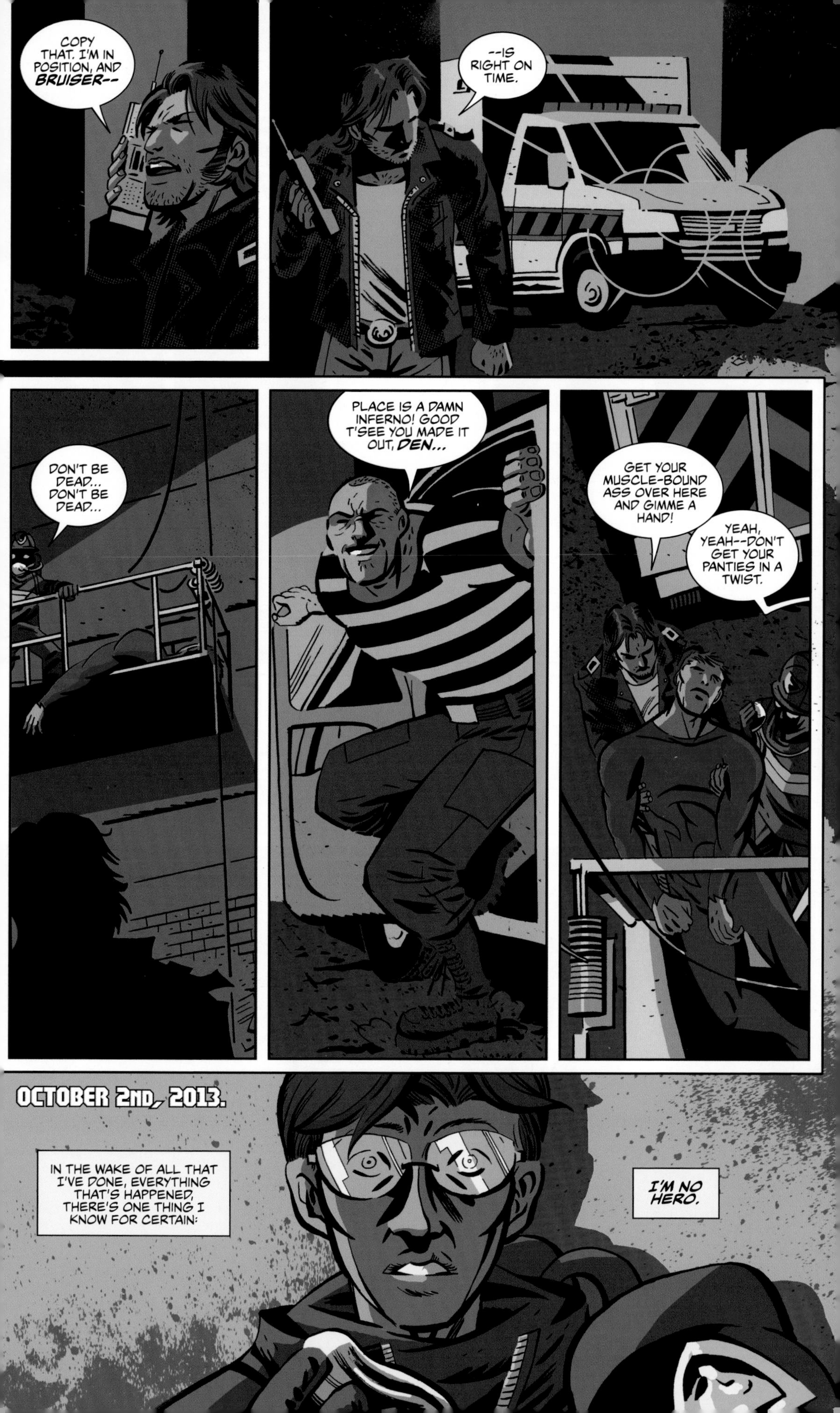
COPY THAT. I'M IN POSITION, AND BRUISER--
--IS RIGHT ON TIME.
DON'T BE DEAD... DON'T BE DEAD...
PLACE IS A DAMN INFERNO! GOOD T'SEE YOU MADE IT OUT, DEN...
GET YOUR MUSCLE-BOUND ASS OVER HERE AND GIMME A HAND!
YEAH, YEAH--DON'T GET YOUR PANTIES IN A TWIST.
OCTOBER 2nd, 2013.
IN THE WAKE OF ALL THAT I'VE DONE, EVERYTHING THAT'S HAPPENED, THERE'S ONE THING I KNOW FOR CERTAIN:
I'M NO HERO.

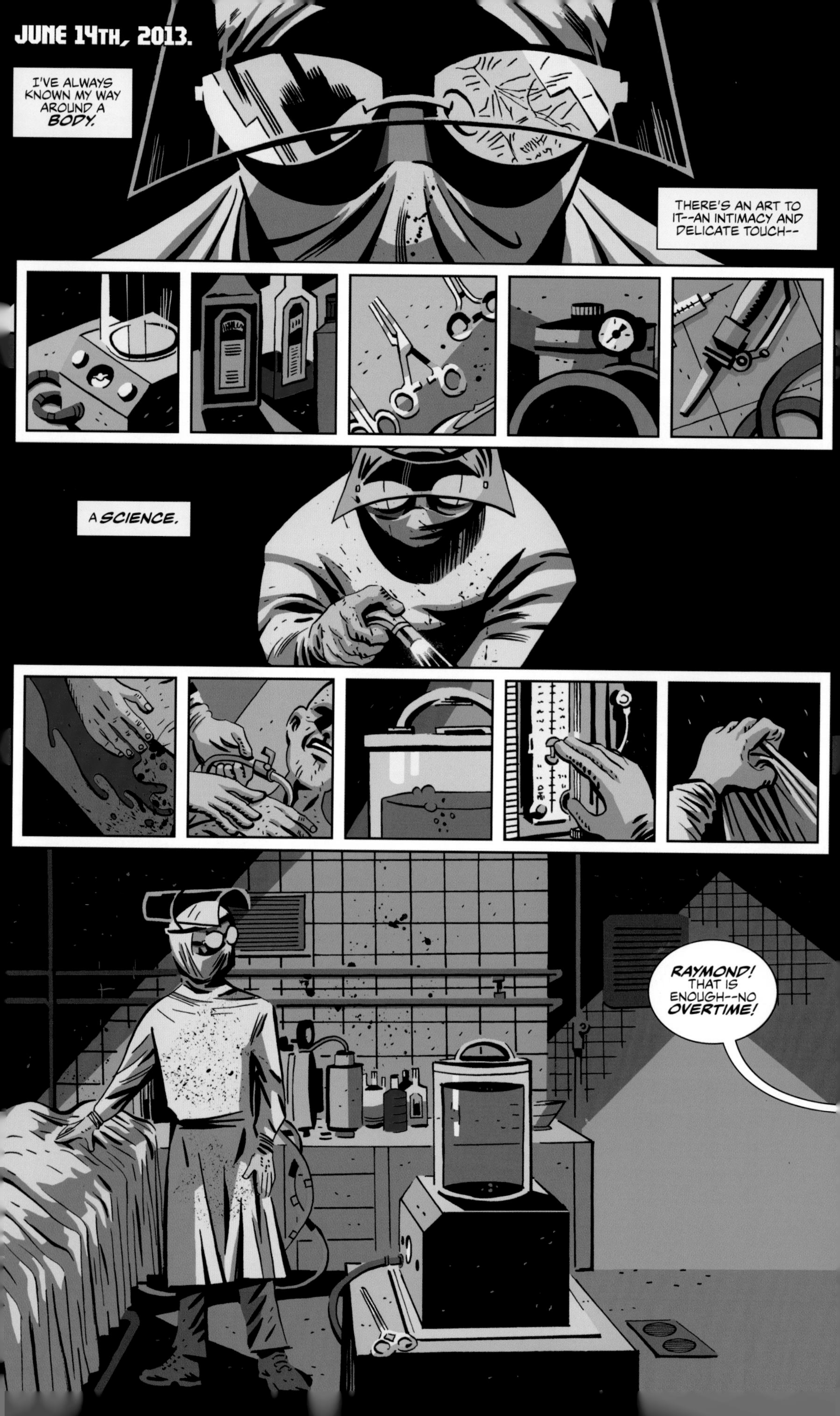
JUNE 14TH, 2013.
I'VE ALWAYS KNOWN MY WAY AROUND A BODY.
THERE'S AN ART TO IT--AN INTIMACY AND DELICATE TOUCH--
A SCIENCE.
RAYMOND! THAT IS ENOUGH--NO OVERTIME!

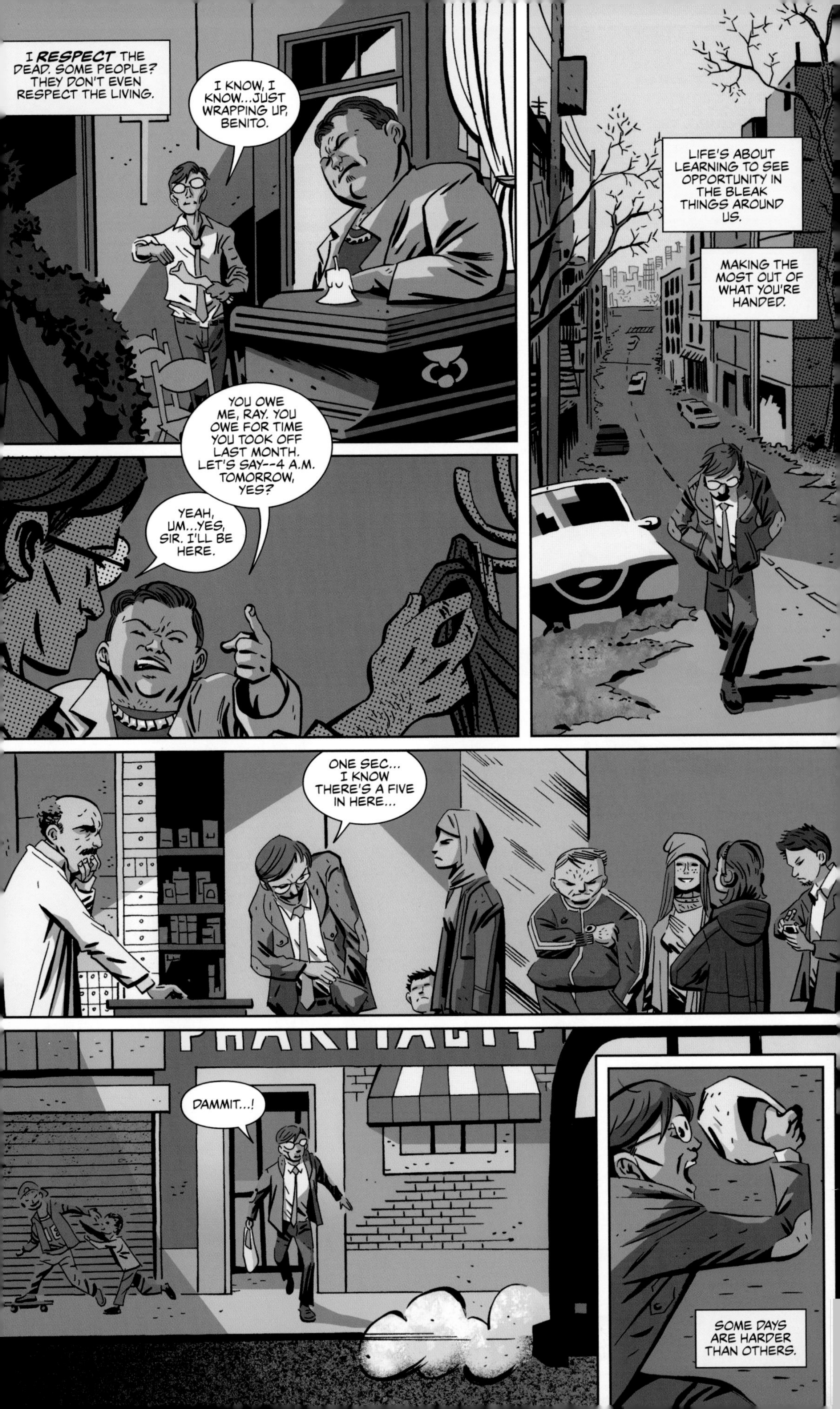

I RESPECT THE DEAD. SOME PEOPLE? THEY DON'T EVEN RESPECT THE LIVING.
I KNOW, I KNOW...JUST WRAPPING UP, BENITO.
YOU OWE ME, RAY. YOU OWE FOR TIME YOU TOOK OFF LAST MONTH. LET'S SAY--4 A.M. TOMORROW, YES?
YEAH, UM...YES, SIR. I'LL BE HERE.
LIFE'S ABOUT LEARNING TO SEE OPPORTUNITY IN THE BLEAK THINGS AROUND US.
MAKING THE MOST OUT OF WHAT YOU'RE HANDED.
ONE SEC... I KNOW THERE'S A FIVE IN HERE...
DAMMIT...!
SOME DAYS ARE HARDER THAN OTHERS.

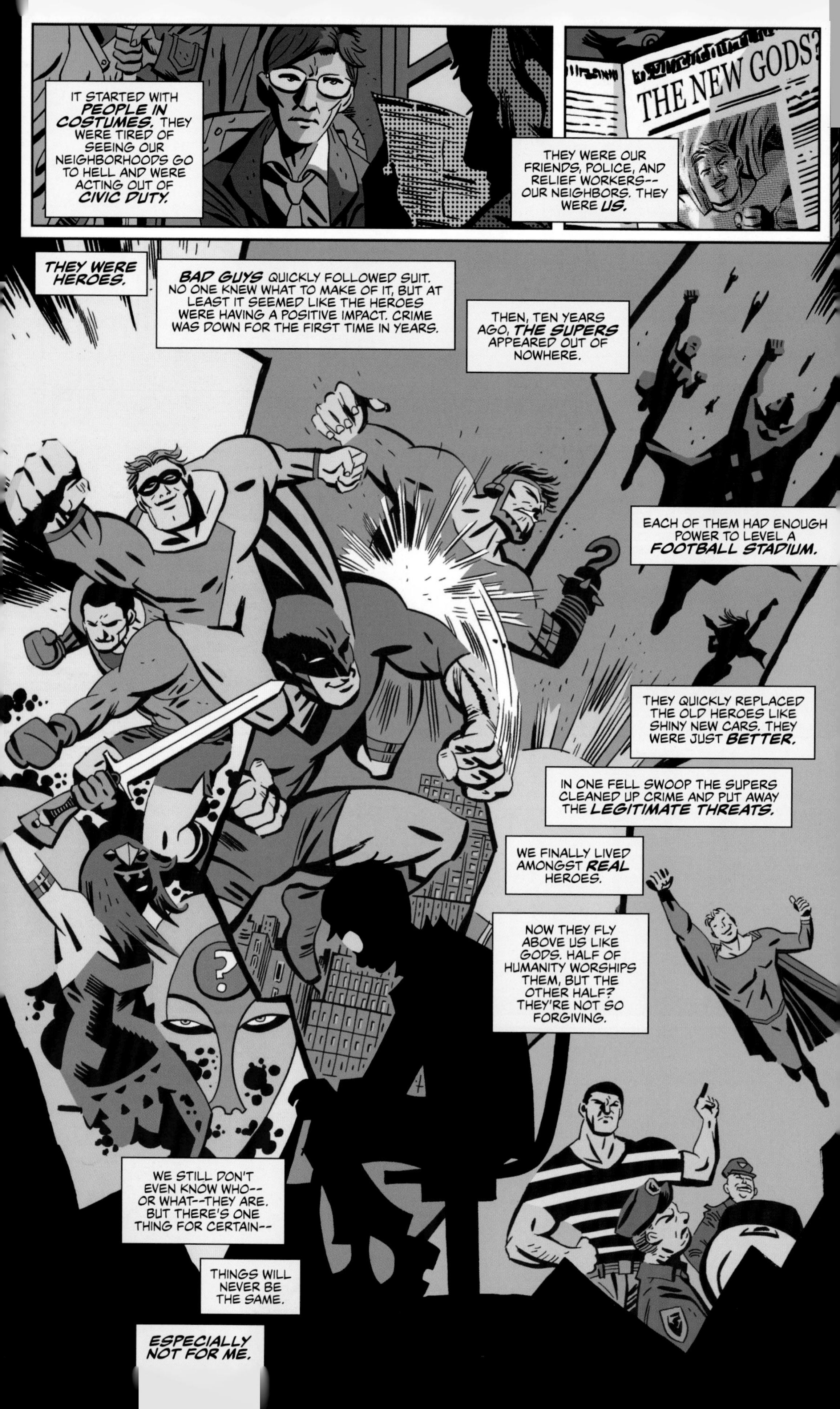
IT STARTED WITH PEOPLE IN COSTUMES. THEY WERE TIRED OF SEEING OUR NEIGHBORHOODS GO TO HELL AND WERE ACTING OUT OF CIVIC DUTY.
THE NEW GODS?
THEY WERE OUR FRIENDS, POLICE, AND RELIEF WORKERS--OUR NEIGHBORS. THEY WERE US.
THEY WERE HEROES.
BAD GUYS QUICKLY FOLLOWED SUIT. NO ONE KNEW WHAT TO MAKE OF IT, BUT AT LEAST IT SEEMED LIKE THE HEROES WERE HAVING A POSITIVE IMPACT. CRIME WAS DOWN FOR THE FIRST TIME IN YEARS.
THEN, TEN YEARS AGO, THE SUPERS APPEARED OUT OF NOWHERE.
EACH OF THEM HAD ENOUGH POWER TO LEVEL A FOOTBALL STADIUM.
THEY QUICKLY REPLACED THE OLD HEROES LIKE SHINY NEW CARS. THEY WERE JUST BETTER.
IN ONE FELL SWOOP THE SUPERS CLEANED UP CRIME AND PUT AWAY THE LEGITIMATE THREATS.
WE FINALLY LIVED AMONGST REAL HEROES.
NOW THEY FLY ABOVE US LIKE GODS. HALF OF HUMANITY WORSHIPS THEM, BUT THE OTHER HALF? THEY'RE NOT SO FORGIVING.
WE STILL DON'T EVEN KNOW WHO--OR WHAT--THEY ARE. BUT THERE'S ONE THING FOR CERTAIN--
THINGS WILL NEVER BE THE SAME.
ESPECIALLY NOT FOR ME.

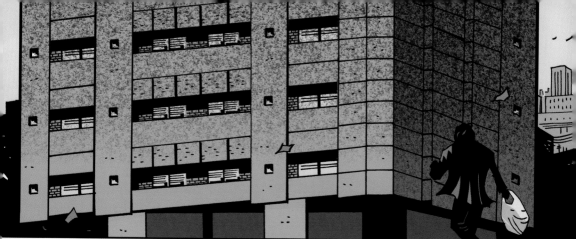

SHANNON!

WHERE ARE YOU?! I'VE GOT YOUR--

I'M IN THE KITCHEN!

I'M SO SORRY I'M LATE, BABY--I GOT YOUR SHOTS, WE GOTTA DO THEM NOW--

RAY, YOU GOTTA CALM DOWN.

I'M *FINE*. I'M MAKING DINNER.

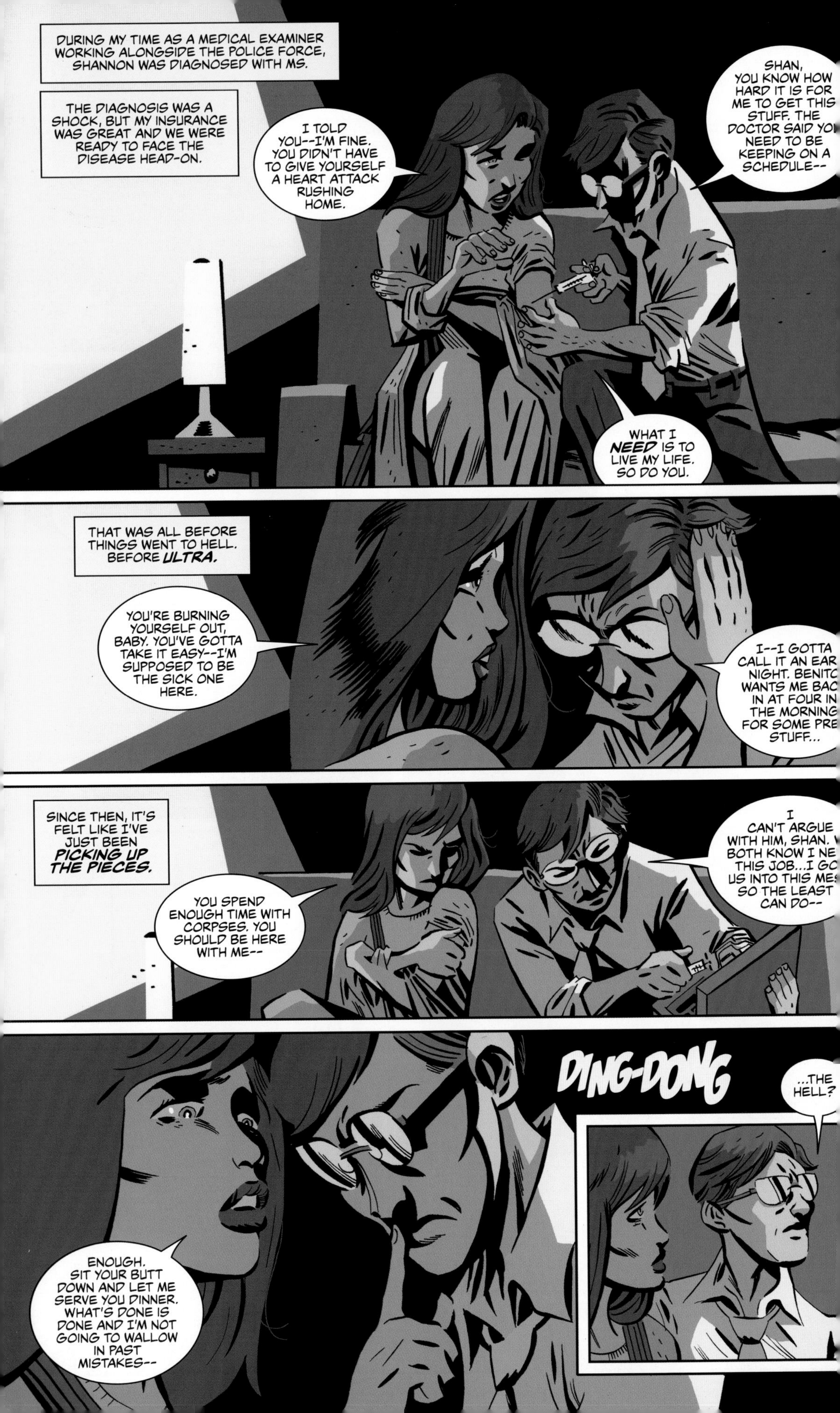
DURING MY TIME AS A MEDICAL EXAMINER WORKING ALONGSIDE THE POLICE FORCE, SHANNON WAS DIAGNOSED WITH MS.
THE DIAGNOSIS WAS A SHOCK, BUT MY INSURANCE WAS GREAT AND WE WERE READY TO FACE THE DISEASE HEAD-ON.
I TOLD YOU--I'M FINE. YOU DIDN'T HAVE TO GIVE YOURSELF A HEART ATTACK RUSHING HOME.
SHAN, YOU KNOW HOW HARD IT IS FOR ME TO GET THIS STUFF. THE DOCTOR SAID YO NEED TO BE KEEPING ON A SCHEDULE--
WHAT I NEED IS TO LIVE MY LIFE. SO DO YOU.
THAT WAS ALL BEFORE THINGS WENT TO HELL. BEFORE ULTRA.
YOU'RE BURNING YOURSELF OUT, BABY. YOU'VE GOTTA TAKE IT EASY--I'M SUPPOSED TO BE THE SICK ONE HERE.
I--I GOTTA CALL IT AN EAR NIGHT. BENITC WANTS ME BAC IN AT FOUR IN THE MORNING FOR SOME PRE STUFF...
SINCE THEN, IT'S FELT LIKE I'VE JUST BEEN PICKING UP THE PIECES.
YOU SPEND ENOUGH TIME WITH CORPSES. YOU SHOULD BE HERE WITH ME--
I CAN'T ARGUE WITH HIM, SHAN. BOTH KNOW I NE THIS JOB...I GO US INTO THIS ME SO THE LEAST CAN DO--
ENOUGH. SIT YOUR BUTT DOWN AND LET ME SERVE YOU DINNER. WHAT'S DONE IS DONE AND I'M NOT GOING TO WALLOW IN PAST MISTAKES--
DING-DONG
...THE HELL?

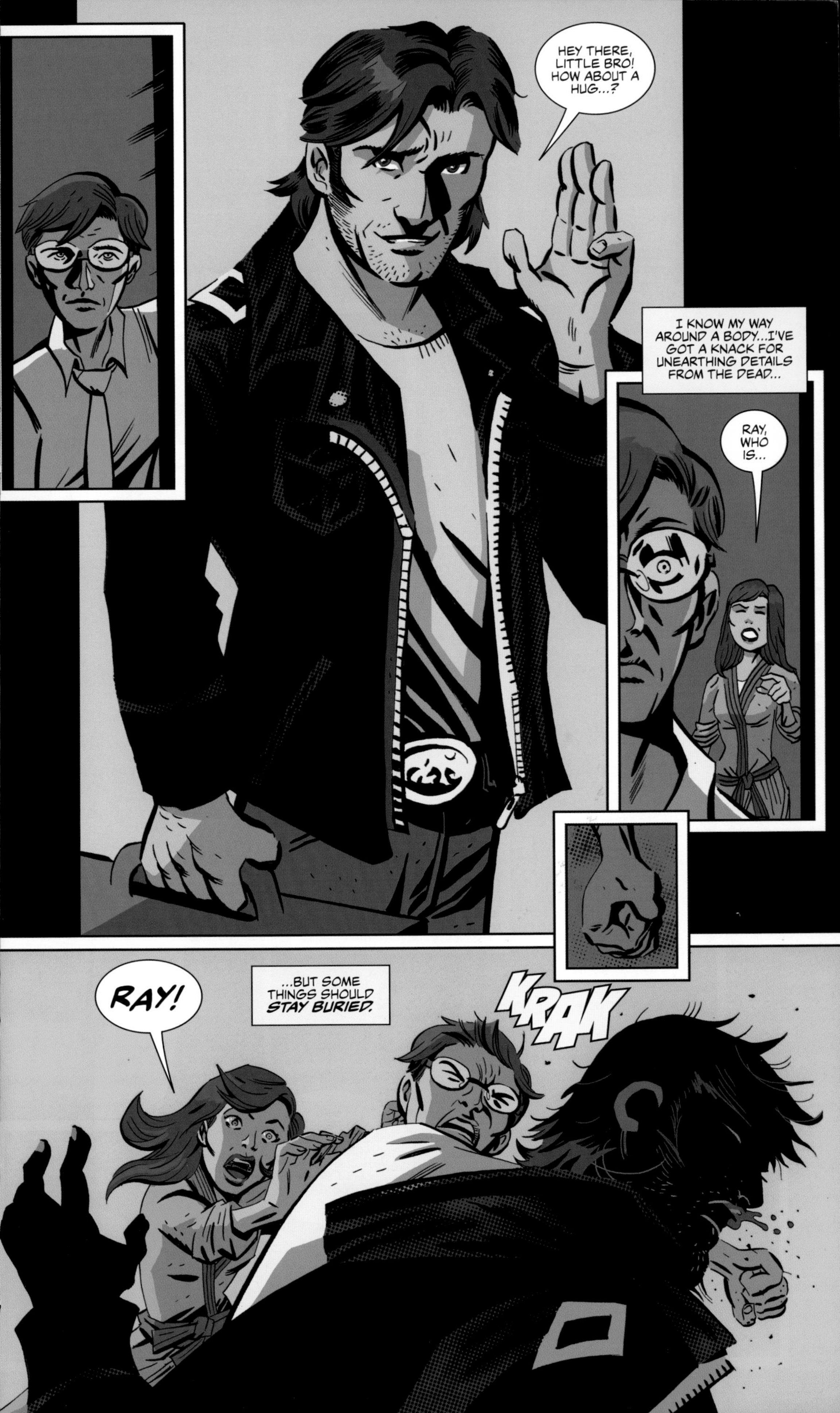
HEY THERE, LITTLE BRO! HOW ABOUT A HUG...?
I KNOW MY WAY AROUND A BODY...I'VE GOT A KNACK FOR UNEARTHING DETAILS FROM THE DEAD...
RAY, WHO IS...
RAY!
...BUT SOME THINGS SHOULD *STAY BURIED.*
KRAK

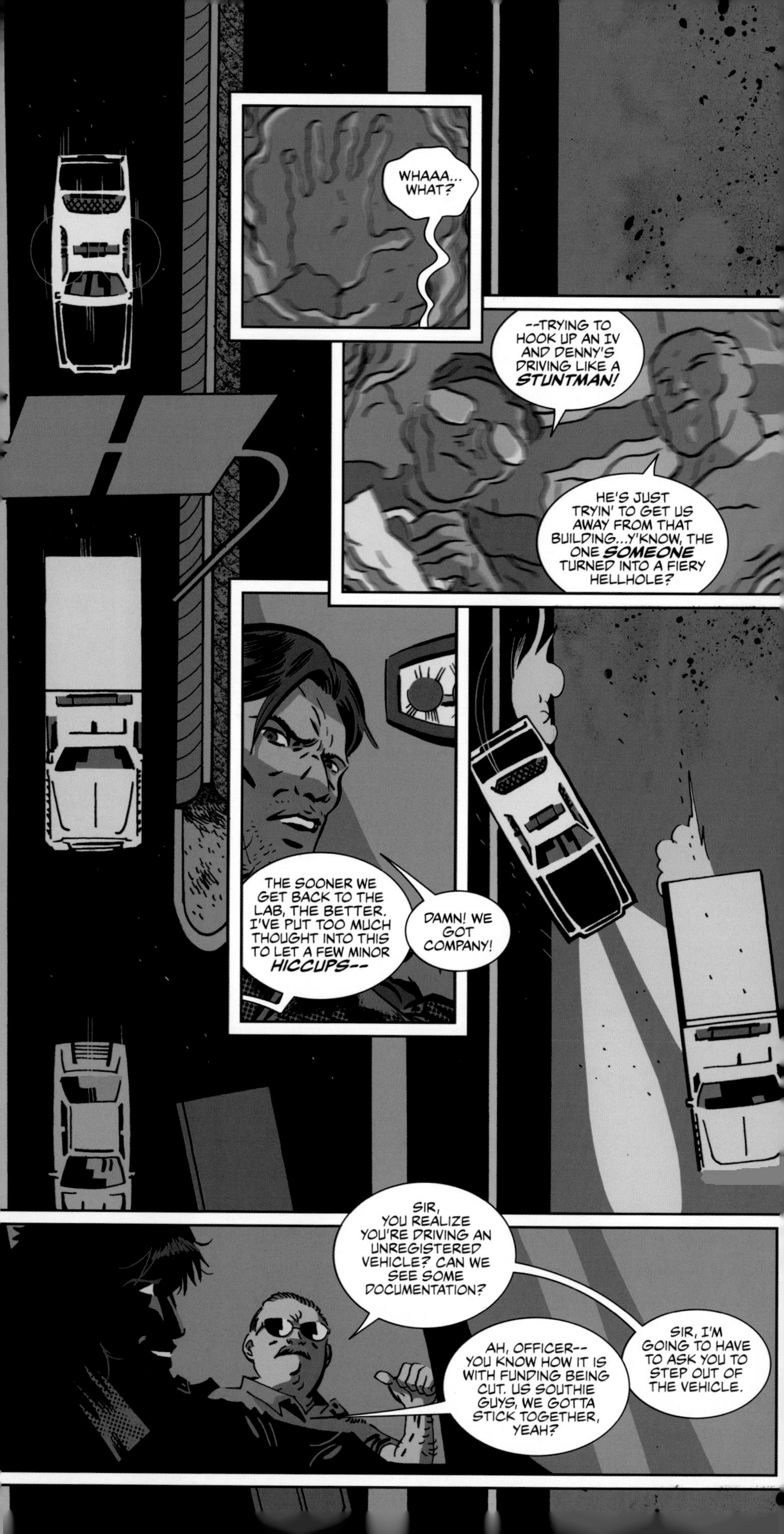
WHAAA... WHAT?
--TRYING TO HOOK UP AN IV AND DENNY'S DRIVING LIKE A STUNTMAN!
HE'S JUST TRYIN' TO GET US AWAY FROM THAT BUILDING...Y'KNOW, THE ONE SOMEONE TURNED INTO A FIERY HELLHOLE?
THE SOONER WE GET BACK TO THE LAB, THE BETTER. I'VE PUT TOO MUCH THOUGHT INTO THIS TO LET A FEW MINOR HICCUPS--
DAMN! WE GOT COMPANY!
SIR, YOU REALIZE YOU'RE DRIVING AN UNREGISTERED VEHICLE? CAN WE SEE SOME DOCUMENTATION?
AH, OFFICER-- YOU KNOW HOW IT IS WITH FUNDING BEING CUT. US SOUTHIE GUYS, WE GOTTA STICK TOGETHER, YEAH?
SIR, I'M GOING TO HAVE TO ASK YOU TO STEP OUT OF THE VEHICLE.

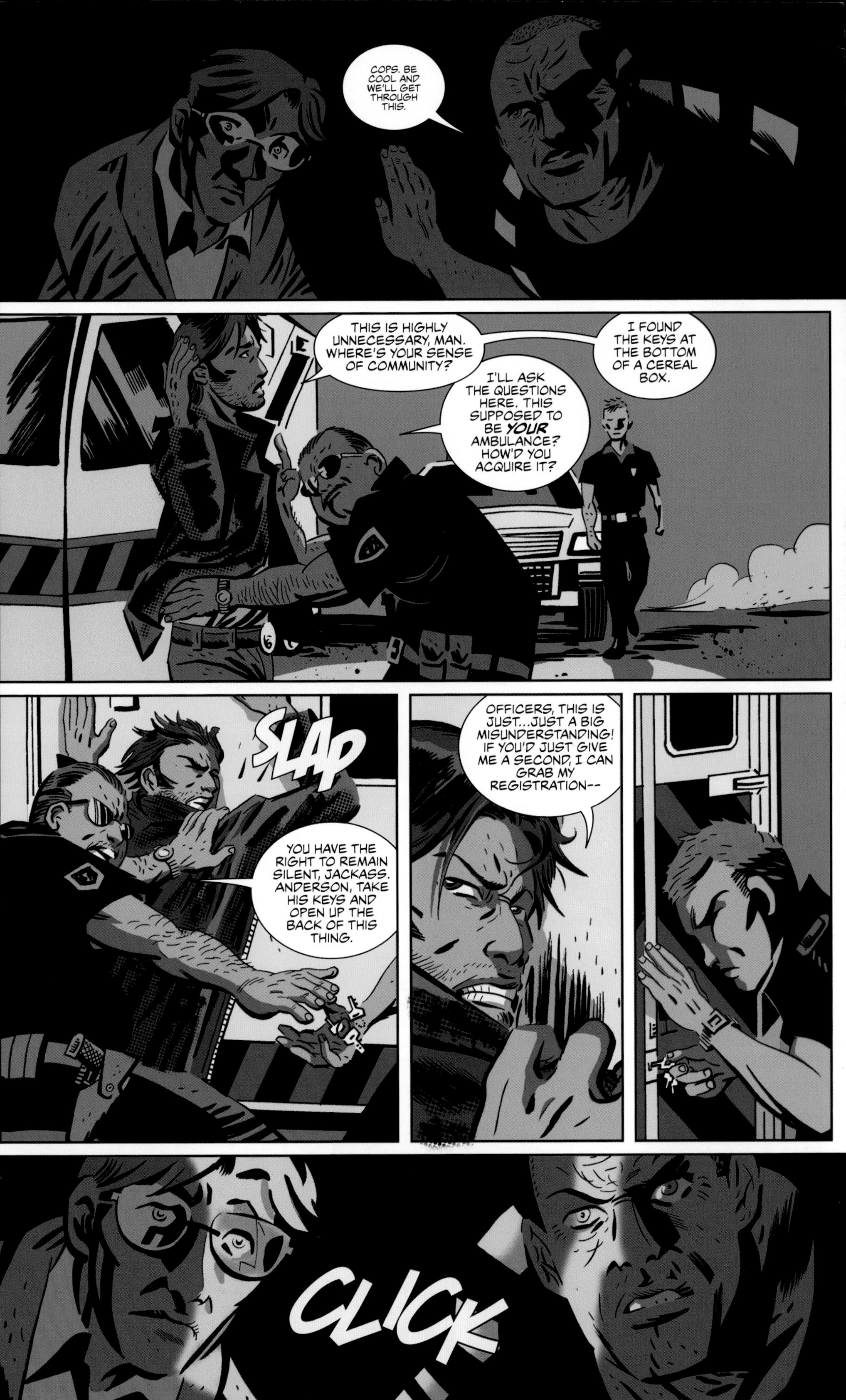
COPS. BE COOL AND WE'LL GET THROUGH THIS.
THIS IS HIGHLY UNNECESSARY, MAN. WHERE'S YOUR SENSE OF COMMUNITY?
I FOUND THE KEYS AT THE BOTTOM OF A CEREAL BOX.
I'LL ASK THE QUESTIONS HERE. THIS SUPPOSED TO BE *YOUR* AMBULANCE? HOW'D YOU ACQUIRE IT?
SLAP
YOU HAVE THE RIGHT TO REMAIN SILENT, JACKASS. ANDERSON, TAKE HIS KEYS AND OPEN UP THE BACK OF THIS THING.
OFFICERS, THIS IS JUST...JUST A BIG MISUNDERSTANDING! IF YOU'D JUST GIVE ME A SECOND, I CAN GRAB MY REGISTRATION--
CLICK

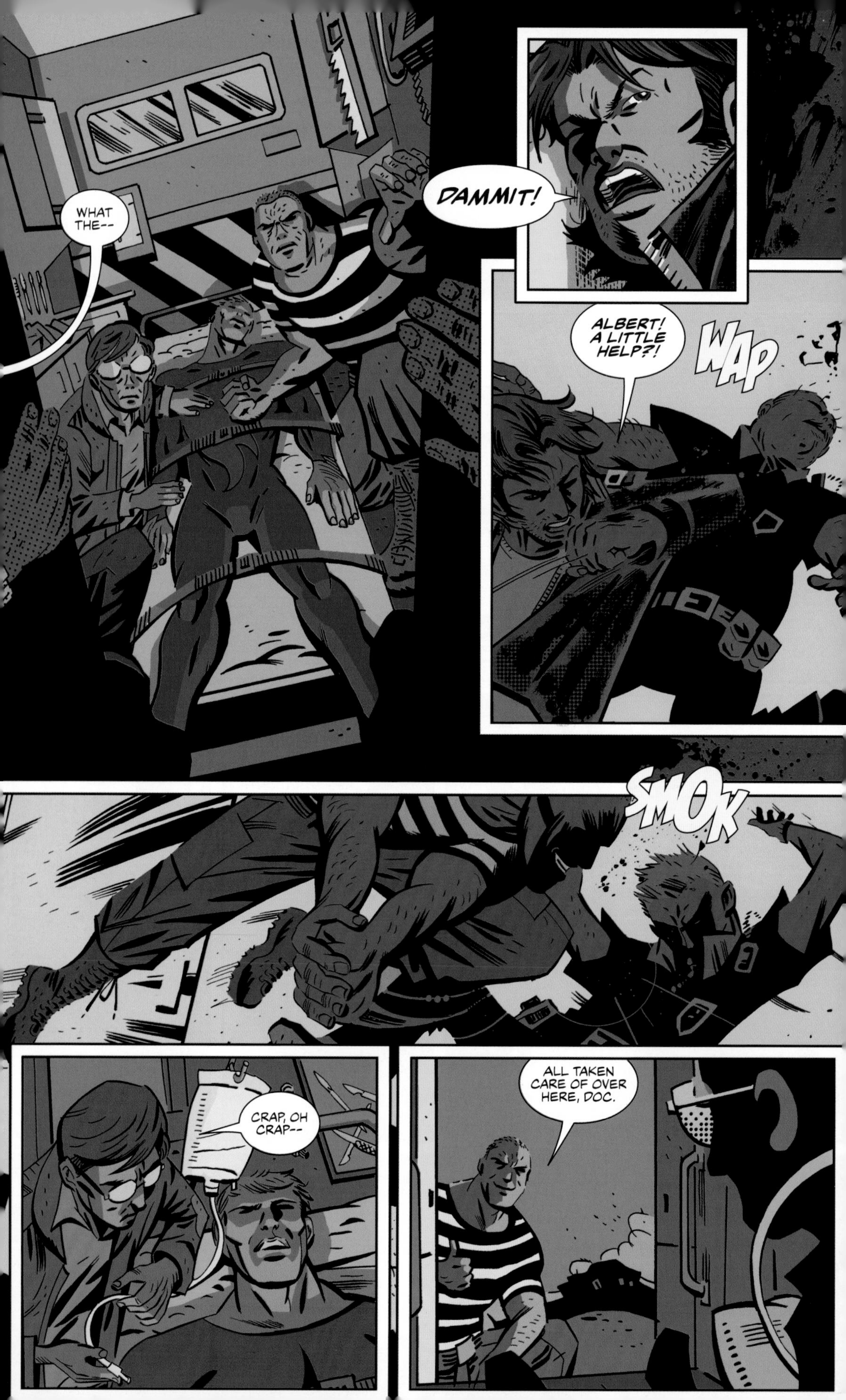
WHAT THE--
DAMMIT!
ALBERT! A LITTLE HELP?!
WAP
SMOK
CRAP, OH CRAP--
ALL TAKEN CARE OF OVER HERE, DOC.

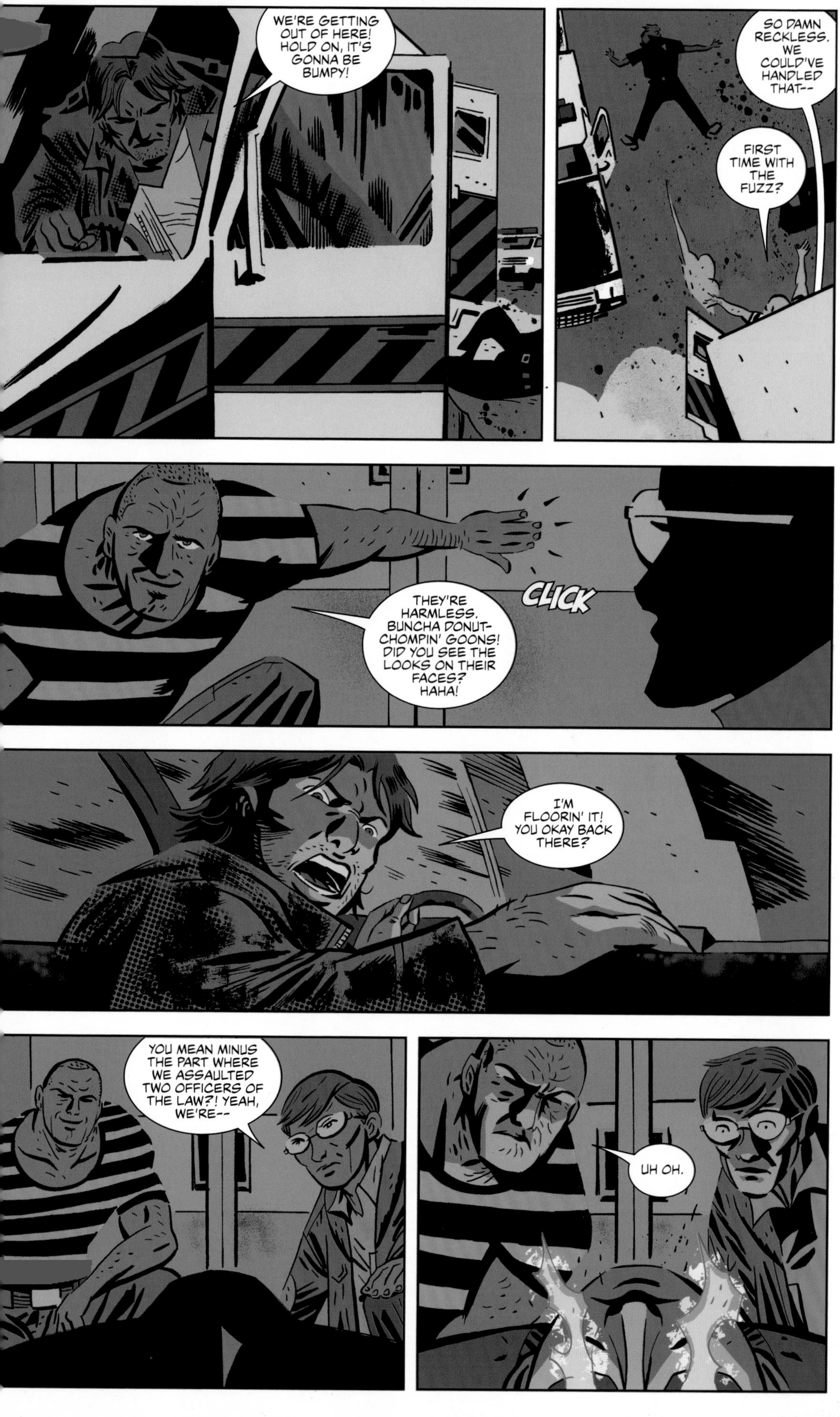
WE'RE GETTING OUT OF HERE! HOLD ON, IT'S GONNA BE BUMPY!
SO DAMN RECKLESS. WE COULD'VE HANDLED THAT--
FIRST TIME WITH THE FUZZ?
CLICK
THEY'RE HARMLESS. BUNCHA DONUT-CHOMPIN' GOONS! DID YOU SEE THE LOOKS ON THEIR FACES? HAHA!
I'M FLOORIN' IT! YOU OKAY BACK THERE?
YOU MEAN MINUS THE PART WHERE WE ASSAULTED TWO OFFICERS OF THE LAW?! YEAH, WE'RE--
UH OH.

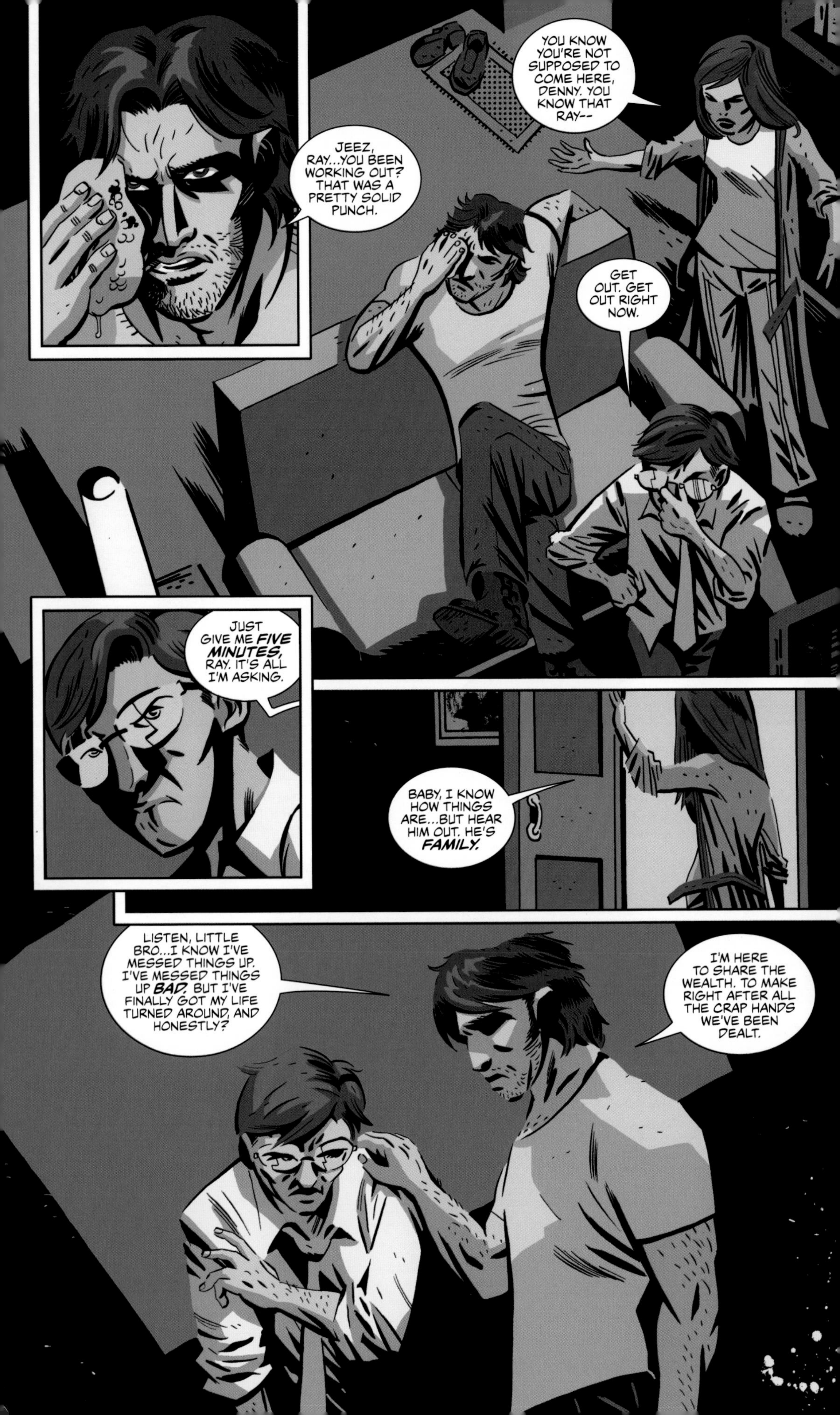
JEEZ, RAY...YOU BEEN WORKING OUT? THAT WAS A PRETTY SOLID PUNCH.
YOU KNOW YOU'RE NOT SUPPOSED TO COME HERE, DENNY. YOU KNOW THAT RAY--
GET OUT. GET OUT RIGHT NOW.
JUST GIVE ME *FIVE MINUTES,* RAY. IT'S ALL I'M ASKING.
BABY, I KNOW HOW THINGS ARE...BUT HEAR HIM OUT. HE'S *FAMILY.*
LISTEN, LITTLE BRO...I KNOW I'VE MESSED THINGS UP. I'VE MESSED THINGS UP *BAD.* BUT I'VE FINALLY GOT MY LIFE TURNED AROUND, AND HONESTLY?
I'M HERE TO SHARE THE WEALTH. TO MAKE RIGHT AFTER ALL THE CRAP HANDS WE'VE BEEN DEALT.

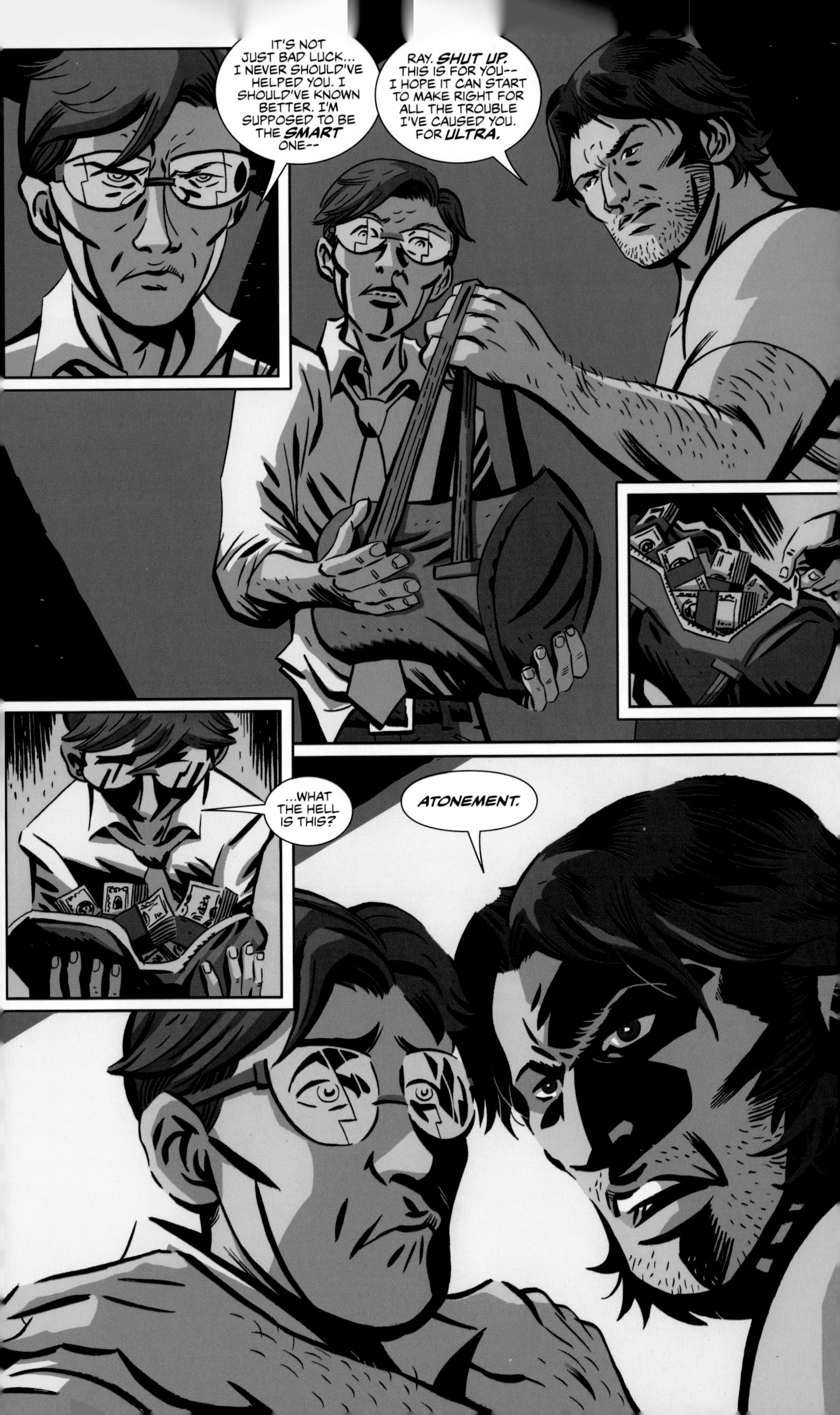
IT'S NOT JUST BAD LUCK... I NEVER SHOULD'VE HELPED YOU. I SHOULD'VE KNOWN BETTER. I'M SUPPOSED TO BE THE SMART ONE--
RAY. SHUT UP. THIS IS FOR YOU-- I HOPE IT CAN START TO MAKE RIGHT FOR ALL THE TROUBLE I'VE CAUSED YOU. FOR ULTRA.
...WHAT THE HELL IS THIS?
ATONEMENT.

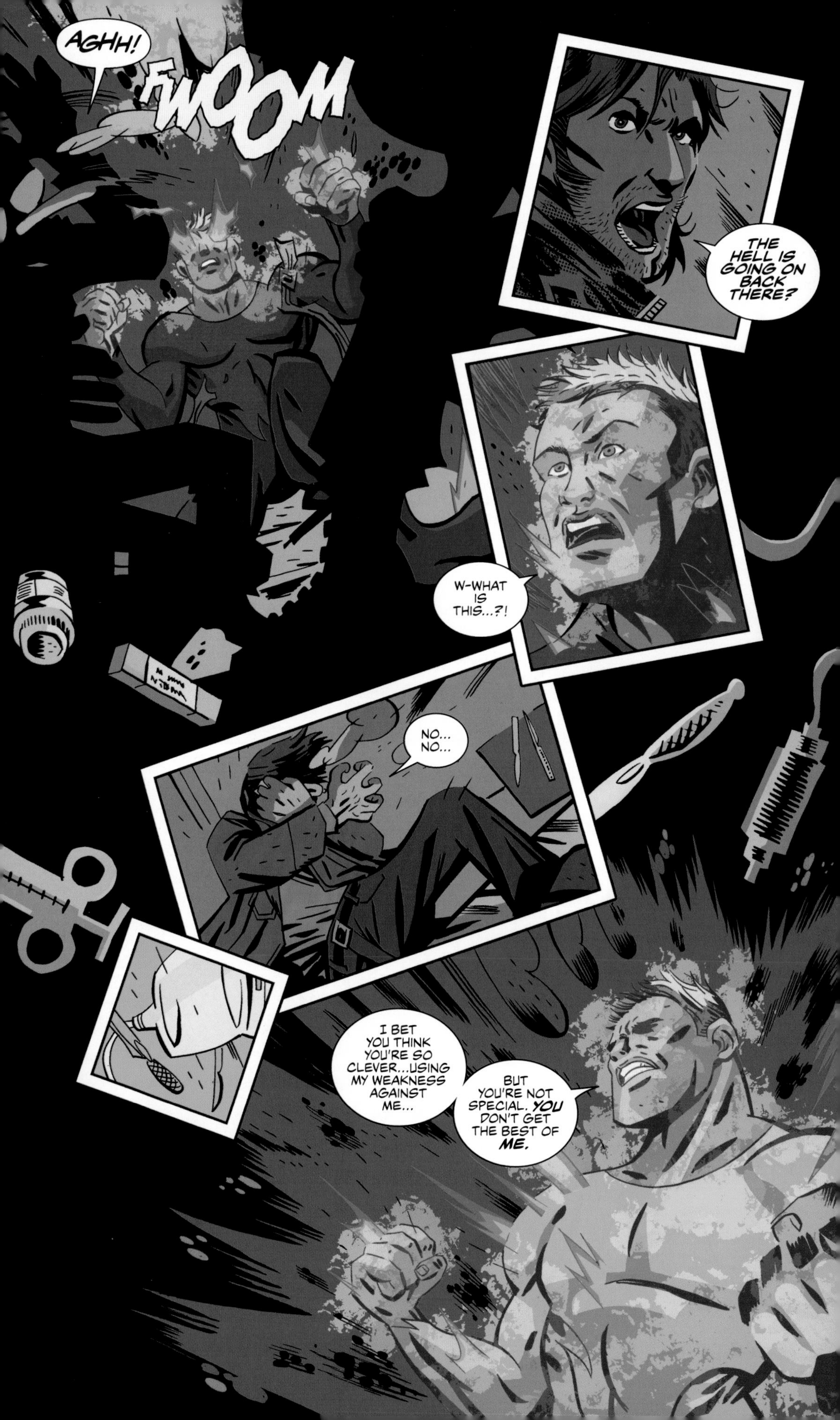
AGHH!
FWOOM
THE HELL IS GOING ON BACK THERE?
W-WHAT IS THIS...?!
NO... NO...
I BET YOU THINK YOU'RE SO CLEVER...USING MY WEAKNESS AGAINST ME...
BUT YOU'RE NOT SPECIAL. *YOU* DON'T GET THE BEST OF *ME.*

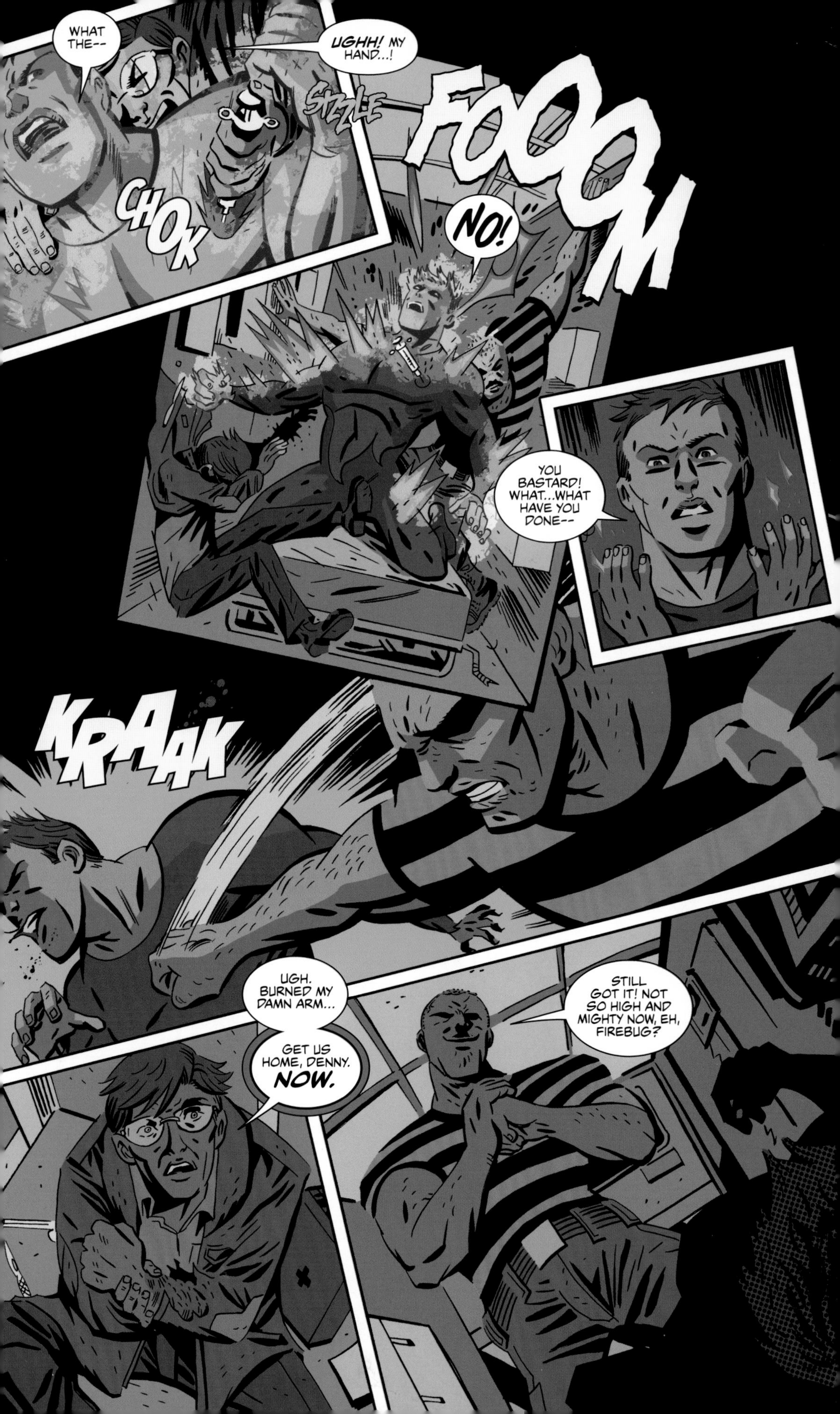
WHAT THE--
UGHH! MY HAND...!
SIZZLE
CHOK
FOOOM
NO!
YOU BASTARD! WHAT...WHAT HAVE YOU DONE--
KRAAK
UGH. BURNED MY DAMN ARM...
GET US HOME, DENNY. NOW.
STILL GOT IT! NOT SO HIGH AND MIGHTY NOW, EH, FIREBUG?

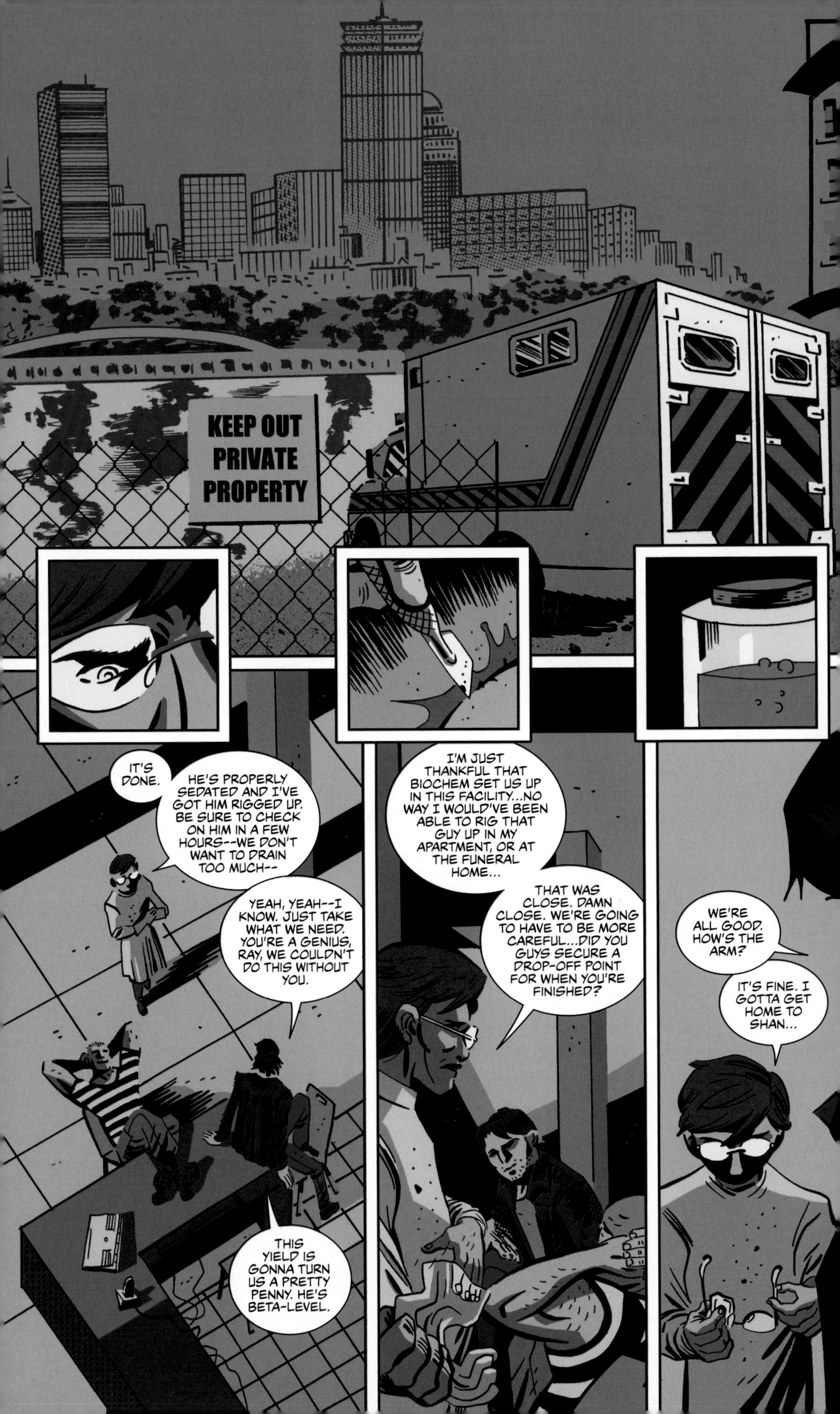
KEEP OUT
PRIVATE
PROPERTY
IT'S DONE.
HE'S PROPERLY SEDATED AND I'VE GOT HIM RIGGED UP. BE SURE TO CHECK ON HIM IN A FEW HOURS--WE DON'T WANT TO DRAIN TOO MUCH--
YEAH, YEAH--I KNOW. JUST TAKE WHAT WE NEED. YOU'RE A GENIUS, RAY, WE COULDN'T DO THIS WITHOUT YOU.
THIS YIELD IS GONNA TURN US A PRETTY PENNY. HE'S BETA-LEVEL.
I'M JUST THANKFUL THAT BIOCHEM SET US UP IN THIS FACILITY...NO WAY I WOULD'VE BEEN ABLE TO RIG THAT GUY UP IN MY APARTMENT, OR AT THE FUNERAL HOME...
THAT WAS CLOSE. DAMN CLOSE. WE'RE GOING TO HAVE TO BE MORE CAREFUL...DID YOU GUYS SECURE A DROP-OFF POINT FOR WHEN YOU'RE FINISHED?
WE'RE ALL GOOD. HOW'S THE ARM?
IT'S FINE. I GOTTA GET HOME TO SHAN...

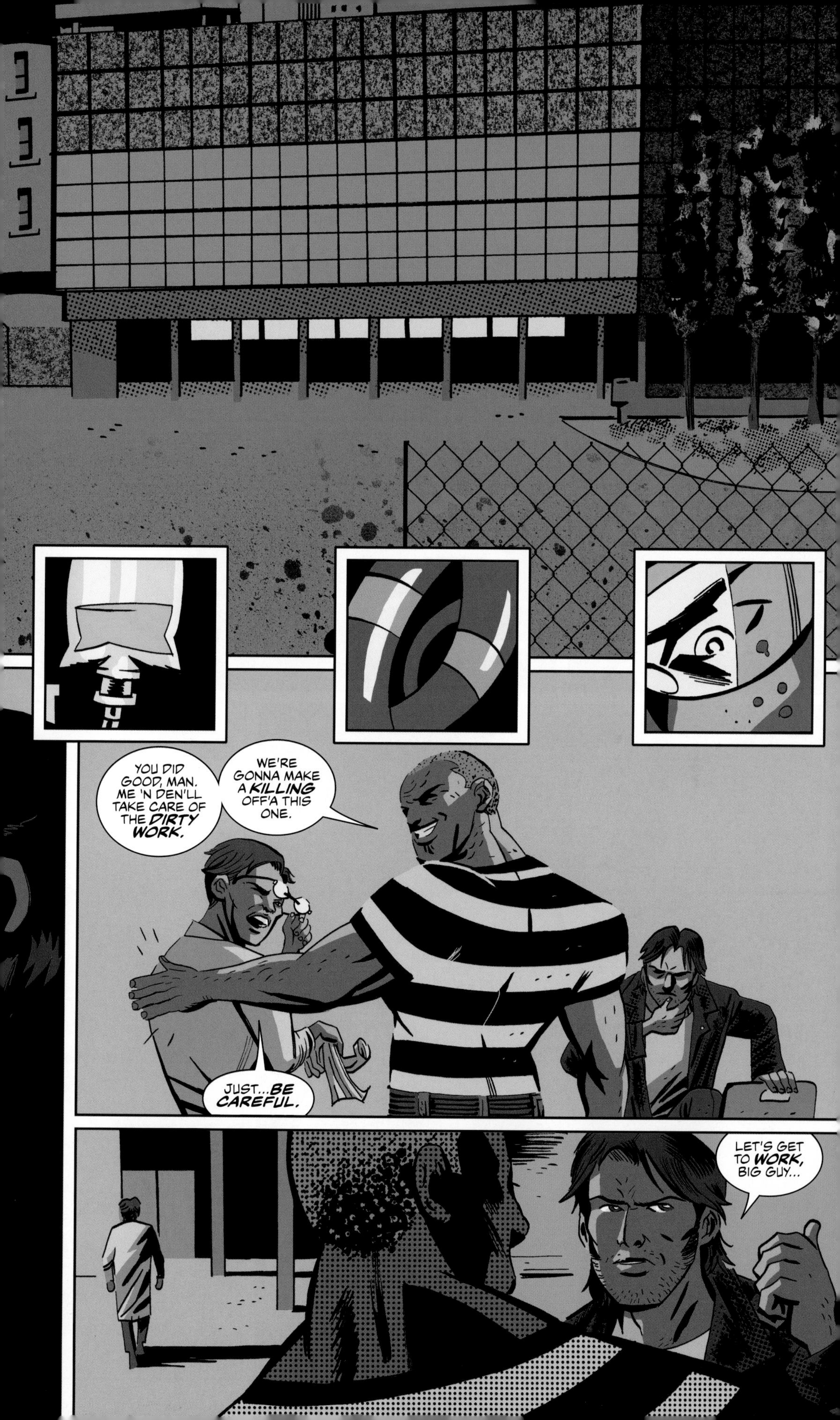
YOU DID GOOD, MAN. ME 'N DEN'LL TAKE CARE OF THE DIRTY WORK.
WE'RE GONNA MAKE A KILLING OFF'A THIS ONE.
JUST...BE CAREFUL.
LET'S GET TO WORK, BIG GUY...

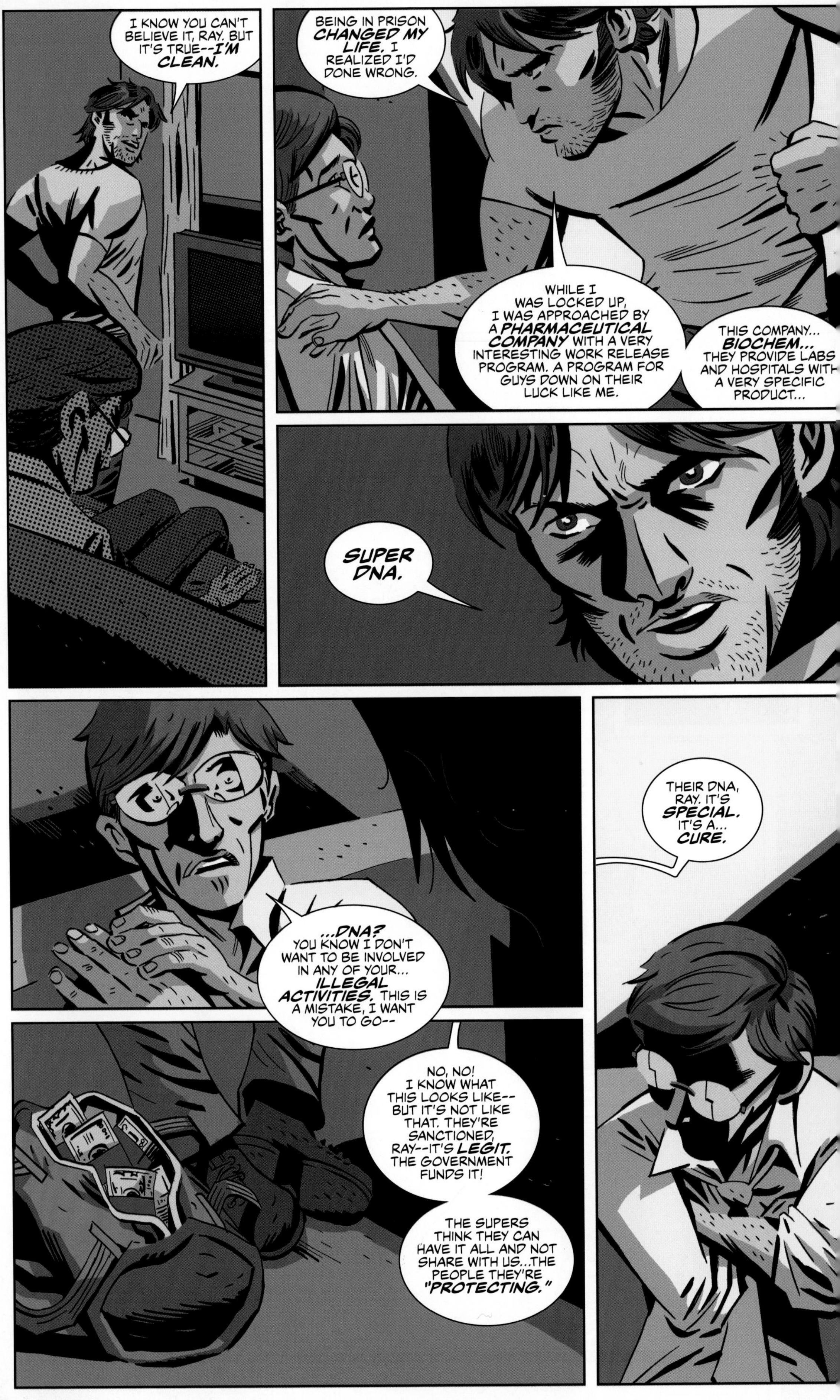

I KNOW YOU CAN'T BELIEVE IT, RAY. BUT IT'S TRUE--I'M CLEAN.
BEING IN PRISON CHANGED MY LIFE. I REALIZED I'D DONE WRONG.
WHILE I WAS LOCKED UP, I WAS APPROACHED BY A PHARMACEUTICAL COMPANY WITH A VERY INTERESTING WORK RELEASE PROGRAM. A PROGRAM FOR GUYS DOWN ON THEIR LUCK LIKE ME.
THIS COMPANY... BIOCHEM... THEY PROVIDE LABS AND HOSPITALS WITH A VERY SPECIFIC PRODUCT...
SUPER DNA.
...DNA? YOU KNOW I DON'T WANT TO BE INVOLVED IN ANY OF YOUR... ILLEGAL ACTIVITIES. THIS IS A MISTAKE, I WANT YOU TO GO--
NO, NO! I KNOW WHAT THIS LOOKS LIKE-- BUT IT'S NOT LIKE THAT. THEY'RE SANCTIONED, RAY--IT'S LEGIT. THE GOVERNMENT FUNDS IT!
THE SUPERS THINK THEY CAN HAVE IT ALL AND NOT SHARE WITH US...THE PEOPLE THEY'RE "PROTECTING."
THEIR DNA, RAY. IT'S SPECIAL. IT'S A... CURE.

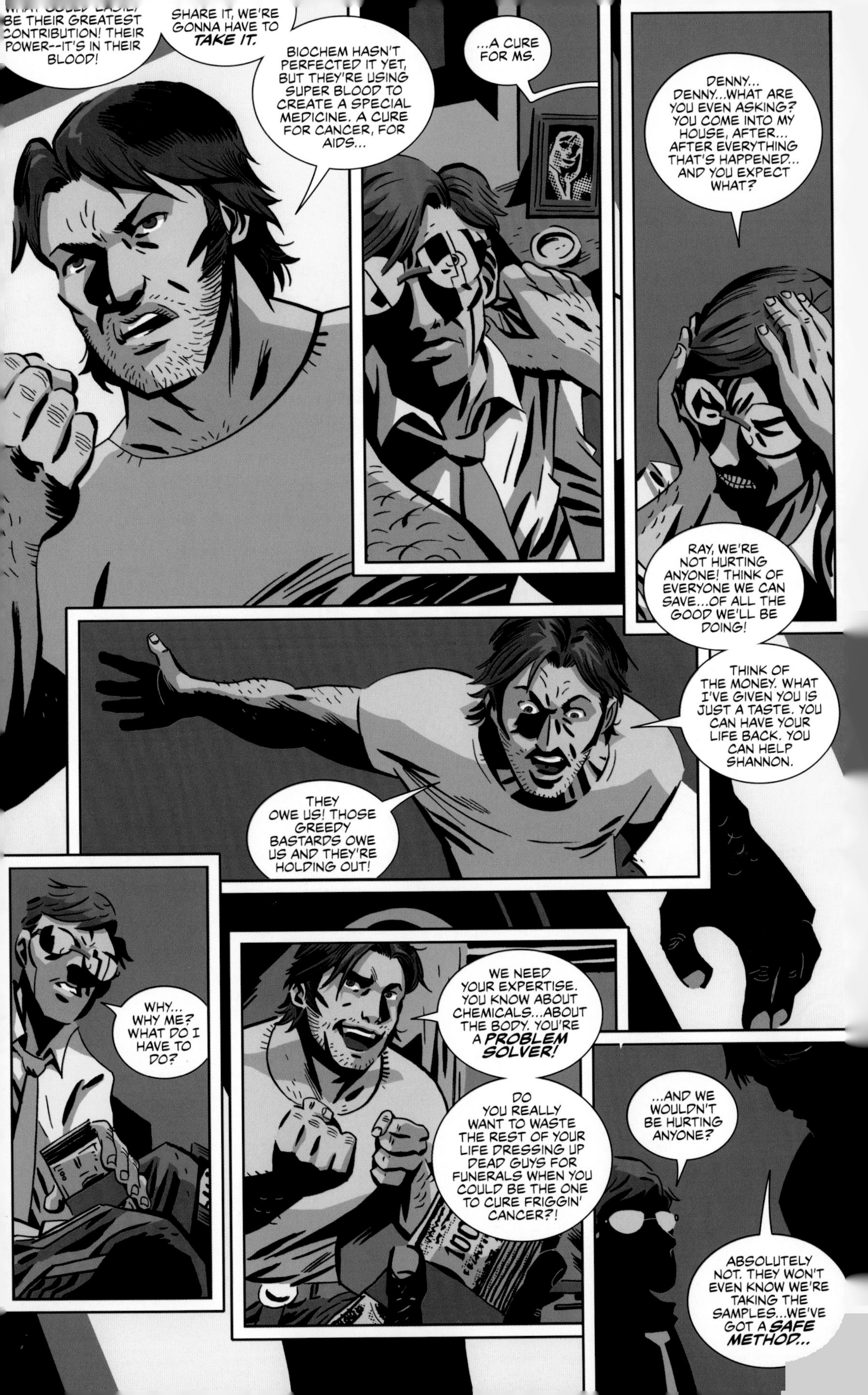

BE THEIR GREATEST CONTRIBUTION! THEIR POWER--IT'S IN THEIR BLOOD!
SHARE IT, WE'RE GONNA HAVE TO *TAKE IT.*
BIOCHEM HASN'T PERFECTED IT YET, BUT THEY'RE USING SUPER BLOOD TO CREATE A SPECIAL MEDICINE. A CURE FOR CANCER, FOR AIDS...
...A CURE FOR MS.
DENNY... DENNY...WHAT ARE YOU EVEN ASKING? YOU COME INTO MY HOUSE, AFTER... AFTER EVERYTHING THAT'S HAPPENED... AND YOU EXPECT WHAT?
RAY, WE'RE NOT HURTING ANYONE! THINK OF EVERYONE WE CAN SAVE...OF ALL THE GOOD WE'LL BE DOING!
THINK OF THE MONEY. WHAT I'VE GIVEN YOU IS JUST A TASTE. YOU CAN HAVE YOUR LIFE BACK. YOU CAN HELP SHANNON.
THEY OWE US! THOSE GREEDY BASTARDS OWE US AND THEY'RE HOLDING OUT!
WHY... WHY ME? WHAT DO I HAVE TO DO?
WE NEED YOUR EXPERTISE. YOU KNOW ABOUT CHEMICALS...ABOUT THE BODY. YOU'RE A ***PROBLEM SOLVER!***
DO YOU REALLY WANT TO WASTE THE REST OF YOUR LIFE DRESSING UP DEAD GUYS FOR FUNERALS WHEN YOU COULD BE THE ONE TO CURE FRIGGIN' CANCER?!
...AND WE WOULDN'T BE HURTING ANYONE?
ABSOLUTELY NOT. THEY WON'T EVEN KNOW WE'RE TAKING THE SAMPLES...WE'VE GOT A ***SAFE METHOD...***

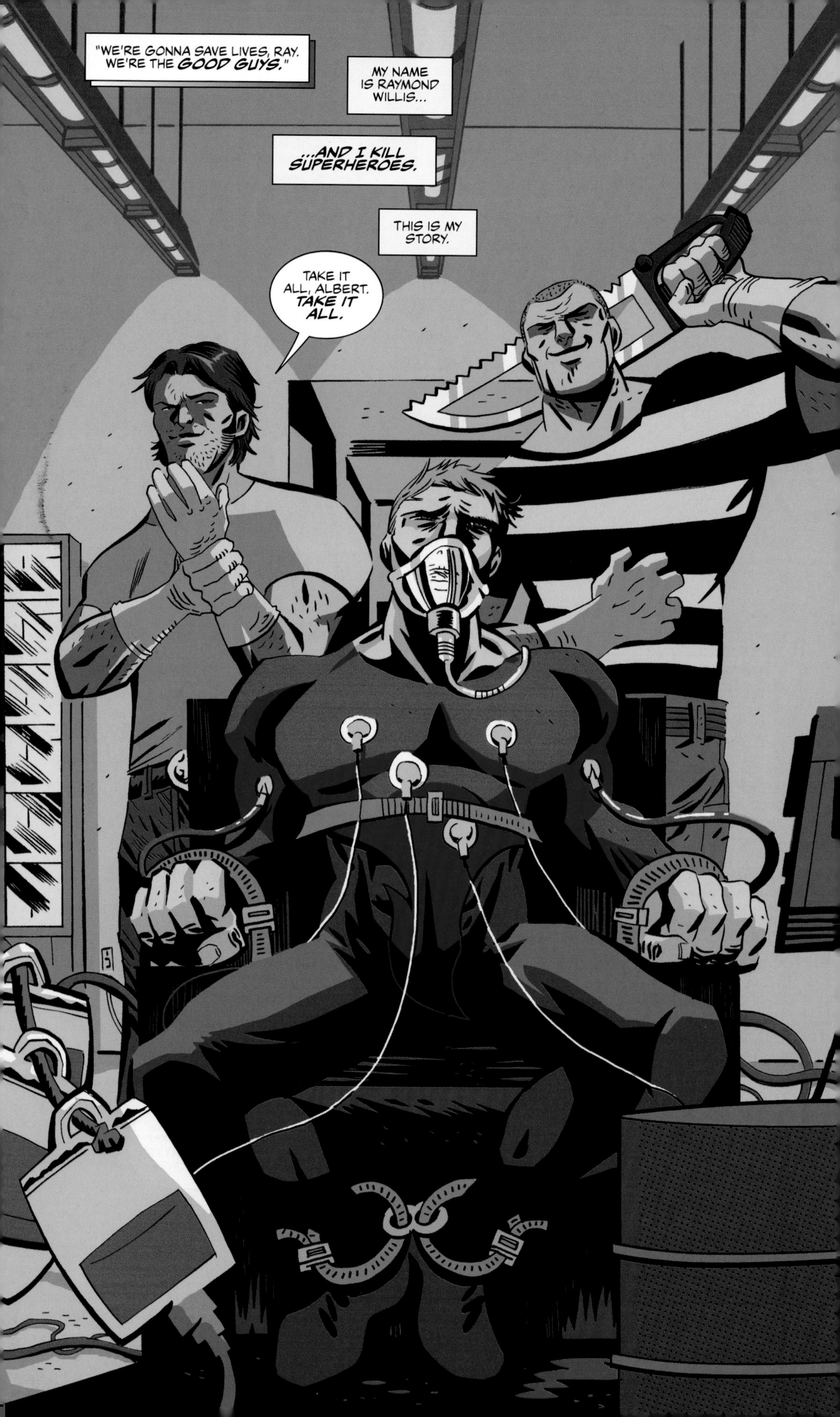
"WE'RE GONNA SAVE LIVES, RAY. WE'RE THE GOOD GUYS."
MY NAME IS RAYMOND WILLIS...
...AND I KILL SUPERHEROES.
THIS IS MY STORY.
TAKE IT ALL, ALBERT. TAKE IT ALL.

chapter two

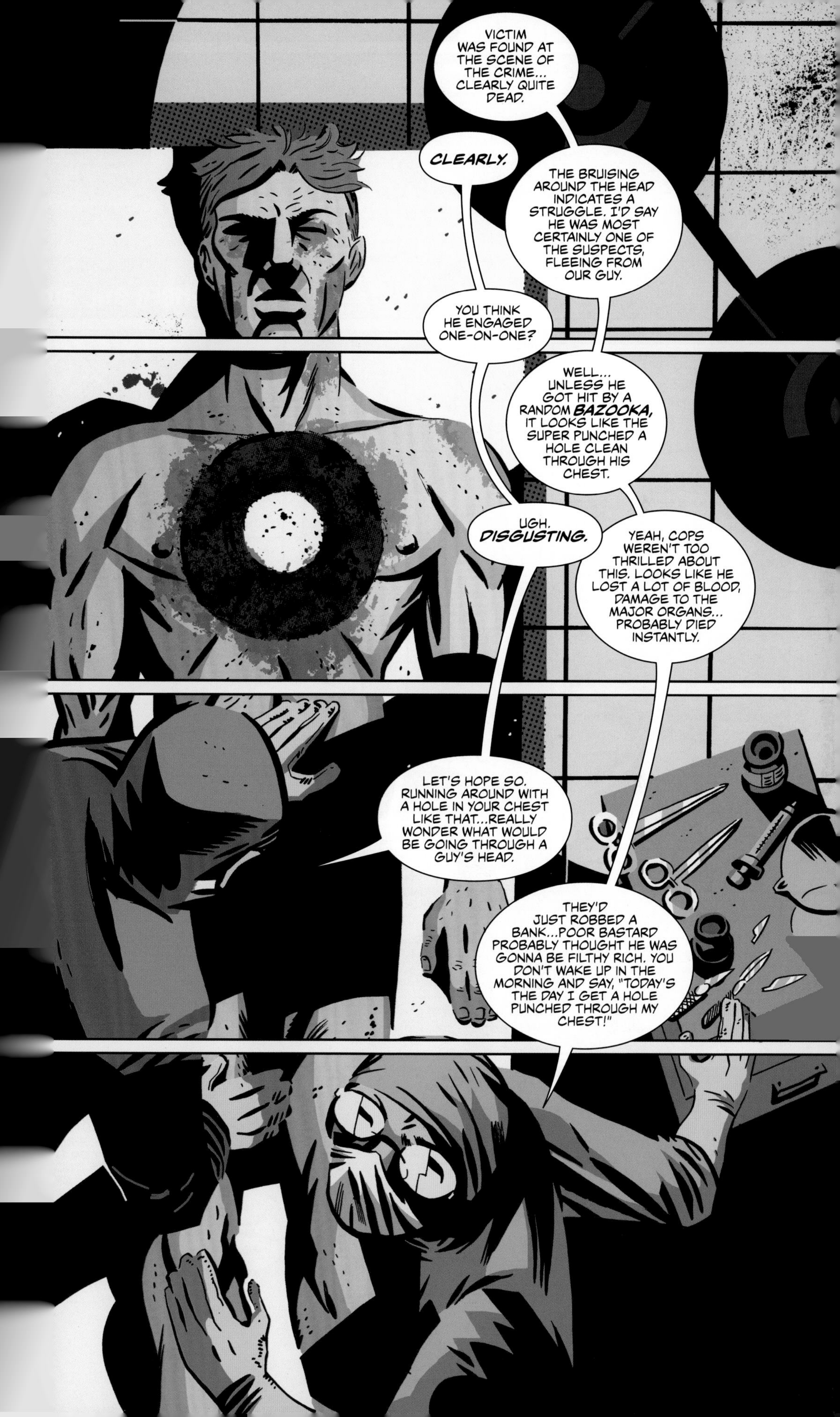
VICTIM WAS FOUND AT THE SCENE OF THE CRIME... CLEARLY QUITE DEAD.
CLEARLY.
THE BRUISING AROUND THE HEAD INDICATES A STRUGGLE. I'D SAY HE WAS MOST CERTAINLY ONE OF THE SUSPECTS, FLEEING FROM OUR GUY.
YOU THINK HE ENGAGED ONE-ON-ONE?
WELL... UNLESS HE GOT HIT BY A RANDOM BAZOOKA, IT LOOKS LIKE THE SUPER PUNCHED A HOLE CLEAN THROUGH HIS CHEST.
UGH. DISGUSTING.
YEAH, COPS WEREN'T TOO THRILLED ABOUT THIS. LOOKS LIKE HE LOST A LOT OF BLOOD, DAMAGE TO THE MAJOR ORGANS... PROBABLY DIED INSTANTLY.
LET'S HOPE SO. RUNNING AROUND WITH A HOLE IN YOUR CHEST LIKE THAT...REALLY WONDER WHAT WOULD BE GOING THROUGH A GUY'S HEAD.
THEY'D JUST ROBBED A BANK...POOR BASTARD PROBABLY THOUGHT HE WAS GONNA BE FILTHY RICH. YOU DON'T WAKE UP IN THE MORNING AND SAY, "TODAY'S THE DAY I GET A HOLE PUNCHED THROUGH MY CHEST!"

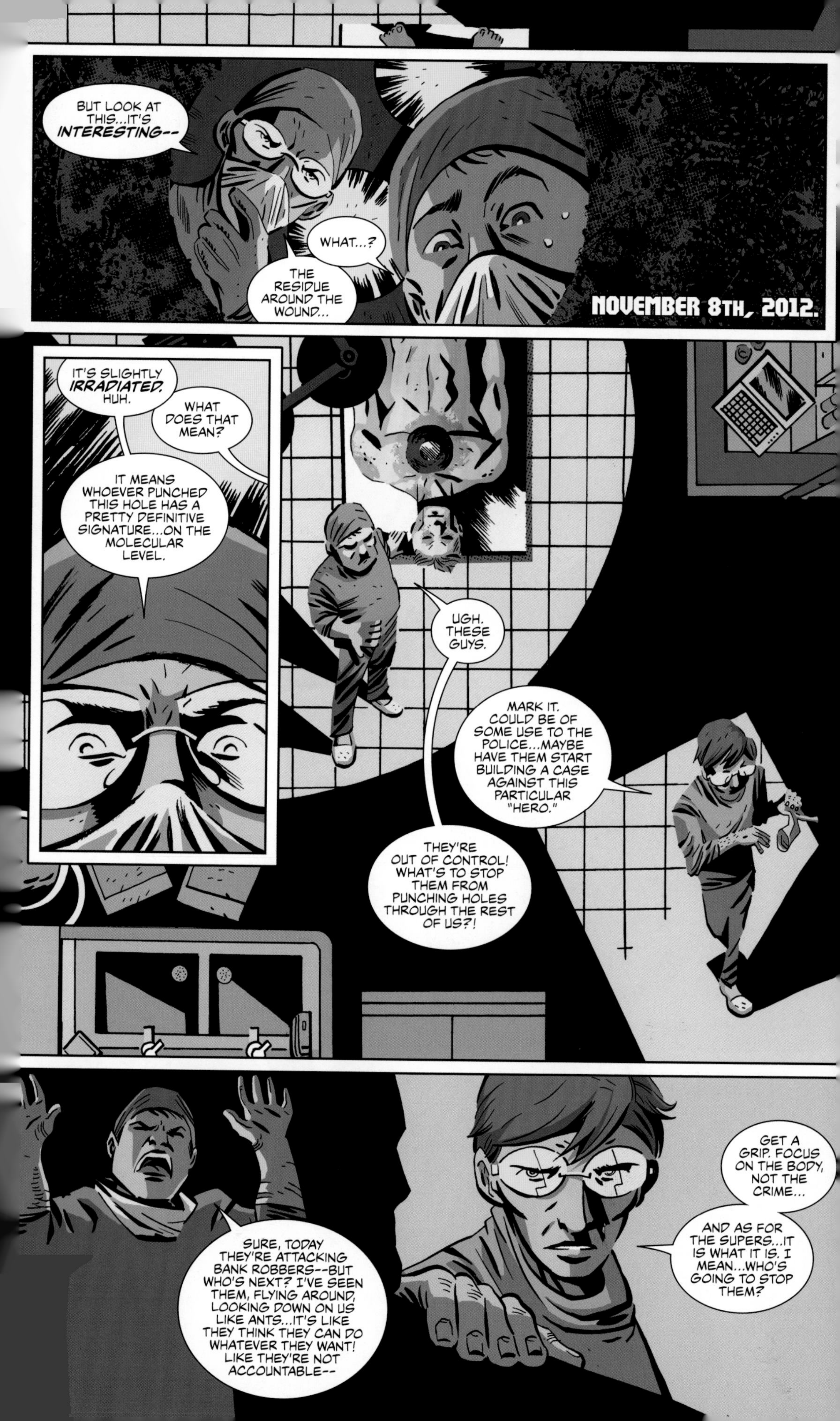

BUT LOOK AT THIS...IT'S INTERESTING--
WHAT...?
THE RESIDUE AROUND THE WOUND...
NOVEMBER 8TH, 2012.
IT'S SLIGHTLY IRRADIATED. HUH.
WHAT DOES THAT MEAN?
IT MEANS WHOEVER PUNCHED THIS HOLE HAS A PRETTY DEFINITIVE SIGNATURE...ON THE MOLECULAR LEVEL.
UGH. THESE GUYS.
THEY'RE OUT OF CONTROL! WHAT'S TO STOP THEM FROM PUNCHING HOLES THROUGH THE REST OF US?!
MARK IT. COULD BE OF SOME USE TO THE POLICE...MAYBE HAVE THEM START BUILDING A CASE AGAINST THIS PARTICULAR "HERO."
SURE, TODAY THEY'RE ATTACKING BANK ROBBERS--BUT WHO'S NEXT? I'VE SEEN THEM, FLYING AROUND, LOOKING DOWN ON US LIKE ANTS...IT'S LIKE THEY THINK THEY CAN DO WHATEVER THEY WANT! LIKE THEY'RE NOT ACCOUNTABLE--
GET A GRIP. FOCUS ON THE BODY, NOT THE CRIME...
AND AS FOR THE SUPERS...IT IS WHAT IT IS. I MEAN...WHO'S GOING TO STOP THEM?

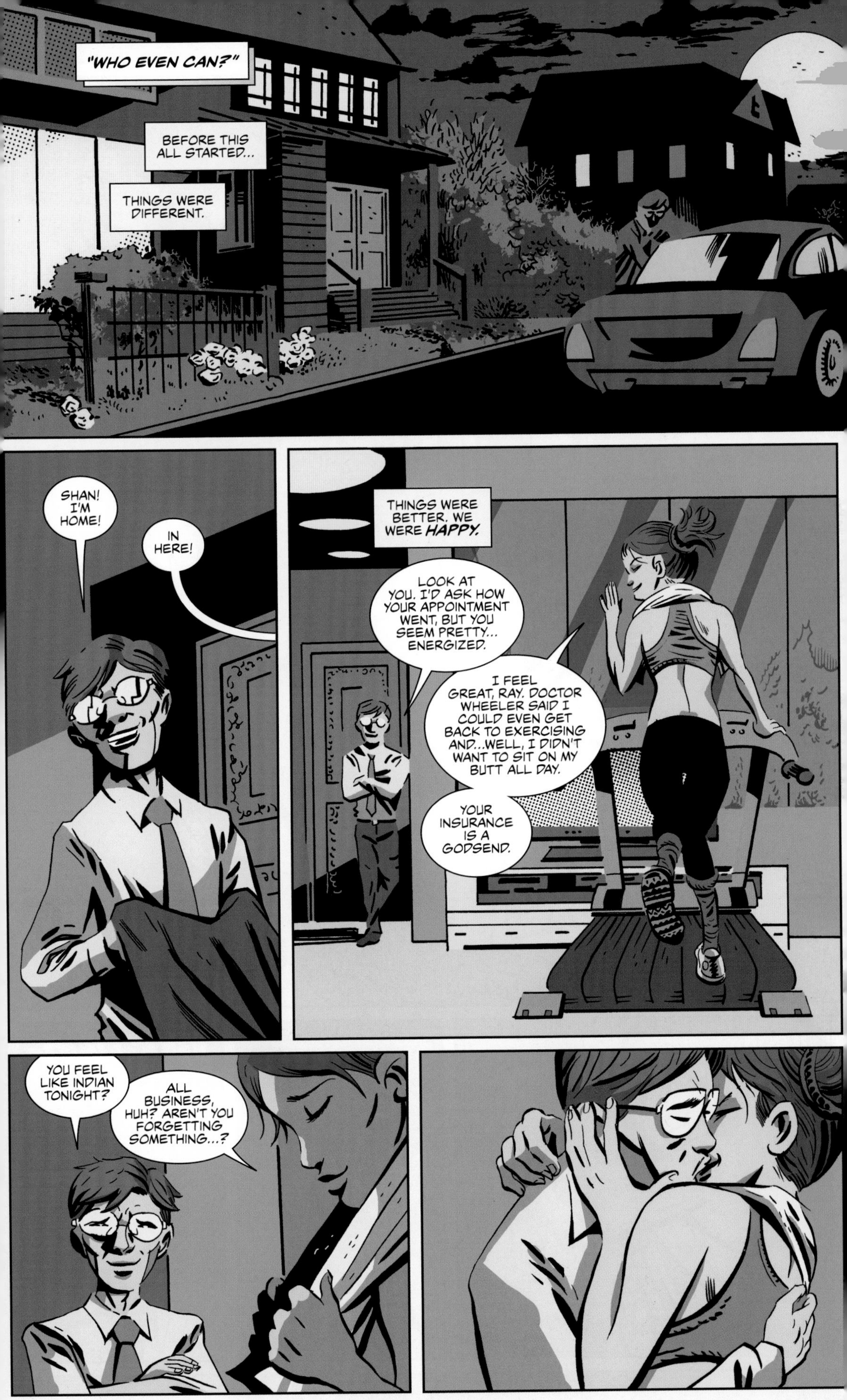
"WHO EVEN CAN?"
BEFORE THIS ALL STARTED...
THINGS WERE DIFFERENT.
SHAN! I'M HOME!
IN HERE!
THINGS WERE BETTER. WE WERE *HAPPY.*
LOOK AT YOU. I'D ASK HOW YOUR APPOINTMENT WENT, BUT YOU SEEM PRETTY... ENERGIZED.
I FEEL GREAT, RAY. DOCTOR WHEELER SAID I COULD EVEN GET BACK TO EXERCISING AND...WELL, I DIDN'T WANT TO SIT ON MY BUTT ALL DAY.
YOUR INSURANCE IS A GODSEND.
YOU FEEL LIKE INDIAN TONIGHT?
ALL BUSINESS, HUH? AREN'T YOU FORGETTING SOMETHING...?

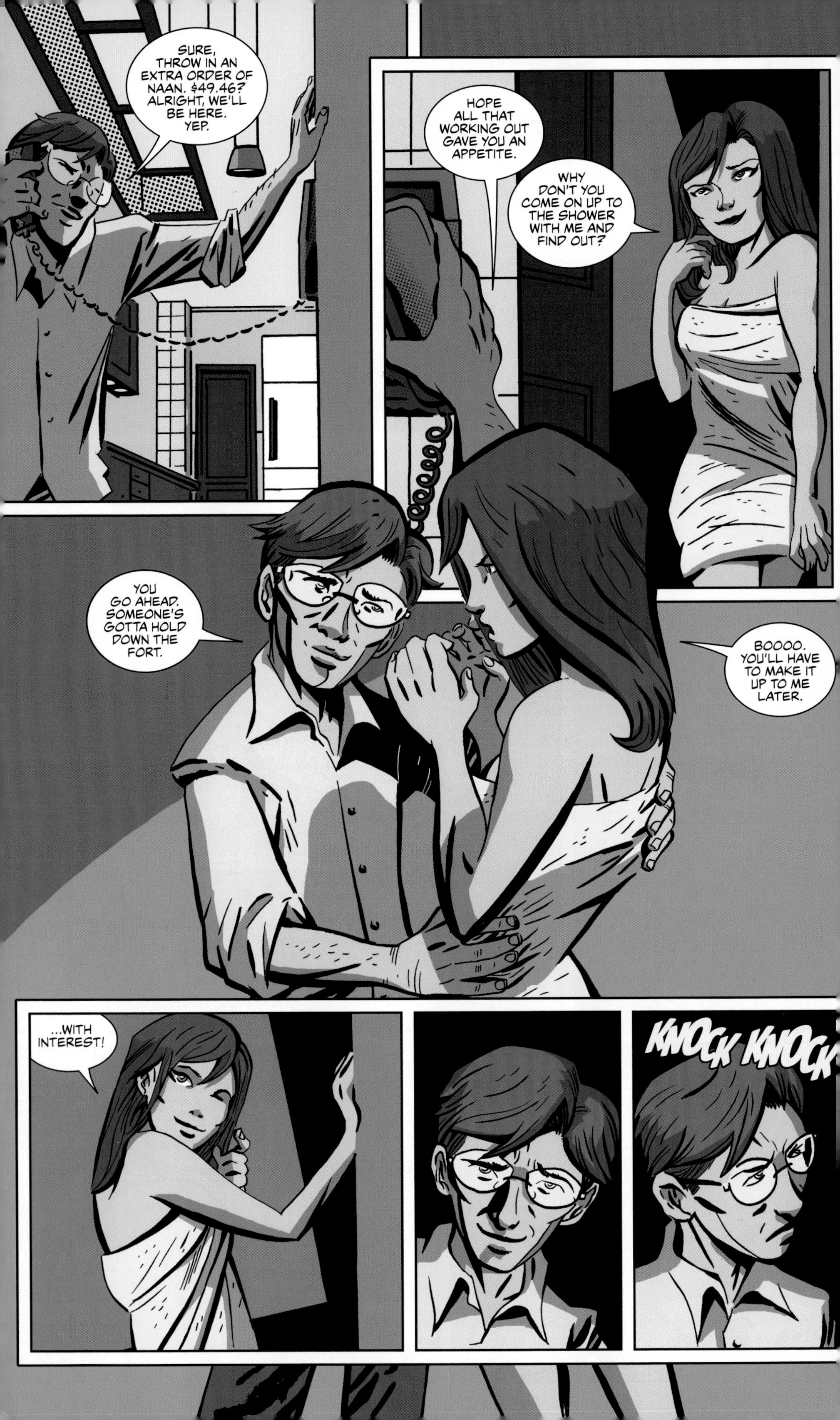
SURE, THROW IN AN EXTRA ORDER OF NAAN. $49.46? ALRIGHT, WE'LL BE HERE. YEP.
HOPE ALL THAT WORKING OUT GAVE YOU AN APPETITE.
WHY DON'T YOU COME ON UP TO THE SHOWER WITH ME AND FIND OUT?
YOU GO AHEAD. SOMEONE'S GOTTA HOLD DOWN THE FORT.
BOOOO. YOU'LL HAVE TO MAKE IT UP TO ME LATER.
...WITH INTEREST!
KNOCK KNOCK

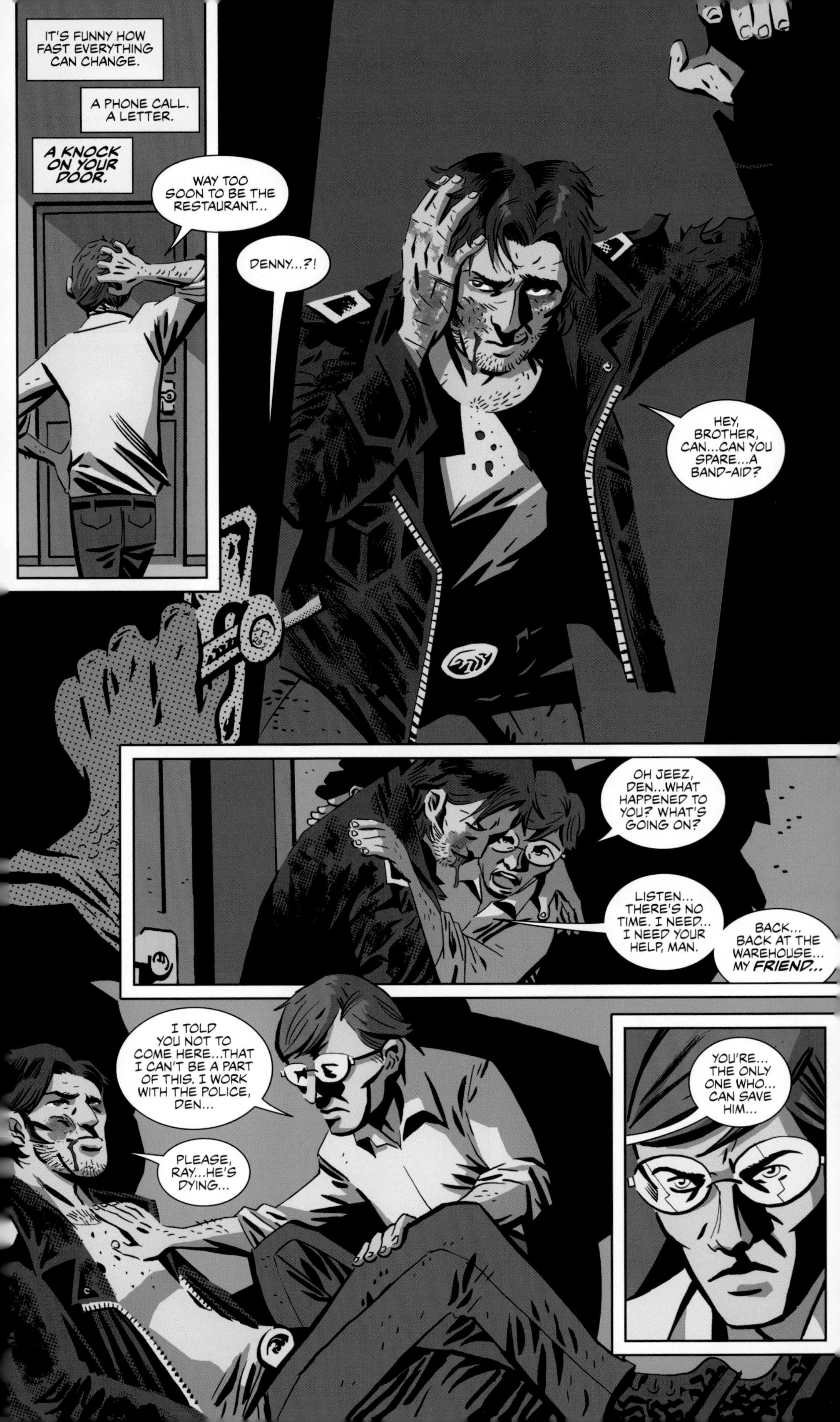
IT'S FUNNY HOW FAST EVERYTHING CAN CHANGE.
A PHONE CALL. A LETTER.
A KNOCK ON YOUR DOOR.
WAY TOO SOON TO BE THE RESTAURANT...
DENNY...?!
HEY, BROTHER, CAN...CAN YOU SPARE...A BAND-AID?
OH JEEZ, DEN...WHAT HAPPENED TO YOU? WHAT'S GOING ON?
LISTEN... THERE'S NO TIME. I NEED... I NEED YOUR HELP, MAN.
BACK... BACK AT THE WAREHOUSE... MY FRIEND...
I TOLD YOU NOT TO COME HERE...THAT I CAN'T BE A PART OF THIS. I WORK WITH THE POLICE, DEN...
PLEASE, RAY...HE'S DYING...
YOU'RE... THE ONLY ONE WHO... CAN SAVE HIM...

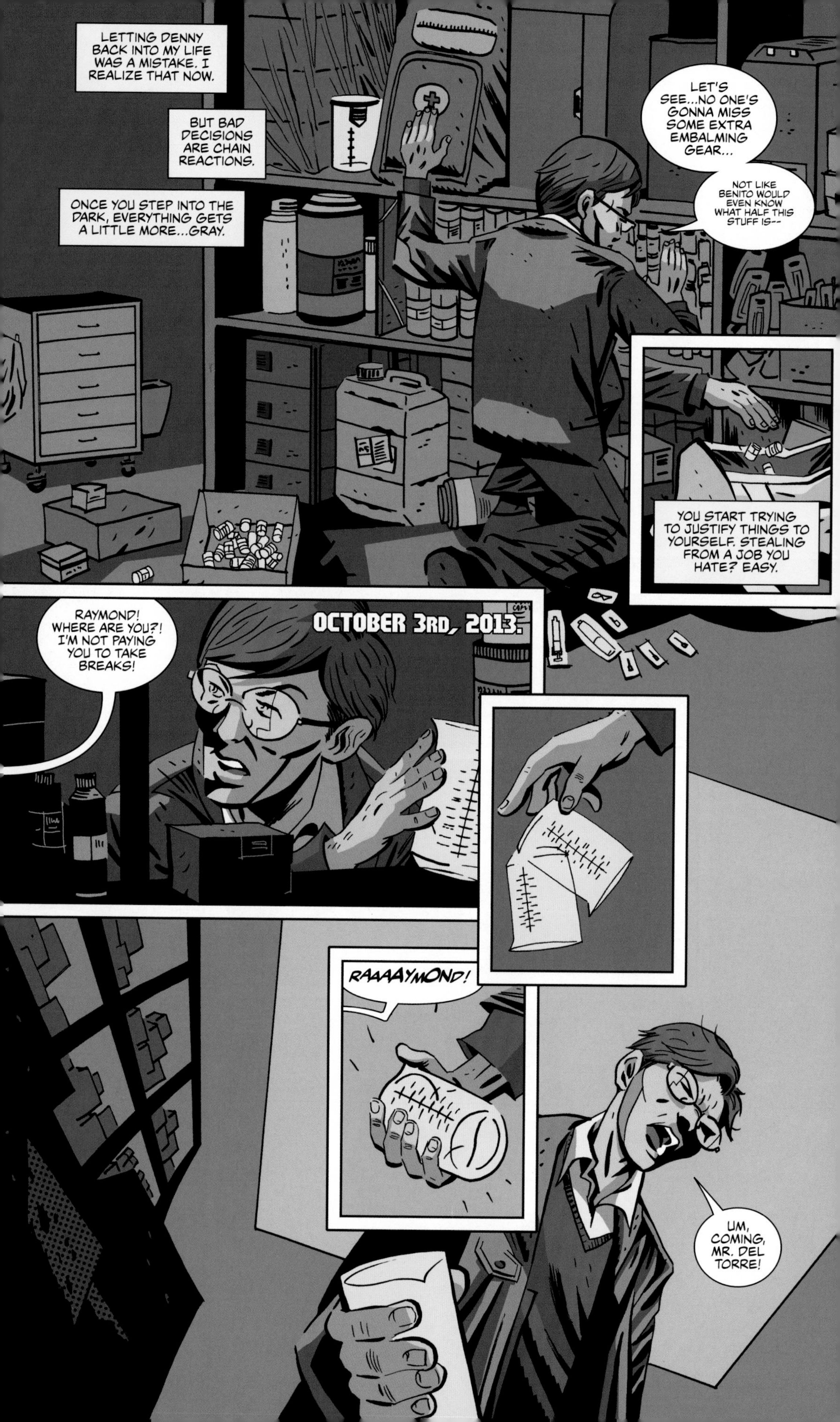

LETTING DENNY BACK INTO MY LIFE WAS A MISTAKE. I REALIZE THAT NOW.
BUT BAD DECISIONS ARE CHAIN REACTIONS.
ONCE YOU STEP INTO THE DARK, EVERYTHING GETS A LITTLE MORE...GRAY.
LET'S SEE...NO ONE'S GONNA MISS SOME EXTRA EMBALMING GEAR...
NOT LIKE BENITO WOULD EVEN KNOW WHAT HALF THIS STUFF IS--
YOU START TRYING TO JUSTIFY THINGS TO YOURSELF. STEALING FROM A JOB YOU HATE? EASY.
OCTOBER 3RD, 2013.
RAYMOND! WHERE ARE YOU?! I'M NOT PAYING YOU TO TAKE BREAKS!
RAAAAYMOND!
UM, COMING, MR. DEL TORRE!

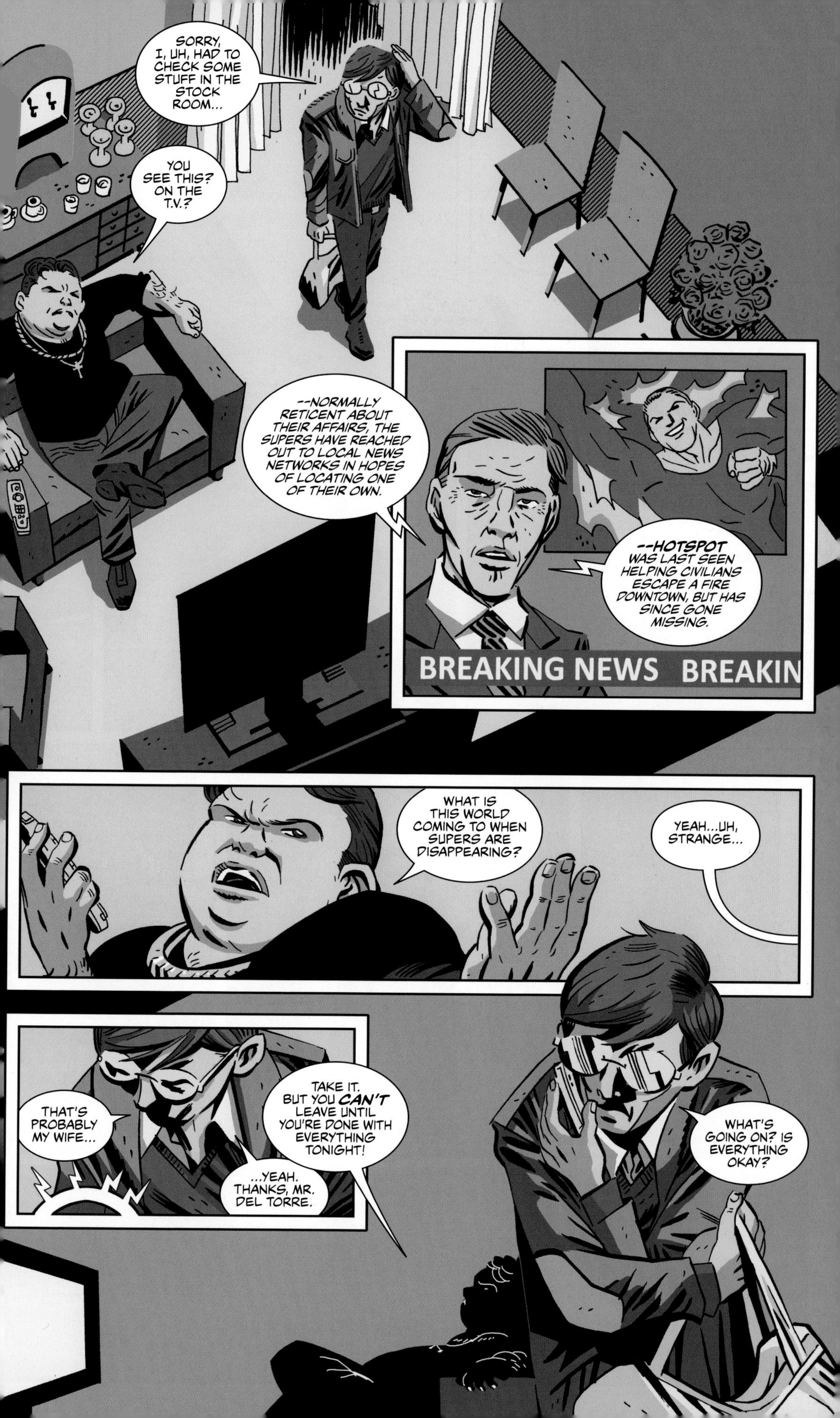
SORRY, I, UH, HAD TO CHECK SOME STUFF IN THE STOCK ROOM...
YOU SEE THIS? ON THE T.V.?
--NORMALLY RETICENT ABOUT THEIR AFFAIRS, THE SUPERS HAVE REACHED OUT TO LOCAL NEWS NETWORKS IN HOPES OF LOCATING ONE OF THEIR OWN.
--HOTSPOT WAS LAST SEEN HELPING CIVILIANS ESCAPE A FIRE DOWNTOWN, BUT HAS SINCE GONE MISSING.
BREAKING NEWS BREAKIN
WHAT IS THIS WORLD COMING TO WHEN SUPERS ARE DISAPPEARING?
YEAH...UH, STRANGE...
THAT'S PROBABLY MY WIFE...
TAKE IT. BUT YOU CAN'T LEAVE UNTIL YOU'RE DONE WITH EVERYTHING TONIGHT!
...YEAH. THANKS, MR. DEL TORRE.
WHAT'S GOING ON? IS EVERYTHING OKAY?

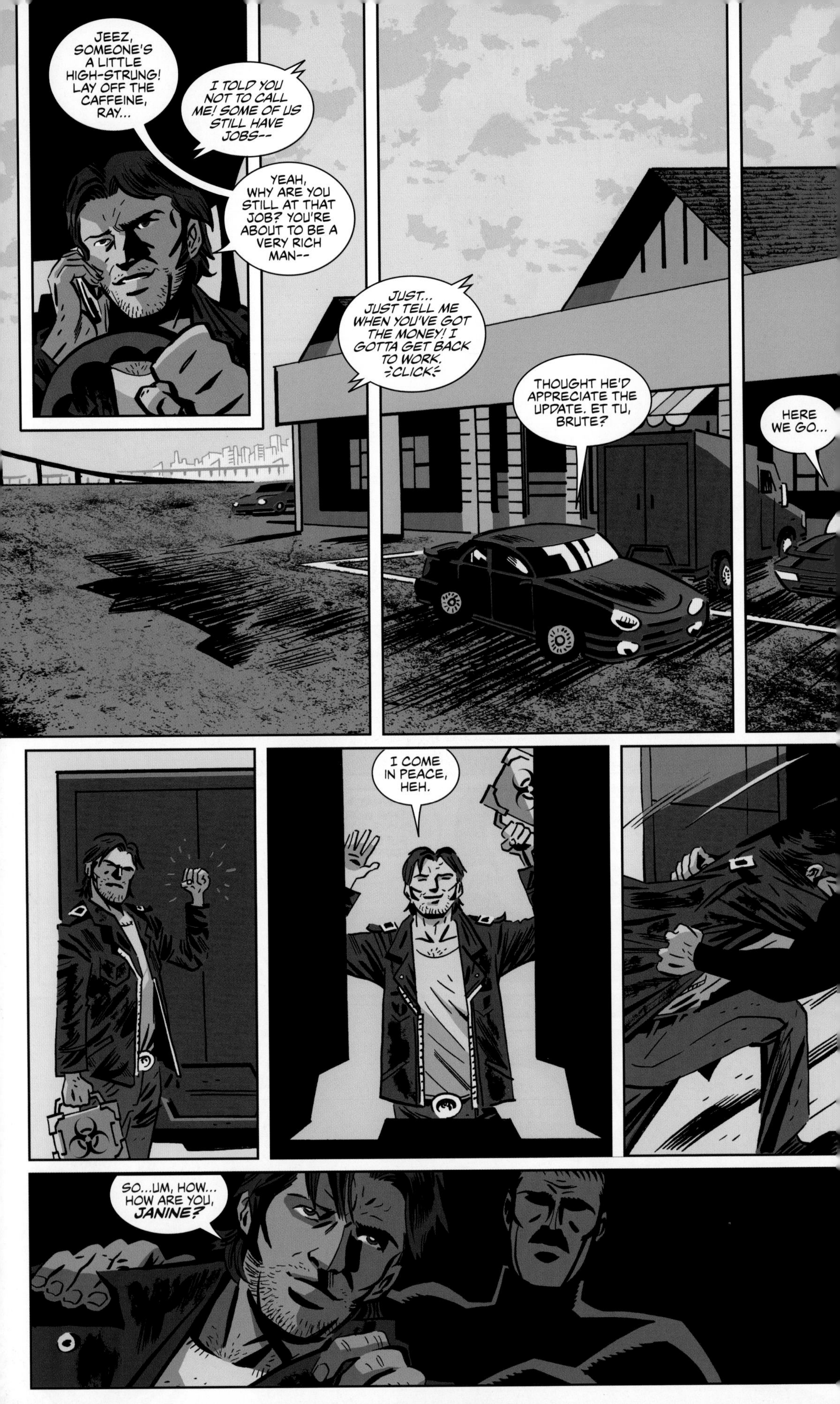
JEEZ, SOMEONE'S A LITTLE HIGH-STRUNG! LAY OFF THE CAFFEINE, RAY...
I TOLD YOU NOT TO CALL ME! SOME OF US STILL HAVE JOBS--
YEAH, WHY ARE YOU STILL AT THAT JOB? YOU'RE ABOUT TO BE A VERY RICH MAN--
JUST... JUST TELL ME WHEN YOU'VE GOT THE MONEY! I GOTTA GET BACK TO WORK. =CLICK=
THOUGHT HE'D APPRECIATE THE UPDATE. ET TU, BRUTE?
HERE WE GO...
I COME IN PEACE, HEH.
SO...UM, HOW... HOW ARE YOU, JANINE?

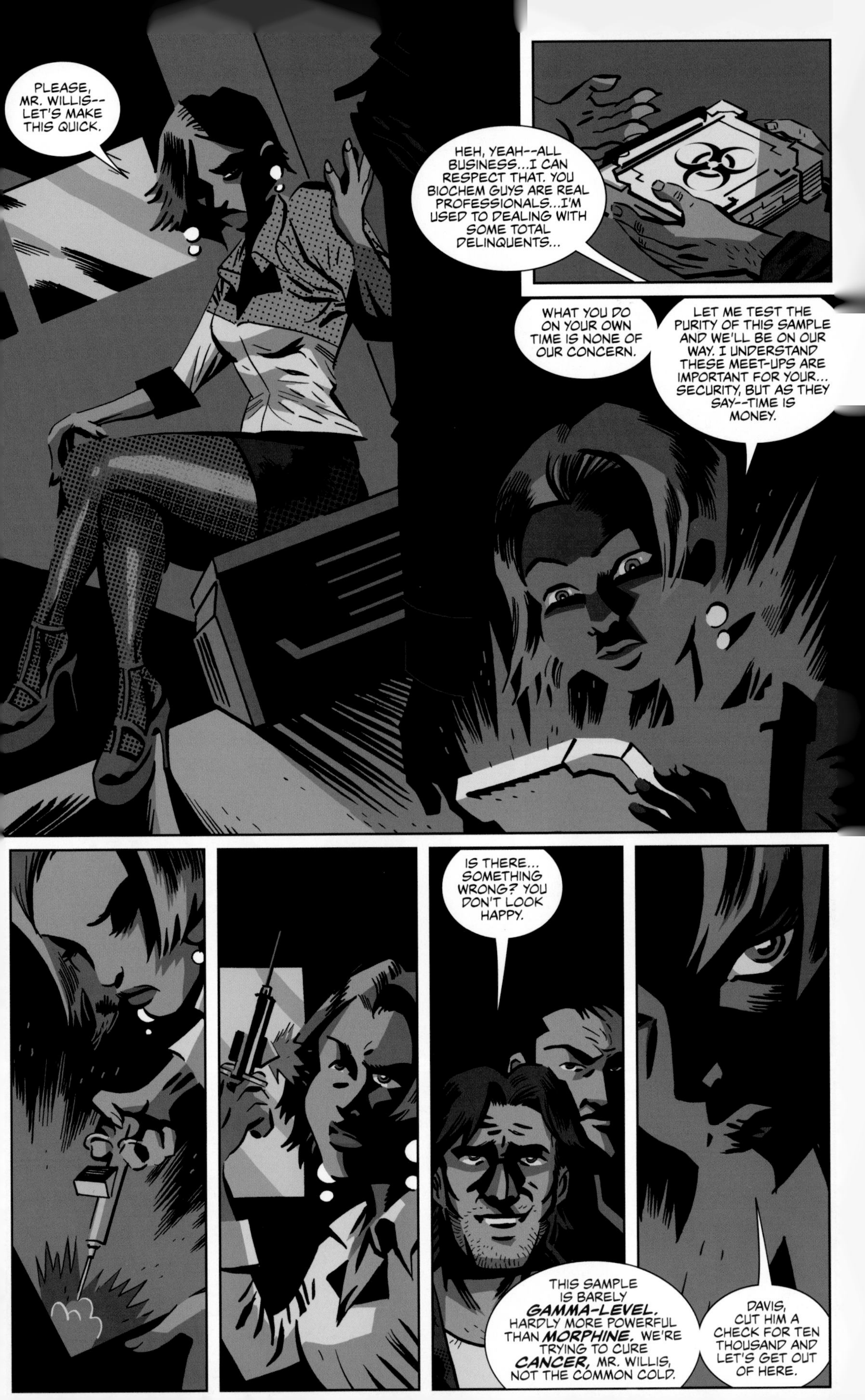
PLEASE, MR. WILLIS-- LET'S MAKE THIS QUICK.
HEH, YEAH--ALL BUSINESS...I CAN RESPECT THAT. YOU BIOCHEM GUYS ARE REAL PROFESSIONALS...I'M USED TO DEALING WITH SOME TOTAL DELINQUENTS...
WHAT YOU DO ON YOUR OWN TIME IS NONE OF OUR CONCERN.
LET ME TEST THE PURITY OF THIS SAMPLE AND WE'LL BE ON OUR WAY. I UNDERSTAND THESE MEET-UPS ARE IMPORTANT FOR YOUR... SECURITY, BUT AS THEY SAY--TIME IS MONEY.
IS THERE... SOMETHING WRONG? YOU DON'T LOOK HAPPY.
THIS SAMPLE IS BARELY GAMMA-LEVEL. HARDLY MORE POWERFUL THAN MORPHINE. WE'RE TRYING TO CURE CANCER, MR. WILLIS, NOT THE COMMON COLD.
DAVIS, CUT HIM A CHECK FOR TEN THOUSAND AND LET'S GET OUT OF HERE.

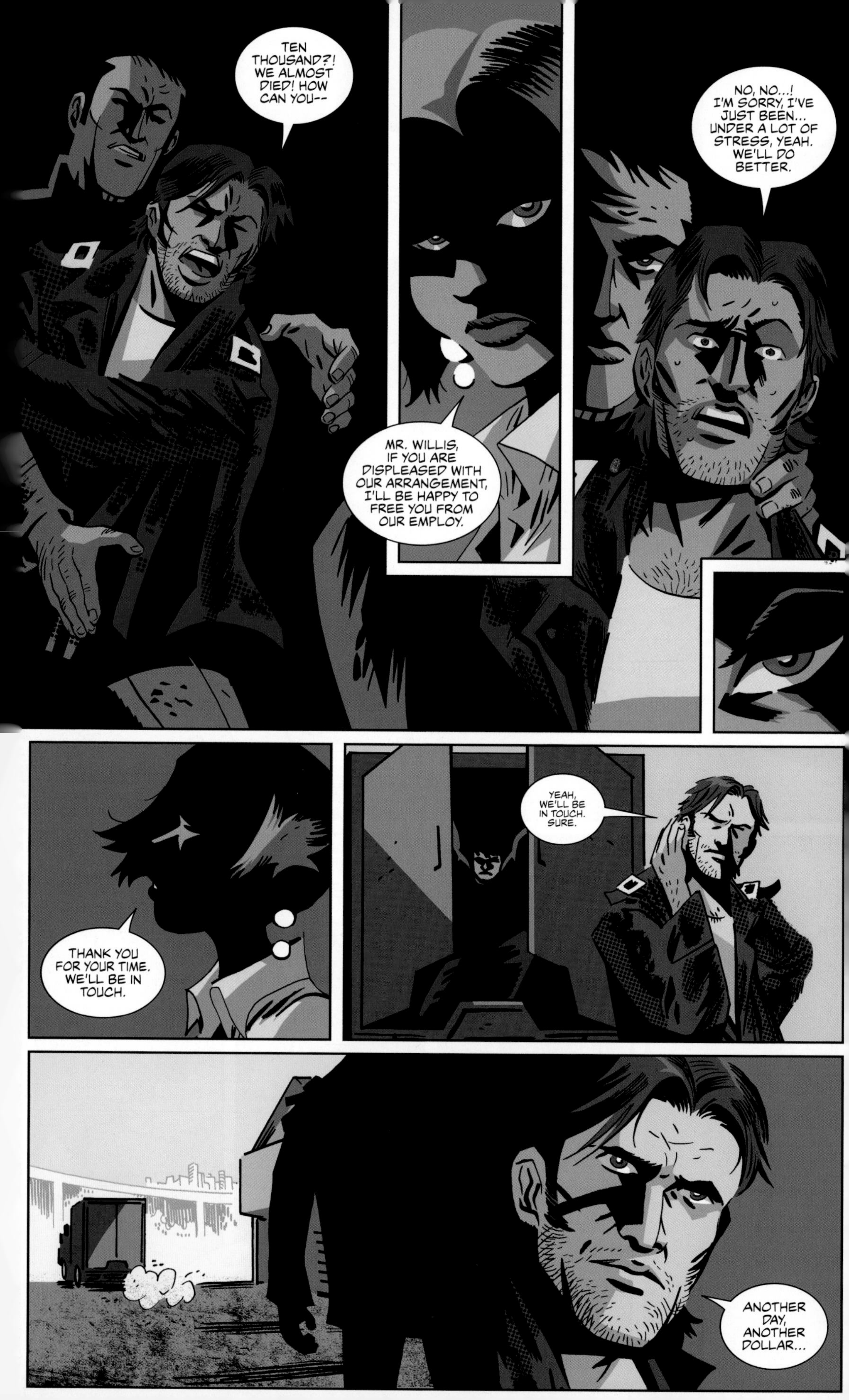
TEN THOUSAND?! WE ALMOST DIED! HOW CAN YOU--
MR. WILLIS, IF YOU ARE DISPLEASED WITH OUR ARRANGEMENT, I'LL BE HAPPY TO FREE YOU FROM OUR EMPLOY.
NO, NO...! I'M SORRY, I'VE JUST BEEN... UNDER A LOT OF STRESS, YEAH. WE'LL DO BETTER.
THANK YOU FOR YOUR TIME. WE'LL BE IN TOUCH.
YEAH, WE'LL BE IN TOUCH. SURE.
ANOTHER DAY, ANOTHER DOLLAR...

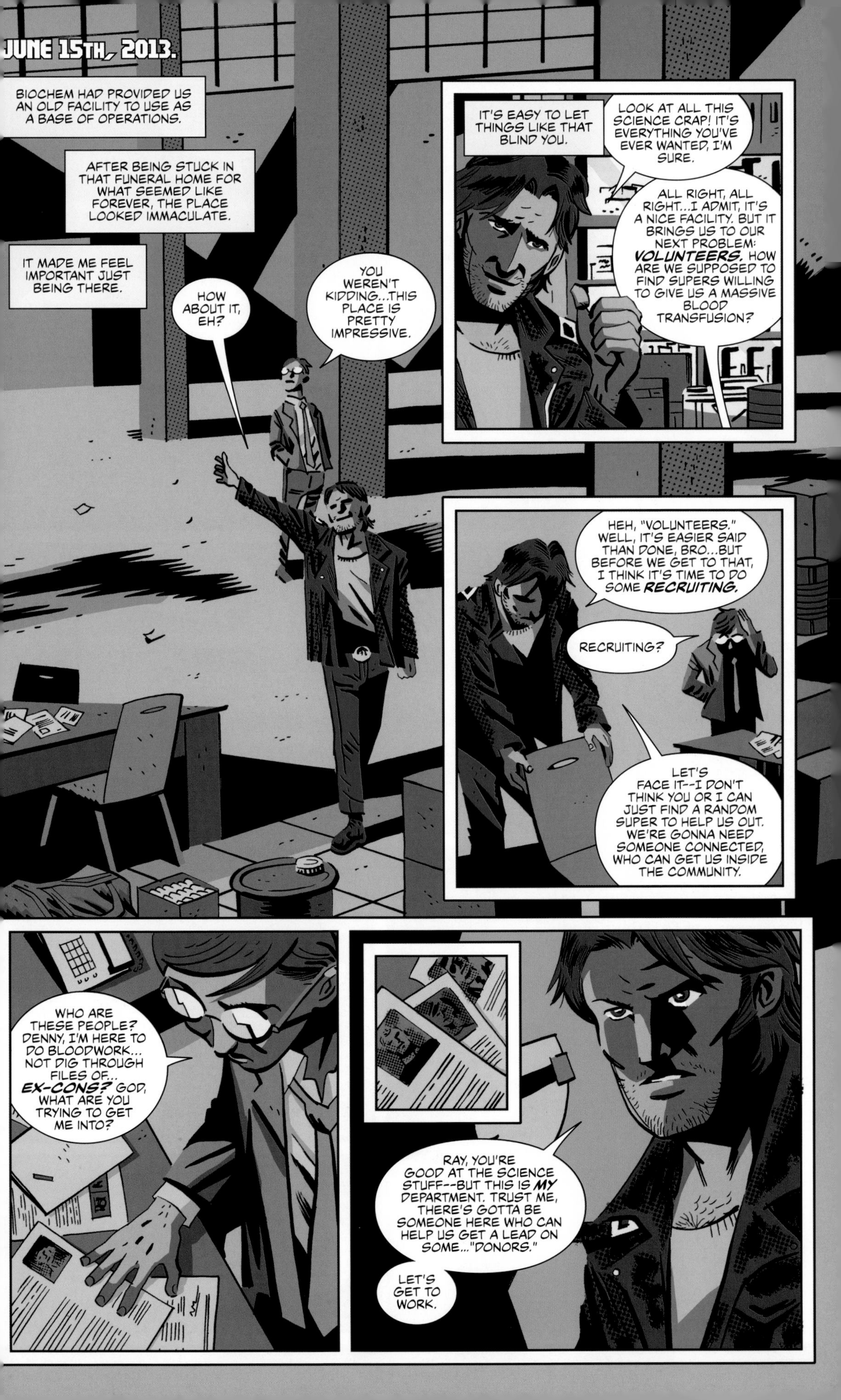

JUNE 15TH, 2013.
BIOCHEM HAD PROVIDED US AN OLD FACILITY TO USE AS A BASE OF OPERATIONS.
AFTER BEING STUCK IN THAT FUNERAL HOME FOR WHAT SEEMED LIKE FOREVER, THE PLACE LOOKED IMMACULATE.
IT MADE ME FEEL IMPORTANT JUST BEING THERE.
HOW ABOUT IT, EH?
YOU WEREN'T KIDDING...THIS PLACE IS PRETTY IMPRESSIVE.
IT'S EASY TO LET THINGS LIKE THAT BLIND YOU.
LOOK AT ALL THIS SCIENCE CRAP! IT'S EVERYTHING YOU'VE EVER WANTED, I'M SURE.
ALL RIGHT, ALL RIGHT...I ADMIT, IT'S A NICE FACILITY. BUT IT BRINGS US TO OUR NEXT PROBLEM: VOLUNTEERS. HOW ARE WE SUPPOSED TO FIND SUPERS WILLING TO GIVE US A MASSIVE BLOOD TRANSFUSION?
HEH, "VOLUNTEERS." WELL, IT'S EASIER SAID THAN DONE, BRO...BUT BEFORE WE GET TO THAT, I THINK IT'S TIME TO DO SOME RECRUITING.
RECRUITING?
LET'S FACE IT--I DON'T THINK YOU OR I CAN JUST FIND A RANDOM SUPER TO HELP US OUT. WE'RE GONNA NEED SOMEONE CONNECTED, WHO CAN GET US INSIDE THE COMMUNITY.
WHO ARE THESE PEOPLE? DENNY, I'M HERE TO DO BLOODWORK... NOT DIG THROUGH FILES OF... EX-CONS? GOD, WHAT ARE YOU TRYING TO GET ME INTO?
RAY, YOU'RE GOOD AT THE SCIENCE STUFF--BUT THIS IS MY DEPARTMENT. TRUST ME, THERE'S GOTTA BE SOMEONE HERE WHO CAN HELP US GET A LEAD ON SOME..."DONORS."
LET'S GET TO WORK.

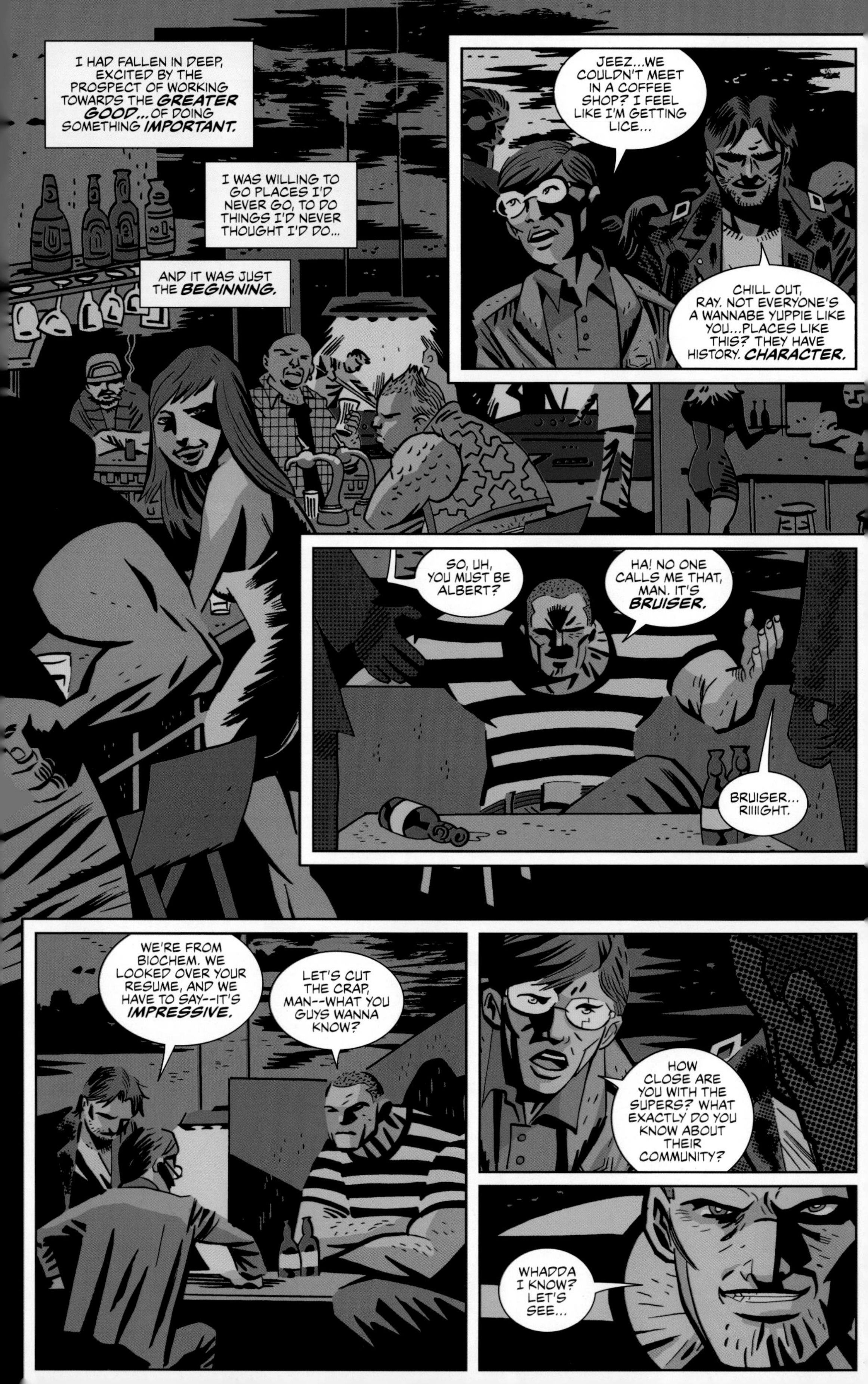
I HAD FALLEN IN DEEP, EXCITED BY THE PROSPECT OF WORKING TOWARDS THE GREATER GOOD...OF DOING SOMETHING IMPORTANT.
I WAS WILLING TO GO PLACES I'D NEVER GO, TO DO THINGS I'D NEVER THOUGHT I'D DO...
AND IT WAS JUST THE BEGINNING.
JEEZ...WE COULDN'T MEET IN A COFFEE SHOP? I FEEL LIKE I'M GETTING LICE...
CHILL OUT, RAY. NOT EVERYONE'S A WANNABE YUPPIE LIKE YOU...PLACES LIKE THIS? THEY HAVE HISTORY. CHARACTER.
SO, UH, YOU MUST BE ALBERT?
HA! NO ONE CALLS ME THAT, MAN. IT'S BRUISER.
BRUISER... RIIIIGHT.
WE'RE FROM BIOCHEM. WE LOOKED OVER YOUR RESUME, AND WE HAVE TO SAY--IT'S IMPRESSIVE.
LET'S CUT THE CRAP, MAN--WHAT YOU GUYS WANNA KNOW?
HOW CLOSE ARE YOU WITH THE SUPERS? WHAT EXACTLY DO YOU KNOW ABOUT THEIR COMMUNITY?
WHADDA I KNOW? LET'S SEE...

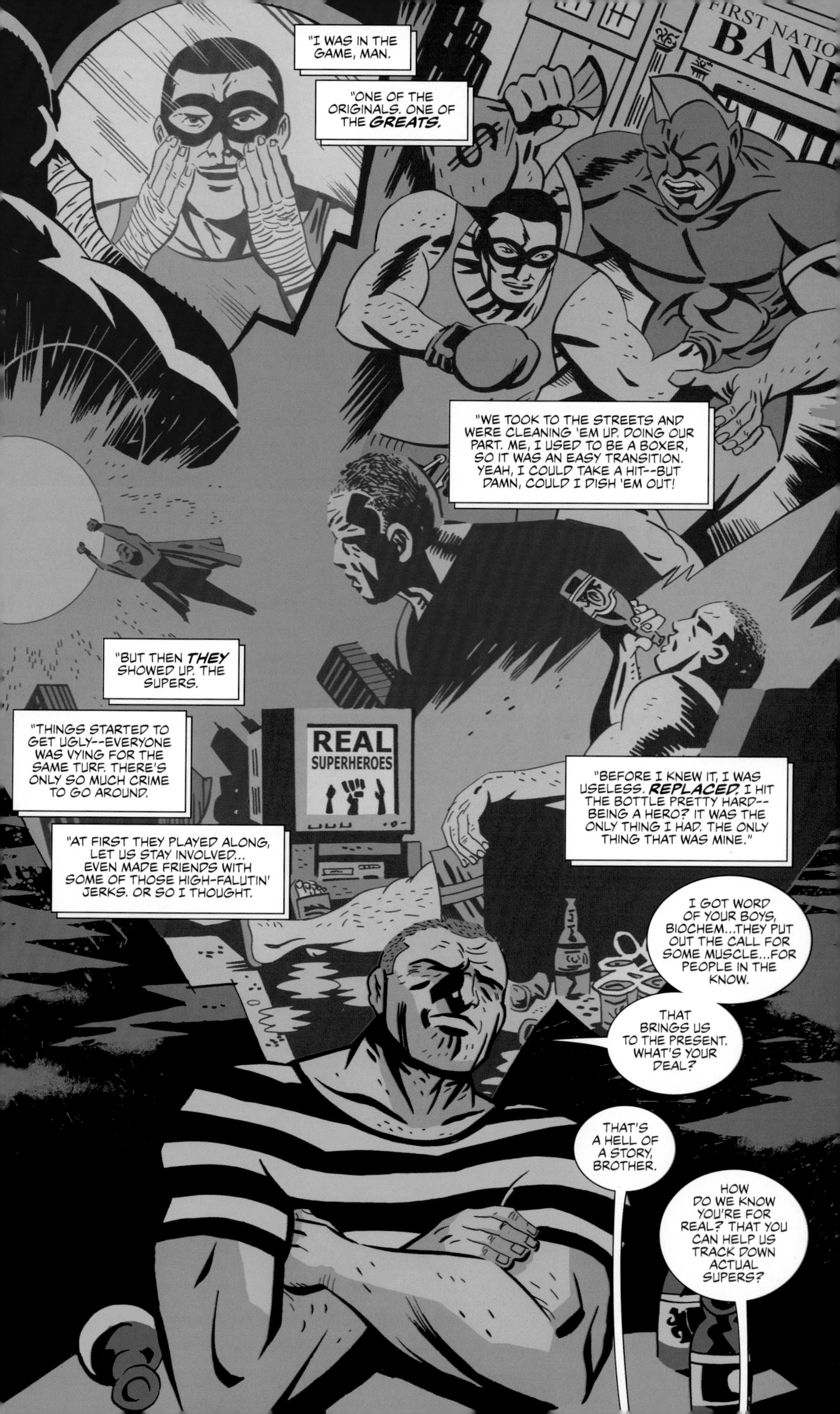
"I WAS IN THE GAME, MAN.
"ONE OF THE ORIGINALS. ONE OF THE GREATS.
FIRST NATIO BANK
"WE TOOK TO THE STREETS AND WERE CLEANING 'EM UP. DOING OUR PART. ME, I USED TO BE A BOXER, SO IT WAS AN EASY TRANSITION. YEAH, I COULD TAKE A HIT--BUT DAMN, COULD I DISH 'EM OUT!
"BUT THEN THEY SHOWED UP. THE SUPERS.
"THINGS STARTED TO GET UGLY--EVERYONE WAS VYING FOR THE SAME TURF. THERE'S ONLY SO MUCH CRIME TO GO AROUND.
REAL SUPERHEROES
"AT FIRST THEY PLAYED ALONG, LET US STAY INVOLVED... EVEN MADE FRIENDS WITH SOME OF THOSE HIGH-FALUTIN' JERKS. OR SO I THOUGHT.
"BEFORE I KNEW IT, I WAS USELESS. REPLACED. I HIT THE BOTTLE PRETTY HARD-- BEING A HERO? IT WAS THE ONLY THING I HAD. THE ONLY THING THAT WAS MINE."
I GOT WORD OF YOUR BOYS, BIOCHEM...THEY PUT OUT THE CALL FOR SOME MUSCLE...FOR PEOPLE IN THE KNOW.
THAT BRINGS US TO THE PRESENT. WHAT'S YOUR DEAL?
THAT'S A HELL OF A STORY, BROTHER.
HOW DO WE KNOW YOU'RE FOR REAL? THAT YOU CAN HELP US TRACK DOWN ACTUAL SUPERS?

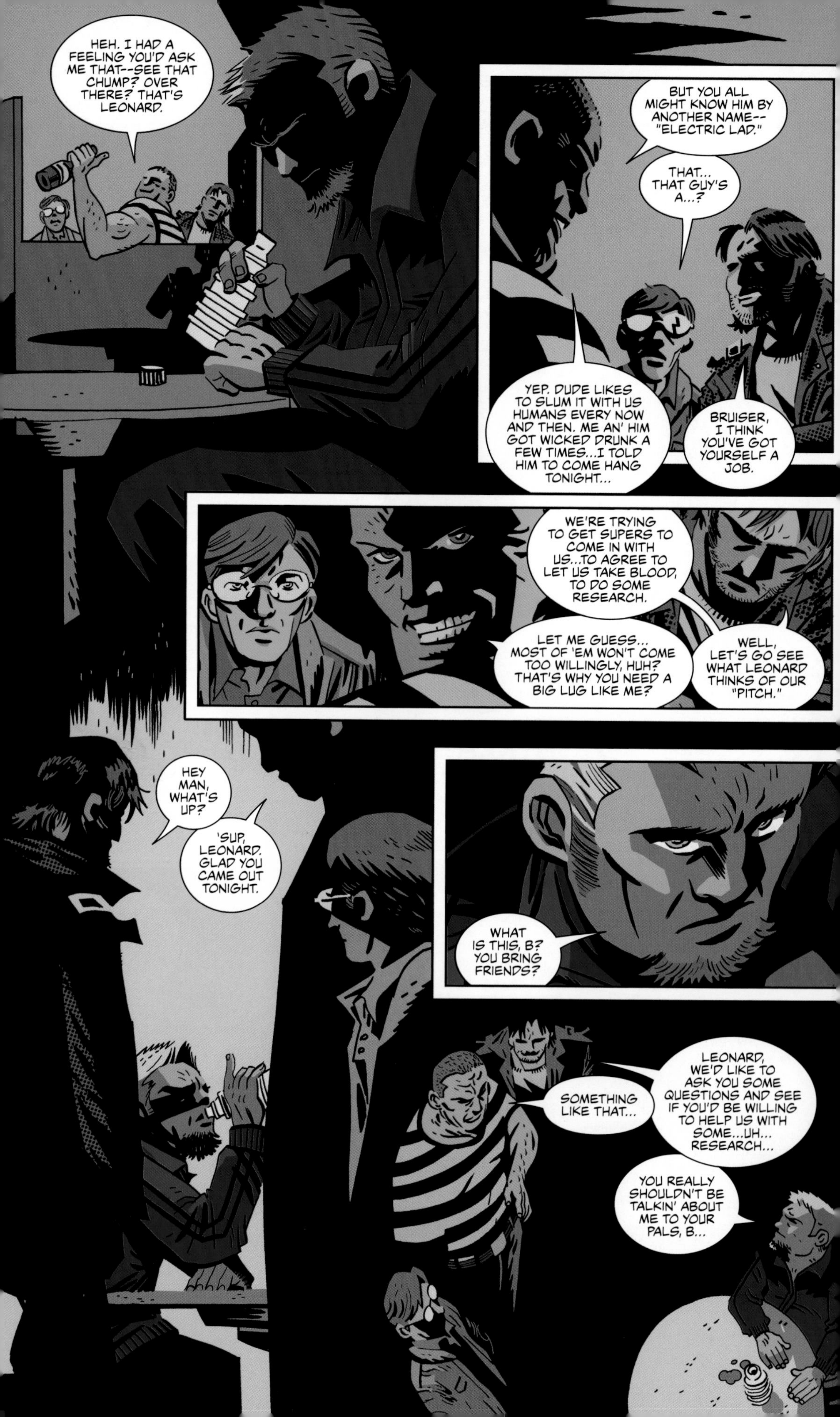
HEH. I HAD A FEELING YOU'D ASK ME THAT--SEE THAT CHUMP? OVER THERE? THAT'S LEONARD.
BUT YOU ALL MIGHT KNOW HIM BY ANOTHER NAME-- "ELECTRIC LAD."
THAT... THAT GUY'S A...?
YEP. DUDE LIKES TO SLUM IT WITH US HUMANS EVERY NOW AND THEN. ME AN' HIM GOT WICKED DRUNK A FEW TIMES...I TOLD HIM TO COME HANG TONIGHT...
BRUISER, I THINK YOU'VE GOT YOURSELF A JOB.
WE'RE TRYING TO GET SUPERS TO COME IN WITH US...TO AGREE TO LET US TAKE BLOOD, TO DO SOME RESEARCH.
LET ME GUESS... MOST OF 'EM WON'T COME TOO WILLINGLY, HUH? THAT'S WHY YOU NEED A BIG LUG LIKE ME?
WELL, LET'S GO SEE WHAT LEONARD THINKS OF OUR "PITCH."
HEY MAN, WHAT'S UP?
'SUP, LEONARD. GLAD YOU CAME OUT TONIGHT.
WHAT IS THIS, B? YOU BRING FRIENDS?
SOMETHING LIKE THAT...
LEONARD, WE'D LIKE TO ASK YOU SOME QUESTIONS AND SEE IF YOU'D BE WILLING TO HELP US WITH SOME...UH... RESEARCH...
YOU REALLY SHOULDN'T BE TALKIN' ABOUT ME TO YOUR PALS, B...

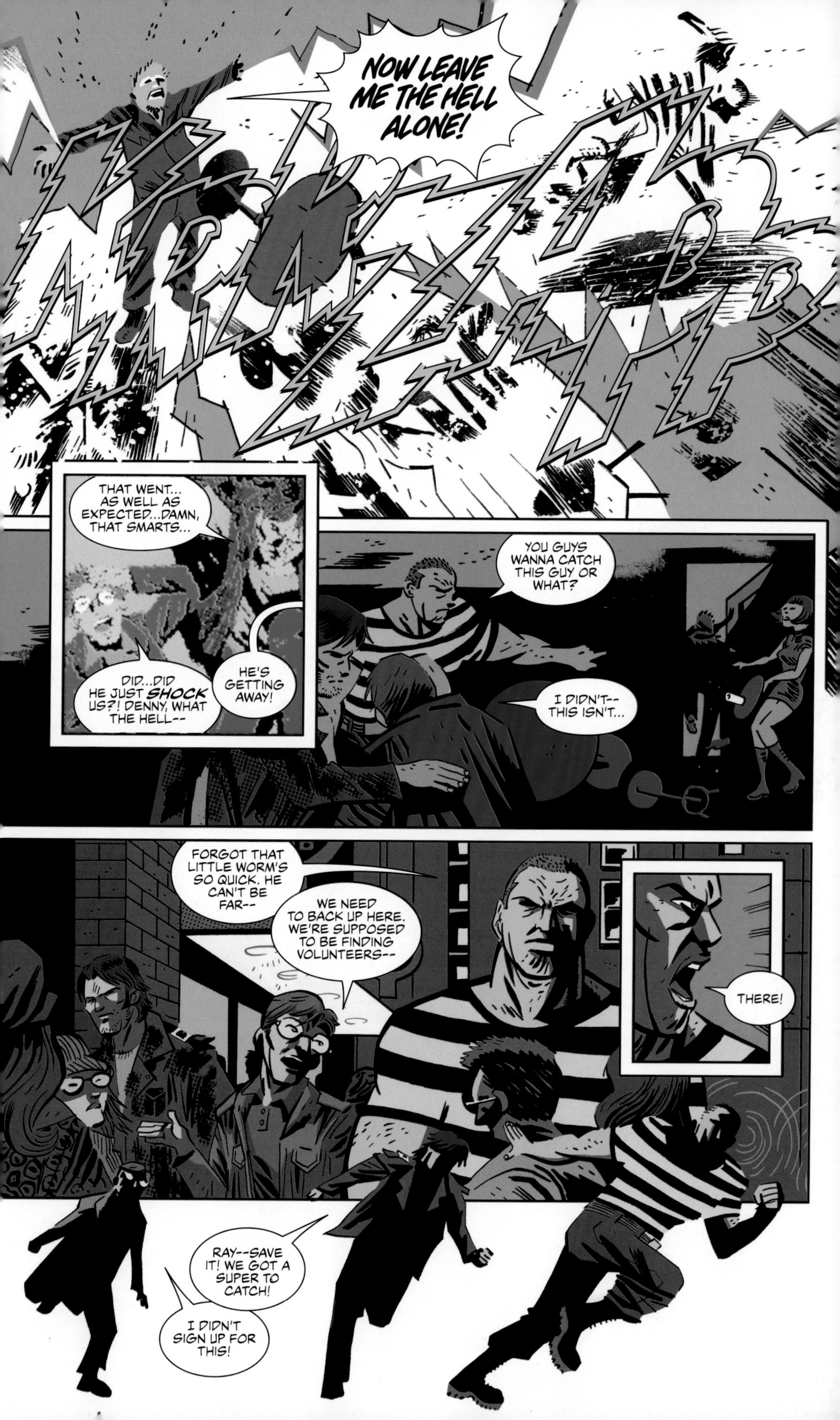
NOW LEAVE ME THE HELL ALONE!
THAT WENT... AS WELL AS EXPECTED...DAMN, THAT SMARTS...
YOU GUYS WANNA CATCH THIS GUY OR WHAT?
DID...DID HE JUST SHOCK US?! DENNY, WHAT THE HELL--
HE'S GETTING AWAY!
I DIDN'T-- THIS ISN'T...
FORGOT THAT LITTLE WORM'S SO QUICK. HE CAN'T BE FAR--
WE NEED TO BACK UP HERE. WE'RE SUPPOSED TO BE FINDING VOLUNTEERS--
THERE!
RAY--SAVE IT! WE GOT A SUPER TO CATCH!
I DIDN'T SIGN UP FOR THIS!

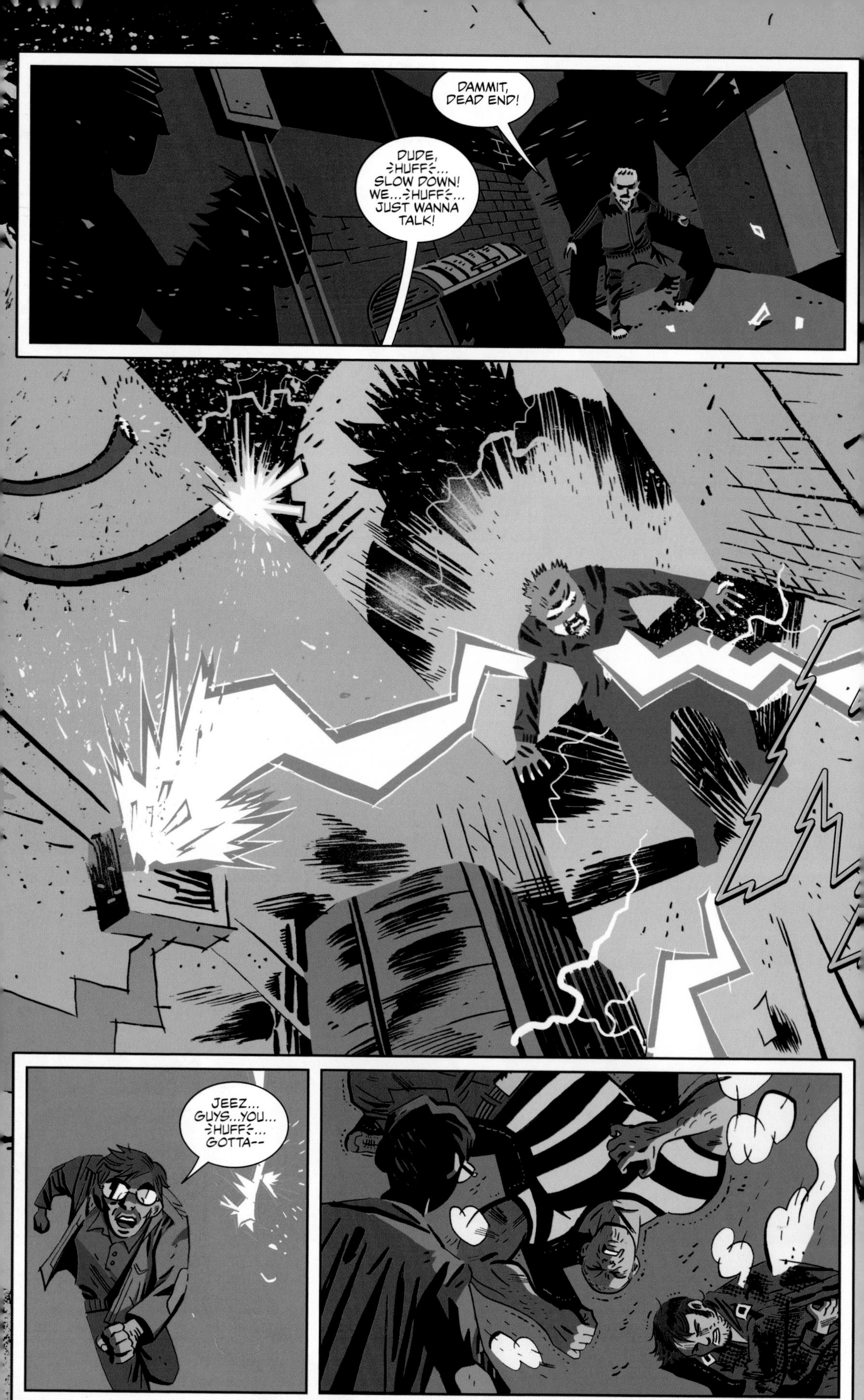

DAMMIT, DEAD END!
DUDE, *HUFF*... SLOW DOWN! WE... *HUFF*... JUST WANNA TALK!
JEEZ... GUYS...YOU... *HUFF*... GOTTA--

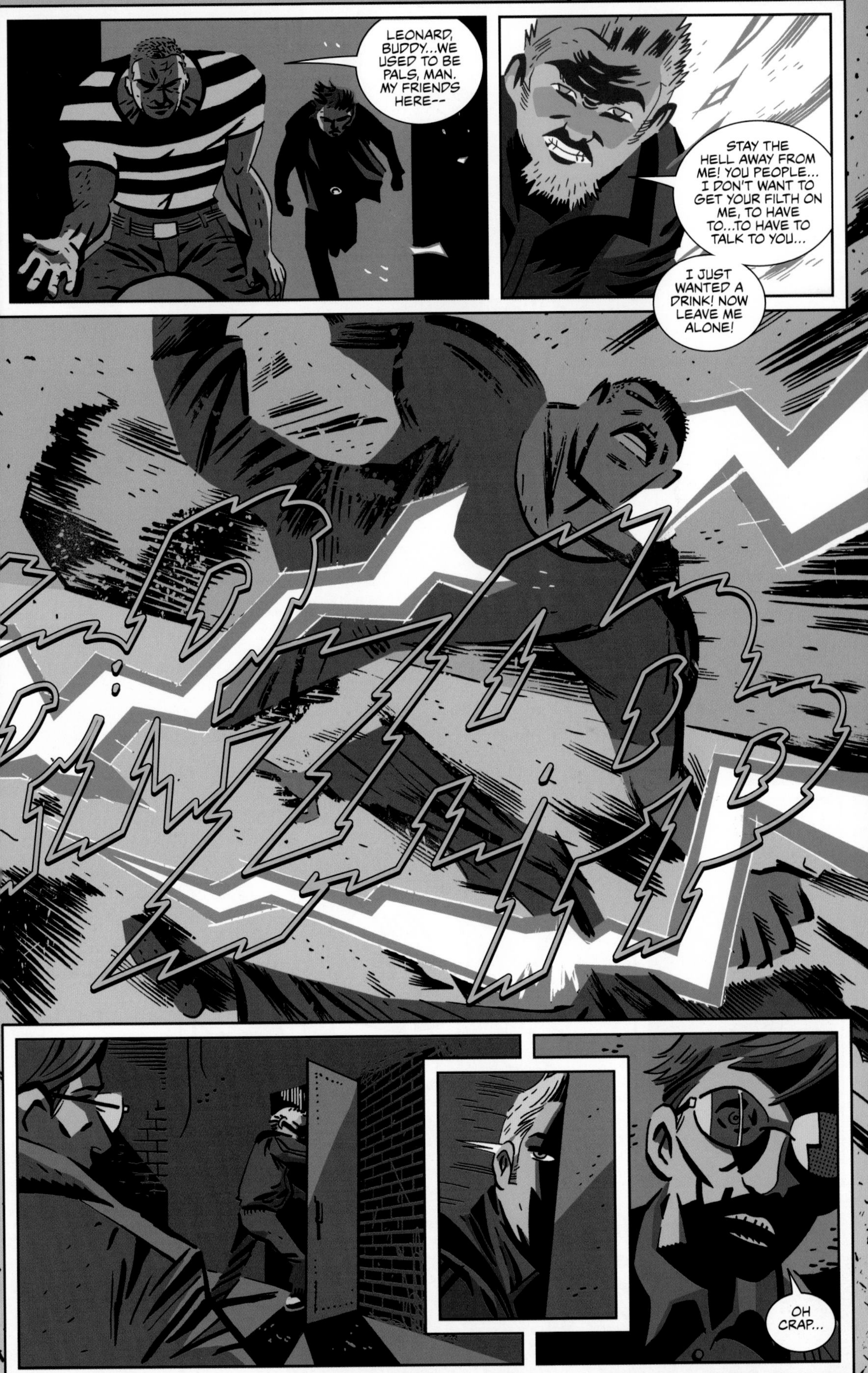
LEONARD, BUDDY...WE USED TO BE PALS, MAN. MY FRIENDS HERE--
STAY THE HELL AWAY FROM ME! YOU PEOPLE... I DON'T WANT TO GET YOUR FILTH ON ME, TO HAVE TO...TO HAVE TO TALK TO YOU...
I JUST WANTED A DRINK! NOW LEAVE ME ALONE!
OH CRAP...

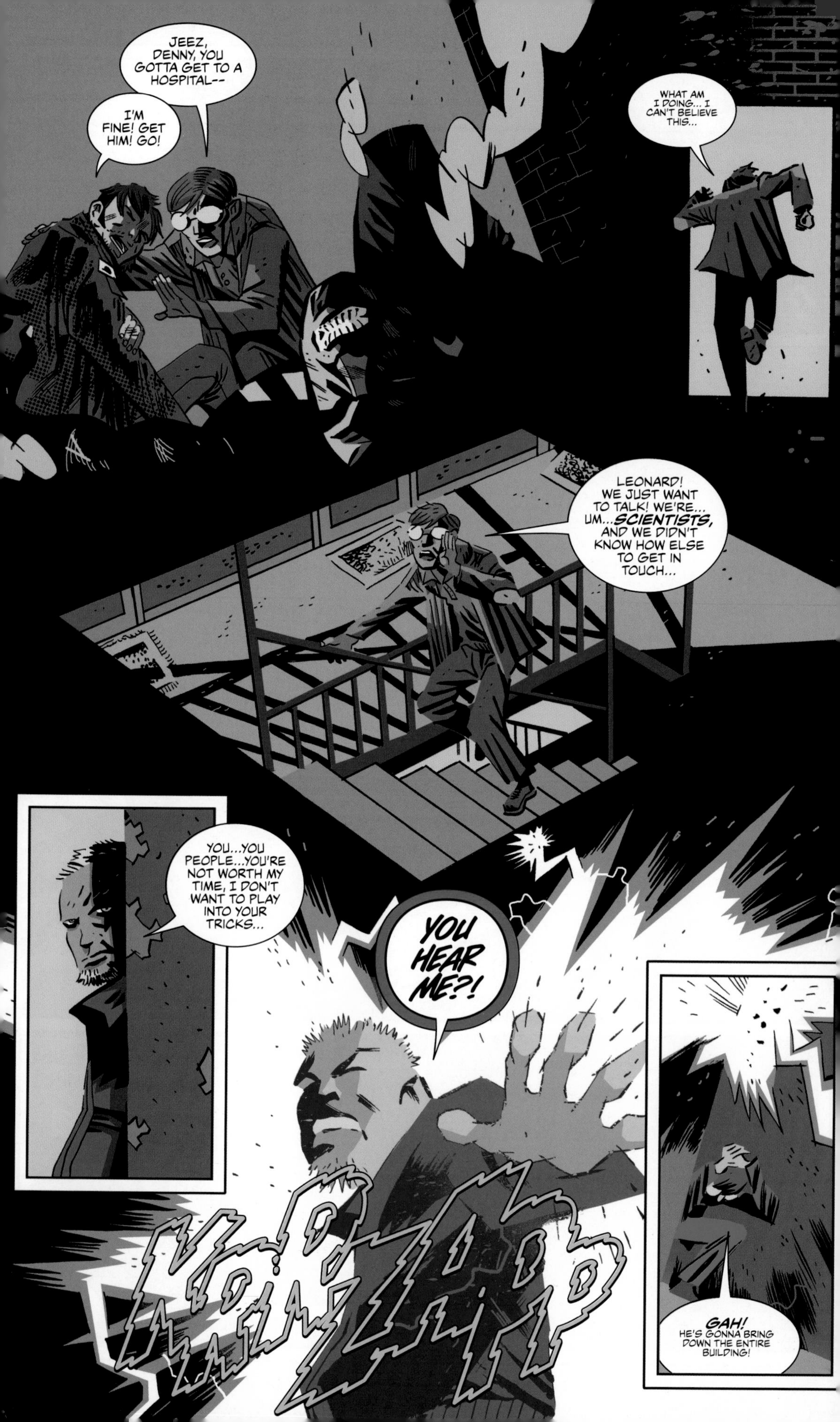
JEEZ, DENNY, YOU GOTTA GET TO A HOSPITAL--
I'M FINE! GET HIM! GO!
WHAT AM I DOING... I CAN'T BELIEVE THIS...
LEONARD! WE JUST WANT TO TALK! WE'RE... UM...SCIENTISTS, AND WE DIDN'T KNOW HOW ELSE TO GET IN TOUCH...
YOU...YOU PEOPLE...YOU'RE NOT WORTH MY TIME, I DON'T WANT TO PLAY INTO YOUR TRICKS...
YOU HEAR ME?!
GAH! HE'S GONNA BRING DOWN THE ENTIRE BUILDING!

YOU ASKED FOR THIS! NOW--

GARRGHH!

YOU DAMN SUPERS! MONSTERS! WE GOTS 'NUFF PROBLEMS IN THIS HOOD WITHOUT YOUR KIND RIPPING UP OUR 'PARTMENTS!

GET OUTTA HERE, YOU FREAK!

MY ONLY CHANCE--

YOU STUPID PEOPLE...

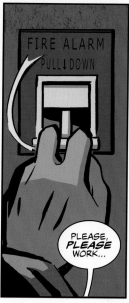

FIRE ALARM
PULL DOWN

PLEASE, *PLEASE* WORK...

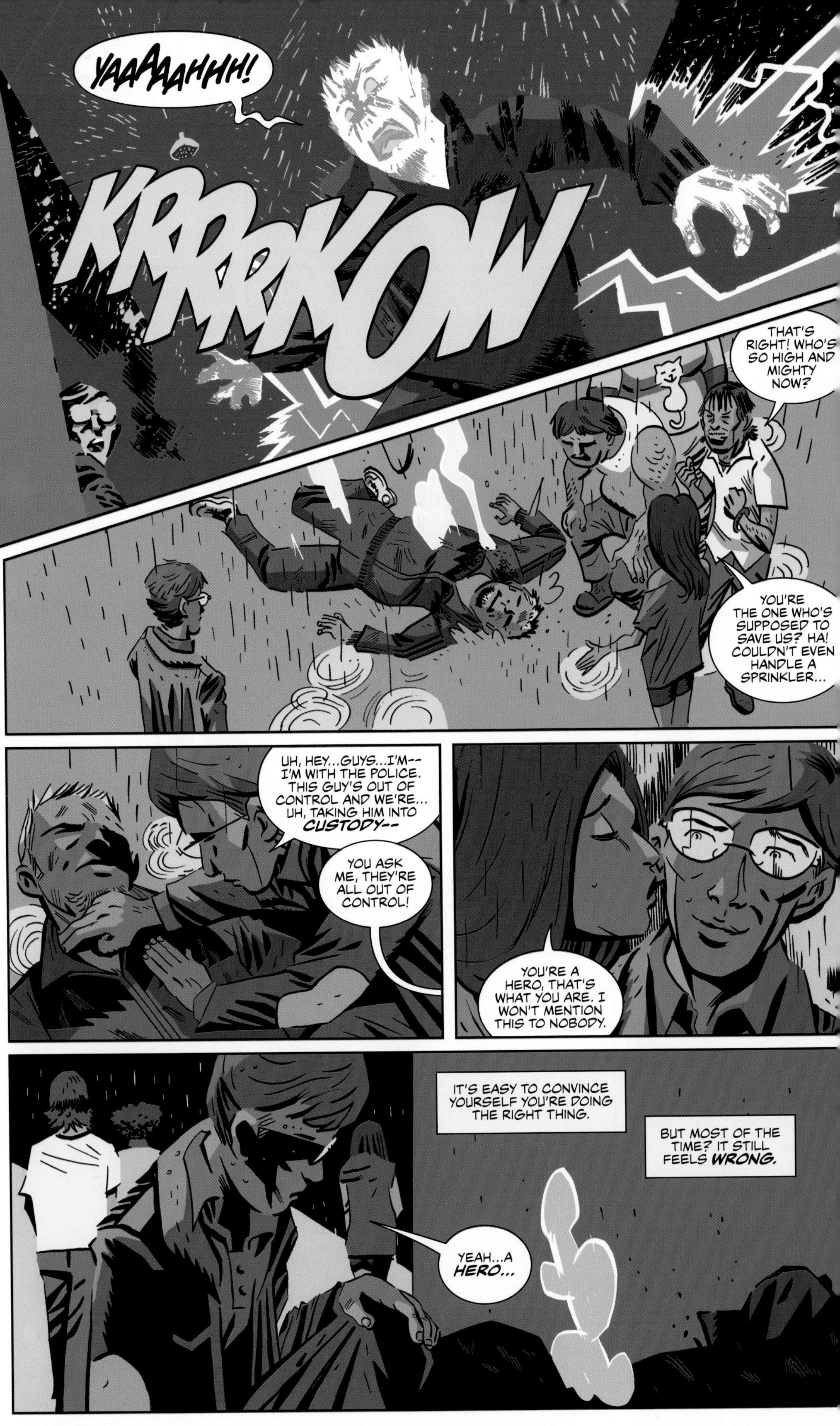
YAAAAAHHH!
KRRRRKOW
THAT'S RIGHT! WHO'S SO HIGH AND MIGHTY NOW?
YOU'RE THE ONE WHO'S SUPPOSED TO SAVE US? HA! COULDN'T EVEN HANDLE A SPRINKLER...
UH, HEY...GUYS...I'M--I'M WITH THE POLICE. THIS GUY'S OUT OF CONTROL AND WE'RE... UH, TAKING HIM INTO CUSTODY--
YOU ASK ME, THEY'RE ALL OUT OF CONTROL!
YOU'RE A HERO, THAT'S WHAT YOU ARE. I WON'T MENTION THIS TO NOBODY.
IT'S EASY TO CONVINCE YOURSELF YOU'RE DOING THE RIGHT THING.
BUT MOST OF THE TIME? IT STILL FEELS WRONG.
YEAH...A HERO...

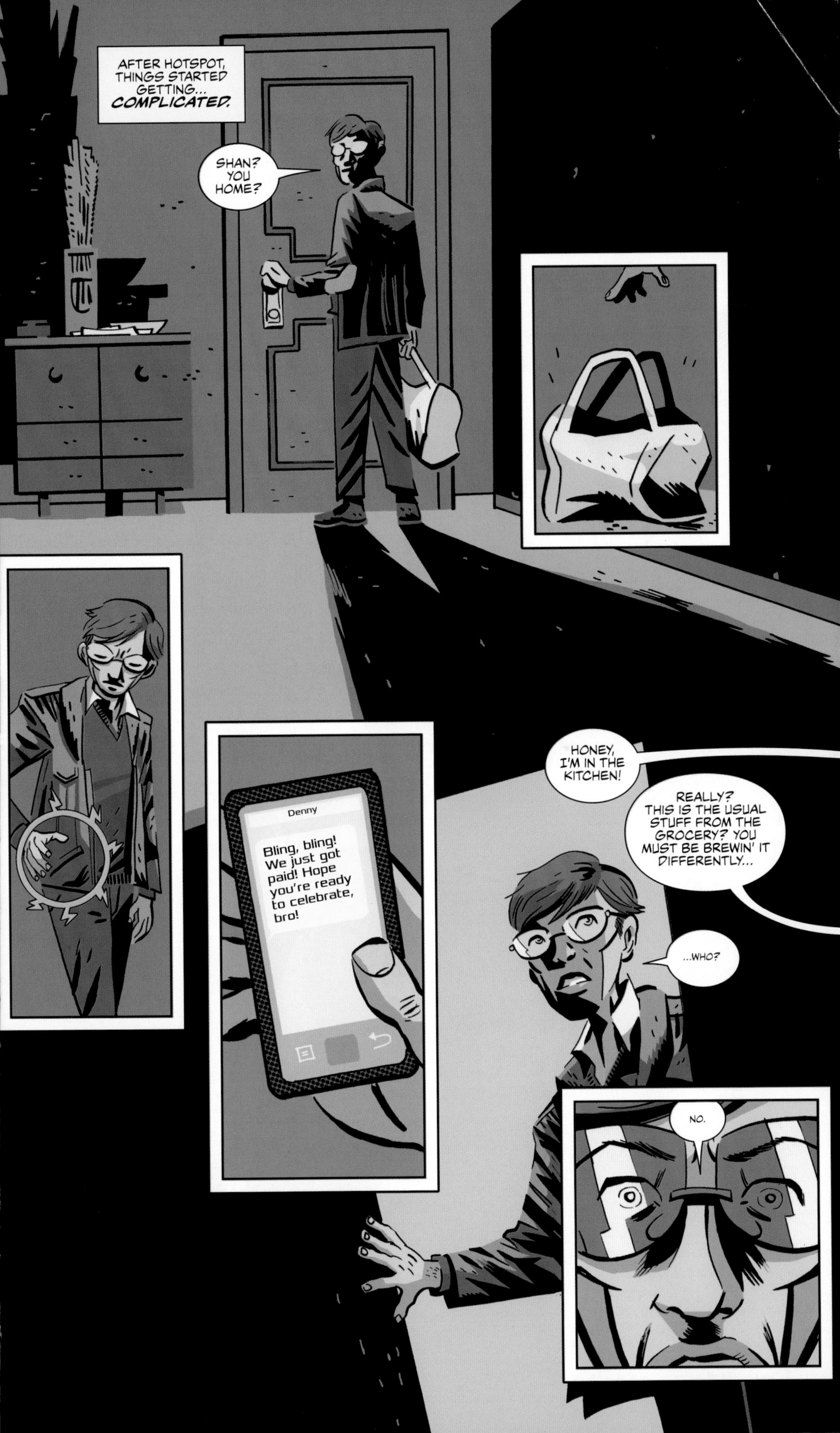
AFTER HOTSPOT, THINGS STARTED GETTING... COMPLICATED.
SHAN? YOU HOME?
Denny
Bling, bling! We just got paid! Hope you're ready to celebrate, bro!
HONEY, I'M IN THE KITCHEN!
REALLY? THIS IS THE USUAL STUFF FROM THE GROCERY? YOU MUST BE BREWIN' IT DIFFERENTLY...
...WHO?
NO.

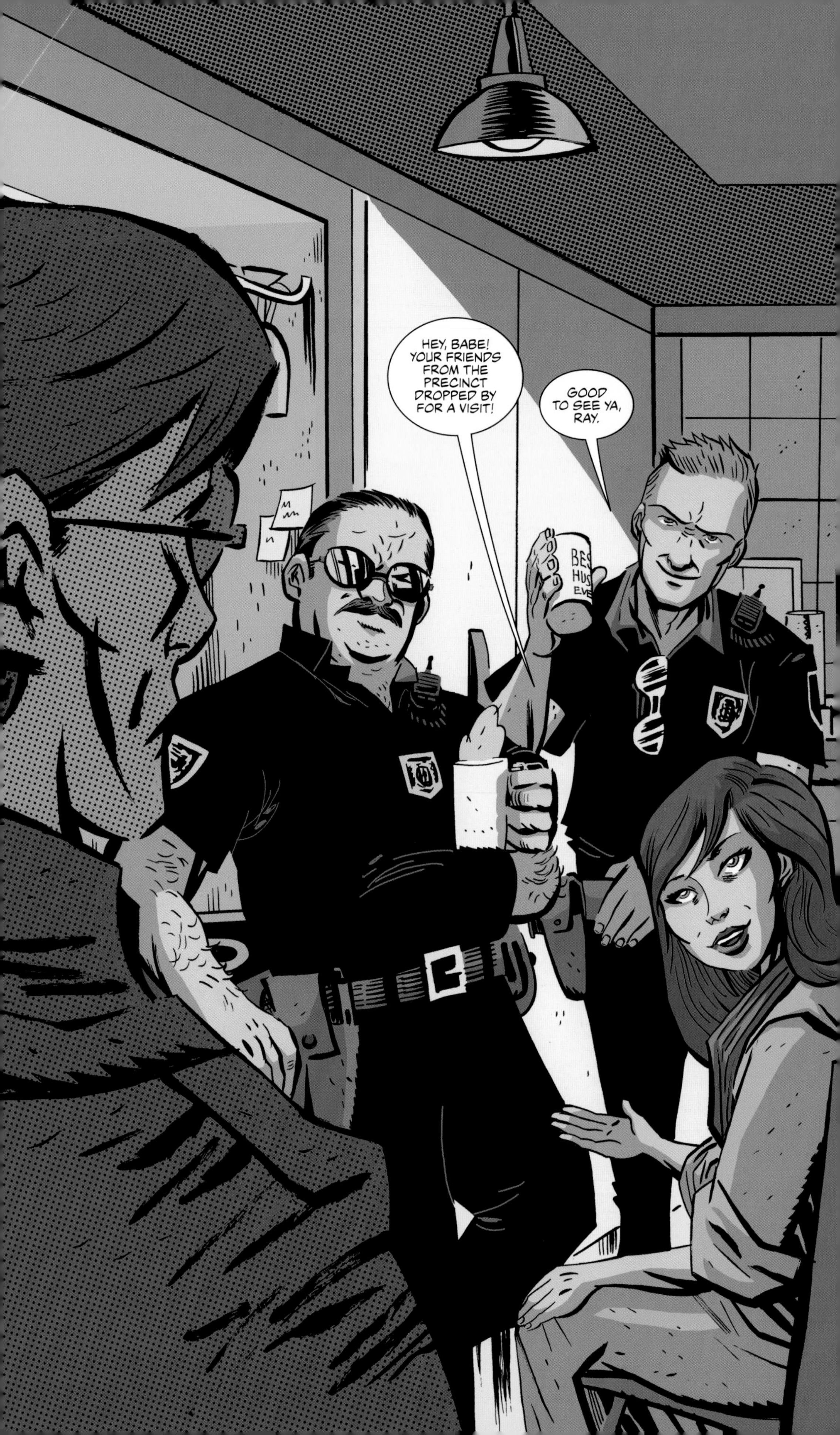
HEY, BABE! YOUR FRIENDS FROM THE PRECINCT DROPPED BY FOR A VISIT!
GOOD TO SEE YA, RAY.

chapter three

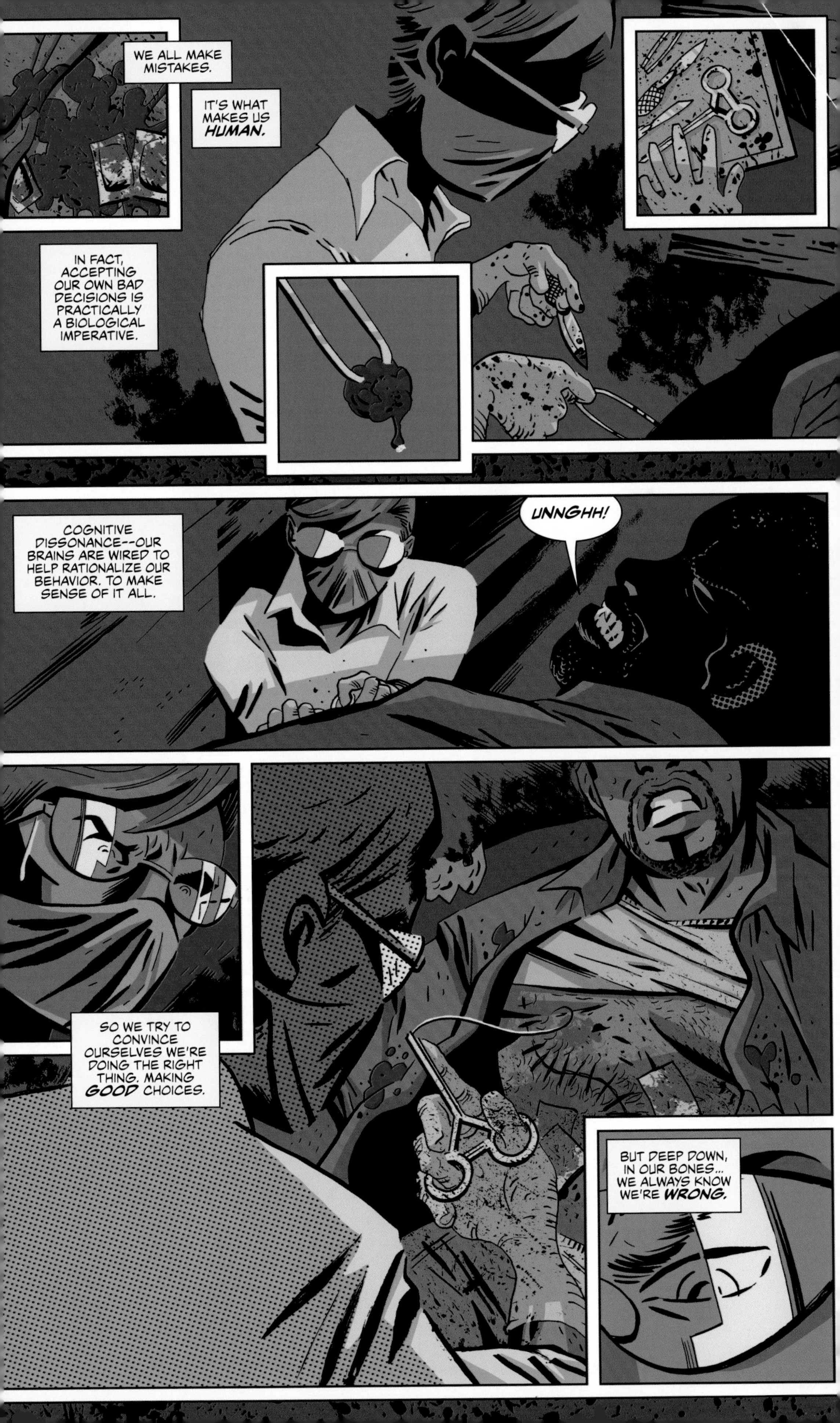
WE ALL MAKE MISTAKES.
IT'S WHAT MAKES US *HUMAN.*
IN FACT, ACCEPTING OUR OWN BAD DECISIONS IS PRACTICALLY A BIOLOGICAL IMPERATIVE.
COGNITIVE DISSONANCE--OUR BRAINS ARE WIRED TO HELP RATIONALIZE OUR BEHAVIOR. TO MAKE SENSE OF IT ALL.
UNNGHH!
SO WE TRY TO CONVINCE OURSELVES WE'RE DOING THE RIGHT THING. MAKING *GOOD* CHOICES.
BUT DEEP DOWN, IN OUR BONES... WE ALWAYS KNOW WE'RE *WRONG.*

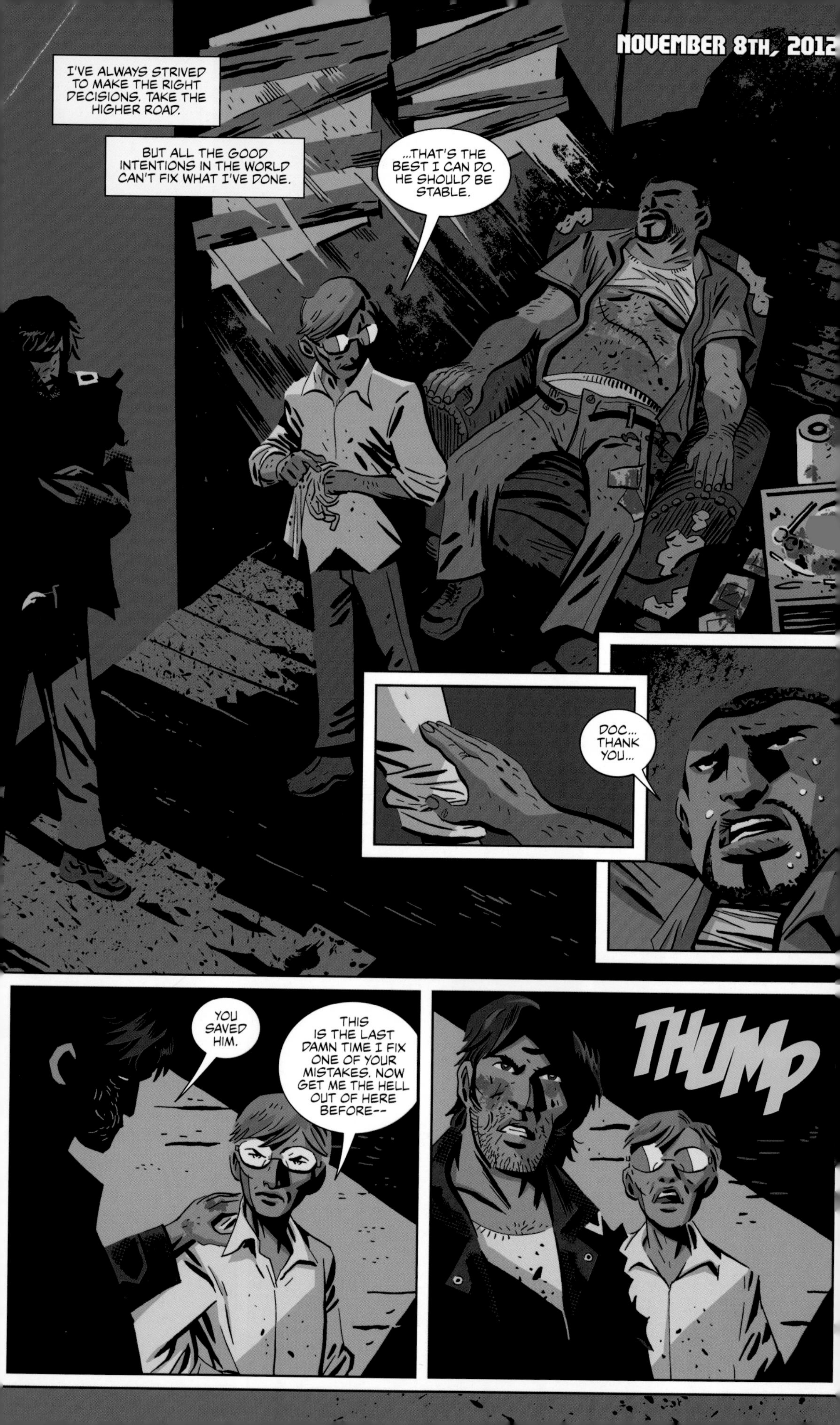
NOVEMBER 8TH, 2012
I'VE ALWAYS STRIVED TO MAKE THE RIGHT DECISIONS. TAKE THE HIGHER ROAD.
BUT ALL THE GOOD INTENTIONS IN THE WORLD CAN'T FIX WHAT I'VE DONE.
...THAT'S THE BEST I CAN DO. HE SHOULD BE STABLE.
DOC... THANK YOU...
YOU SAVED HIM.
THIS IS THE LAST DAMN TIME I FIX ONE OF YOUR MISTAKES. NOW GET ME THE HELL OUT OF HERE BEFORE--
THUMP

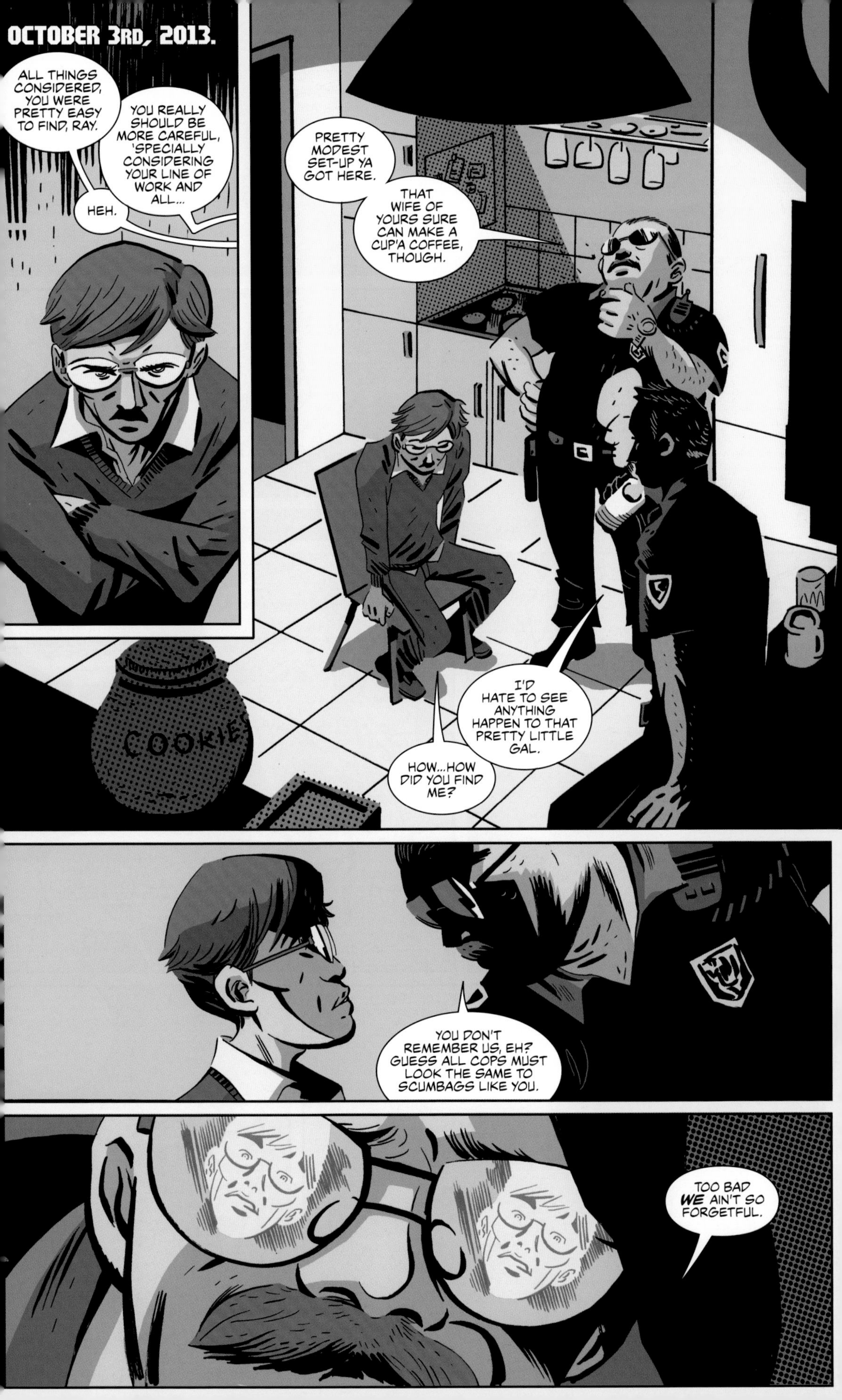

OCTOBER 3RD, 2013.
ALL THINGS CONSIDERED, YOU WERE PRETTY EASY TO FIND, RAY.
HEH.
YOU REALLY SHOULD BE MORE CAREFUL, 'SPECIALLY CONSIDERING YOUR LINE OF WORK AND ALL...
PRETTY MODEST SET-UP YA GOT HERE.
THAT WIFE OF YOURS SURE CAN MAKE A CUP'A COFFEE, THOUGH.
I'D HATE TO SEE ANYTHING HAPPEN TO THAT PRETTY LITTLE GAL.
HOW...HOW DID YOU FIND ME?
COOKIES
YOU DON'T REMEMBER US, EH? GUESS ALL COPS MUST LOOK THE SAME TO SCUMBAGS LIKE YOU.
TOO BAD WE AIN'T SO FORGETFUL.

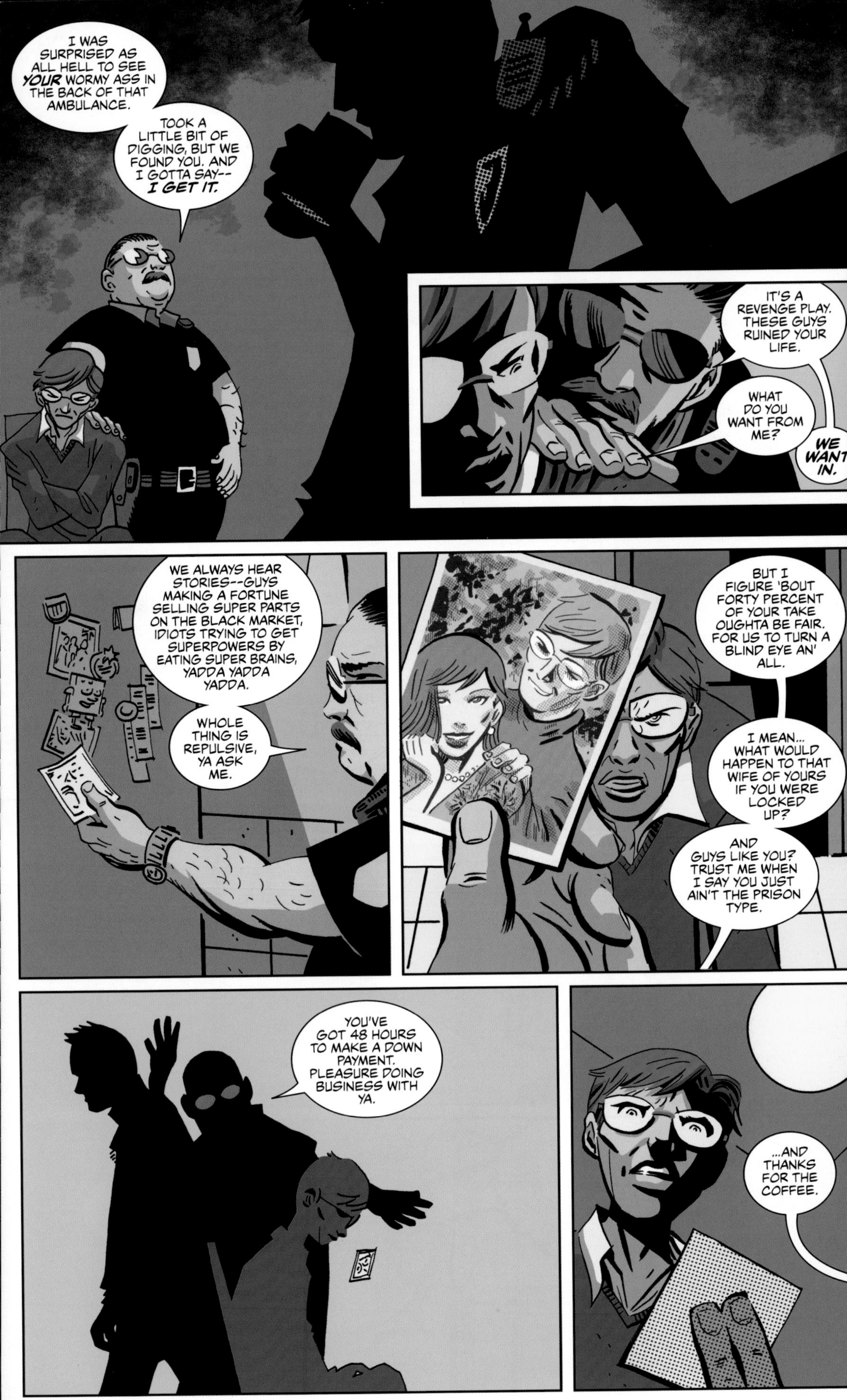
I WAS SURPRISED AS ALL HELL TO SEE *YOUR* WORMY ASS IN THE BACK OF THAT AMBULANCE.
TOOK A LITTLE BIT OF DIGGING, BUT WE FOUND YOU. AND I GOTTA SAY-- *I GET IT.*
IT'S A REVENGE PLAY. THESE GUYS RUINED YOUR LIFE.
WHAT DO YOU WANT FROM ME?
WE WANT IN.
WE ALWAYS HEAR STORIES--GUYS MAKING A FORTUNE SELLING SUPER PARTS ON THE BLACK MARKET, IDIOTS TRYING TO GET SUPERPOWERS BY EATING SUPER BRAINS, YADDA YADDA YADDA.
WHOLE THING IS REPULSIVE, YA ASK ME.
BUT I FIGURE 'BOUT FORTY PERCENT OF YOUR TAKE OUGHTA BE FAIR. FOR US TO TURN A BLIND EYE AN' ALL.
I MEAN... WHAT WOULD HAPPEN TO THAT WIFE OF YOURS IF YOU WERE LOCKED UP?
AND GUYS LIKE YOU? TRUST ME WHEN I SAY YOU JUST AIN'T THE PRISON TYPE.
YOU'VE GOT 48 HOURS TO MAKE A DOWN PAYMENT. PLEASURE DOING BUSINESS WITH YA.
...AND THANKS FOR THE COFFEE.

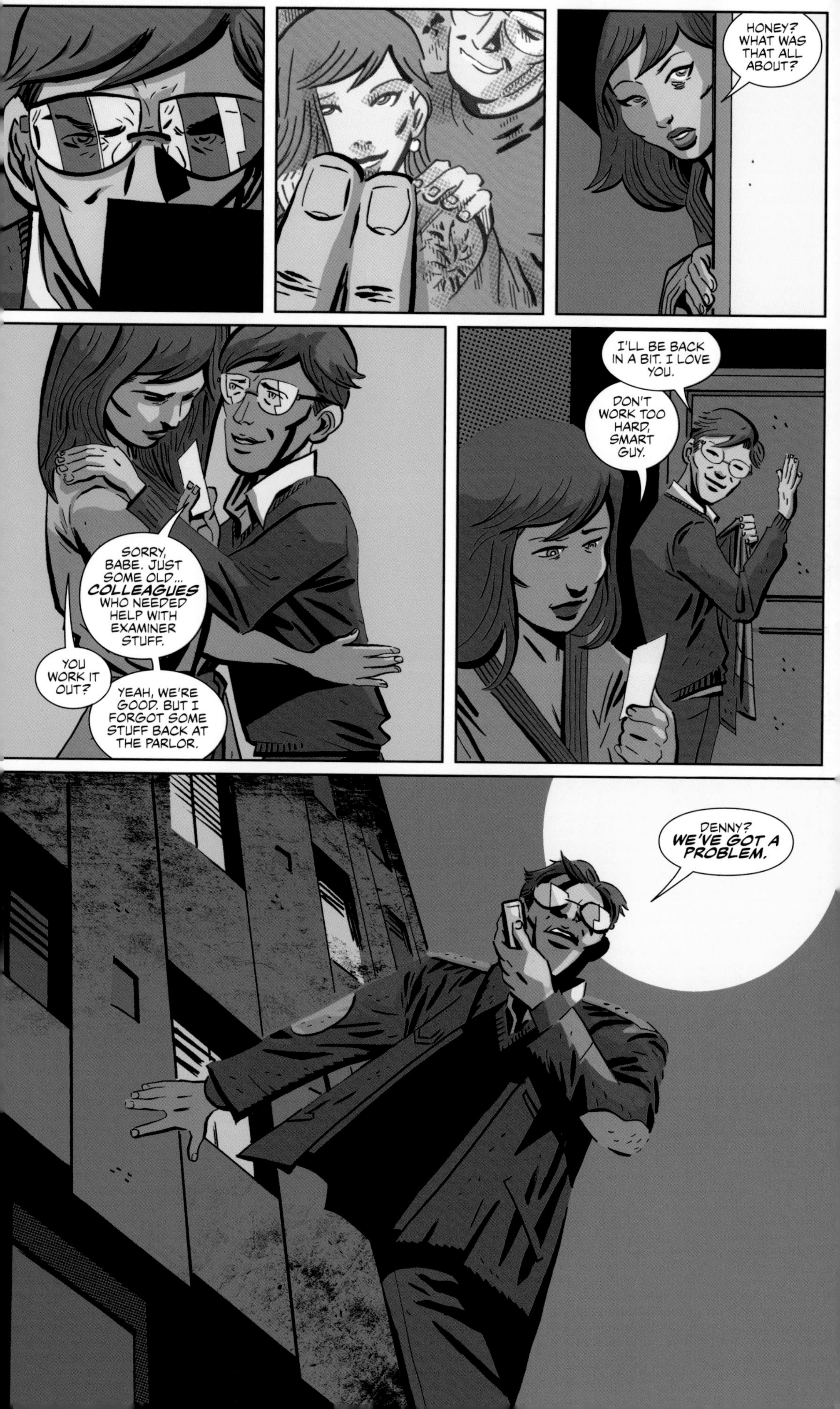
HONEY? WHAT WAS THAT ALL ABOUT?
SORRY, BABE. JUST SOME OLD... COLLEAGUES WHO NEEDED HELP WITH EXAMINER STUFF.
YOU WORK IT OUT?
YEAH, WE'RE GOOD. BUT I FORGOT SOME STUFF BACK AT THE PARLOR.
I'LL BE BACK IN A BIT. I LOVE YOU.
DON'T WORK TOO HARD, SMART GUY.
DENNY? WE'VE GOT A PROBLEM.

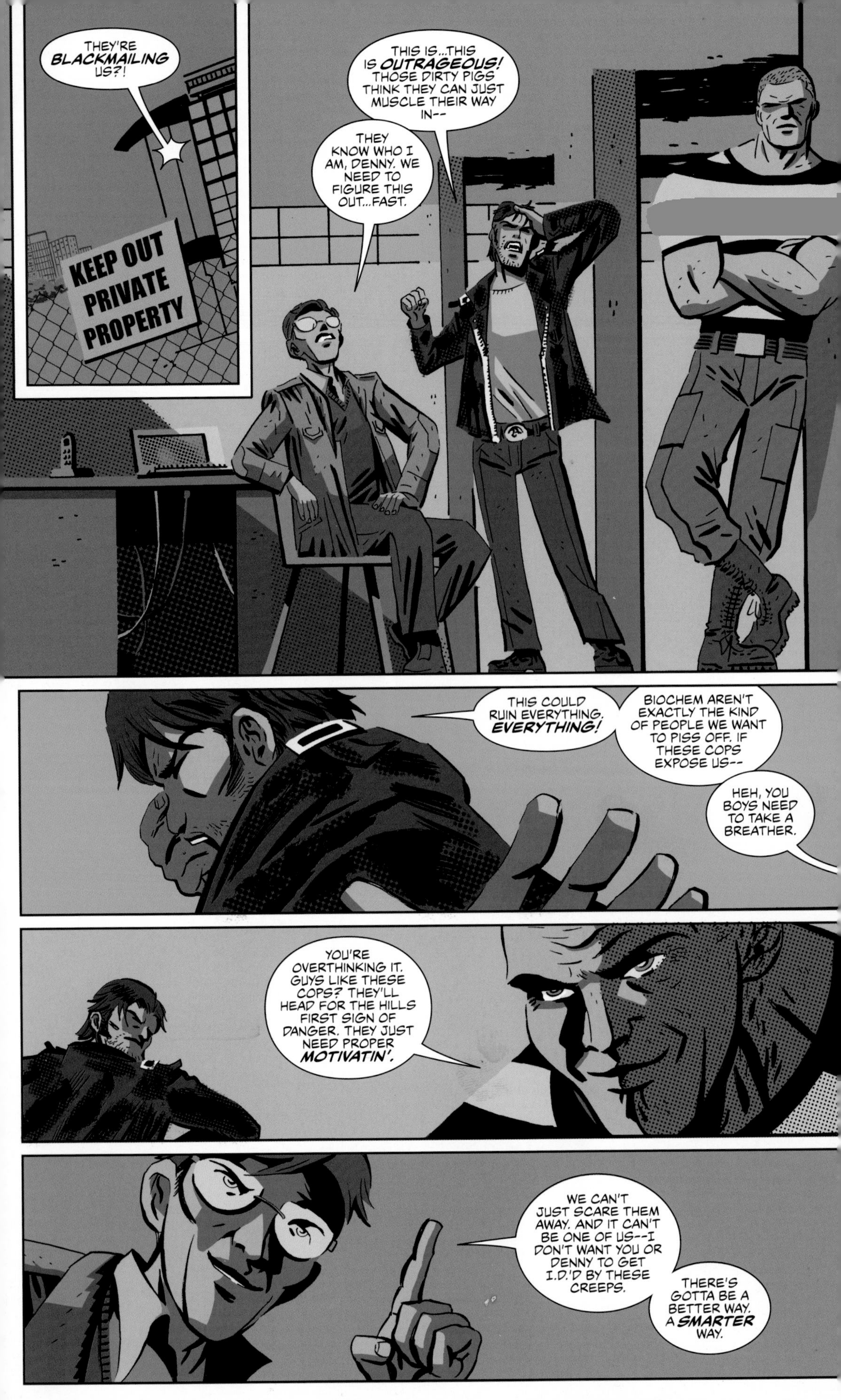
THEY'RE BLACKMAILING US?!
THIS IS...THIS IS OUTRAGEOUS! THOSE DIRTY PIGS THINK THEY CAN JUST MUSCLE THEIR WAY IN--
THEY KNOW WHO I AM, DENNY. WE NEED TO FIGURE THIS OUT...FAST.
KEEP OUT PRIVATE PROPERTY
THIS COULD RUIN EVERYTHING. EVERYTHING!
BIOCHEM AREN'T EXACTLY THE KIND OF PEOPLE WE WANT TO PISS OFF. IF THESE COPS EXPOSE US--
HEH, YOU BOYS NEED TO TAKE A BREATHER.
YOU'RE OVERTHINKING IT. GUYS LIKE THESE COPS? THEY'LL HEAD FOR THE HILLS FIRST SIGN OF DANGER. THEY JUST NEED PROPER MOTIVATIN'.
WE CAN'T JUST SCARE THEM AWAY. AND IT CAN'T BE ONE OF US--I DON'T WANT YOU OR DENNY TO GET I.D.'D BY THESE CREEPS.
THERE'S GOTTA BE A BETTER WAY. A SMARTER WAY.

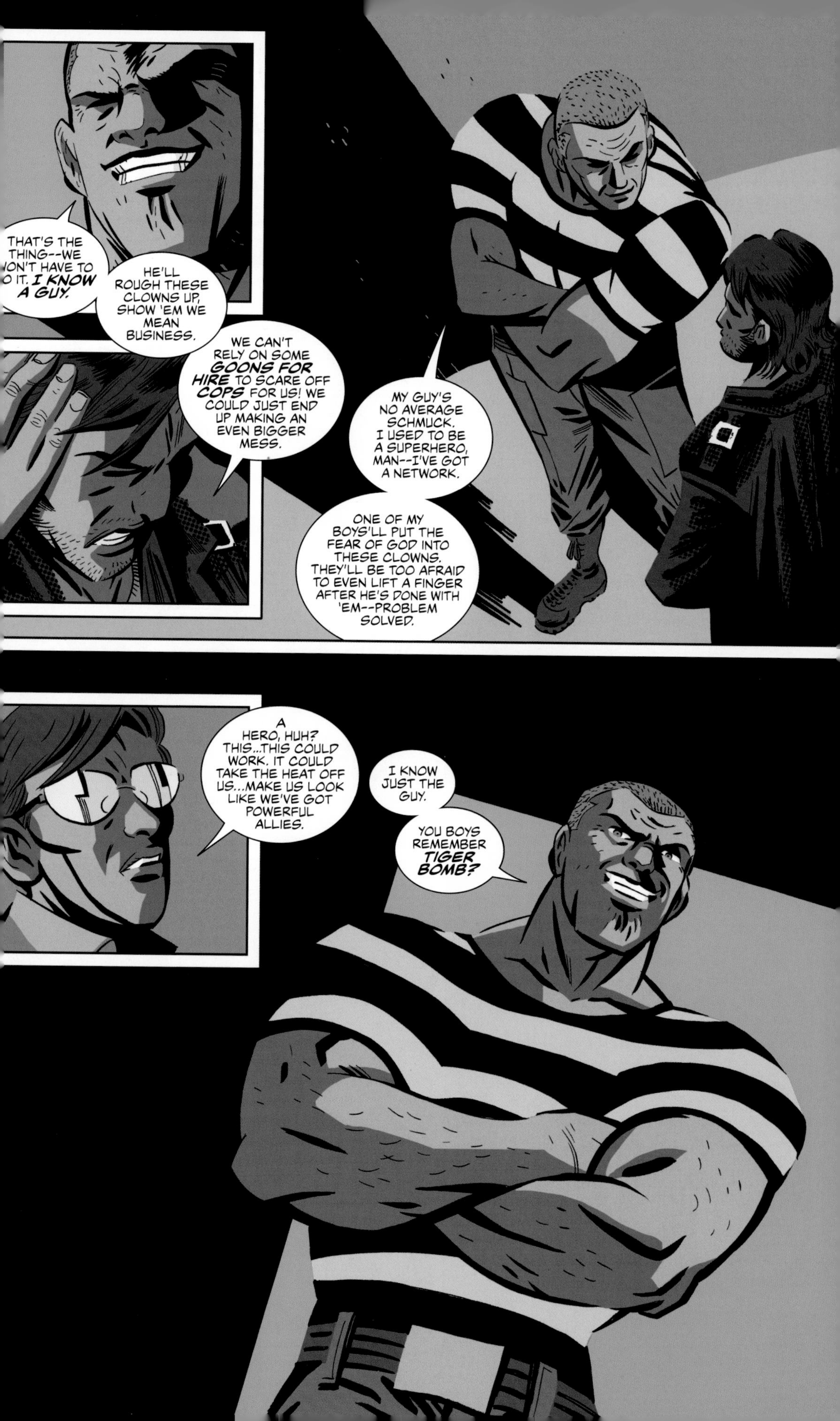

THAT'S THE THING--WE WON'T HAVE TO DO IT. I KNOW A GUY.
HE'LL ROUGH THESE CLOWNS UP, SHOW 'EM WE MEAN BUSINESS.
WE CAN'T RELY ON SOME GOONS FOR HIRE TO SCARE OFF COPS FOR US! WE COULD JUST END UP MAKING AN EVEN BIGGER MESS.
MY GUY'S NO AVERAGE SCHMUCK. I USED TO BE A SUPERHERO, MAN--I'VE GOT A NETWORK.
ONE OF MY BOYS'LL PUT THE FEAR OF GOD INTO THESE CLOWNS. THEY'LL BE TOO AFRAID TO EVEN LIFT A FINGER AFTER HE'S DONE WITH 'EM--PROBLEM SOLVED.
A HERO, HUH? THIS...THIS COULD WORK. IT COULD TAKE THE HEAT OFF US...MAKE US LOOK LIKE WE'VE GOT POWERFUL ALLIES.
I KNOW JUST THE GUY.
YOU BOYS REMEMBER TIGER BOMB?

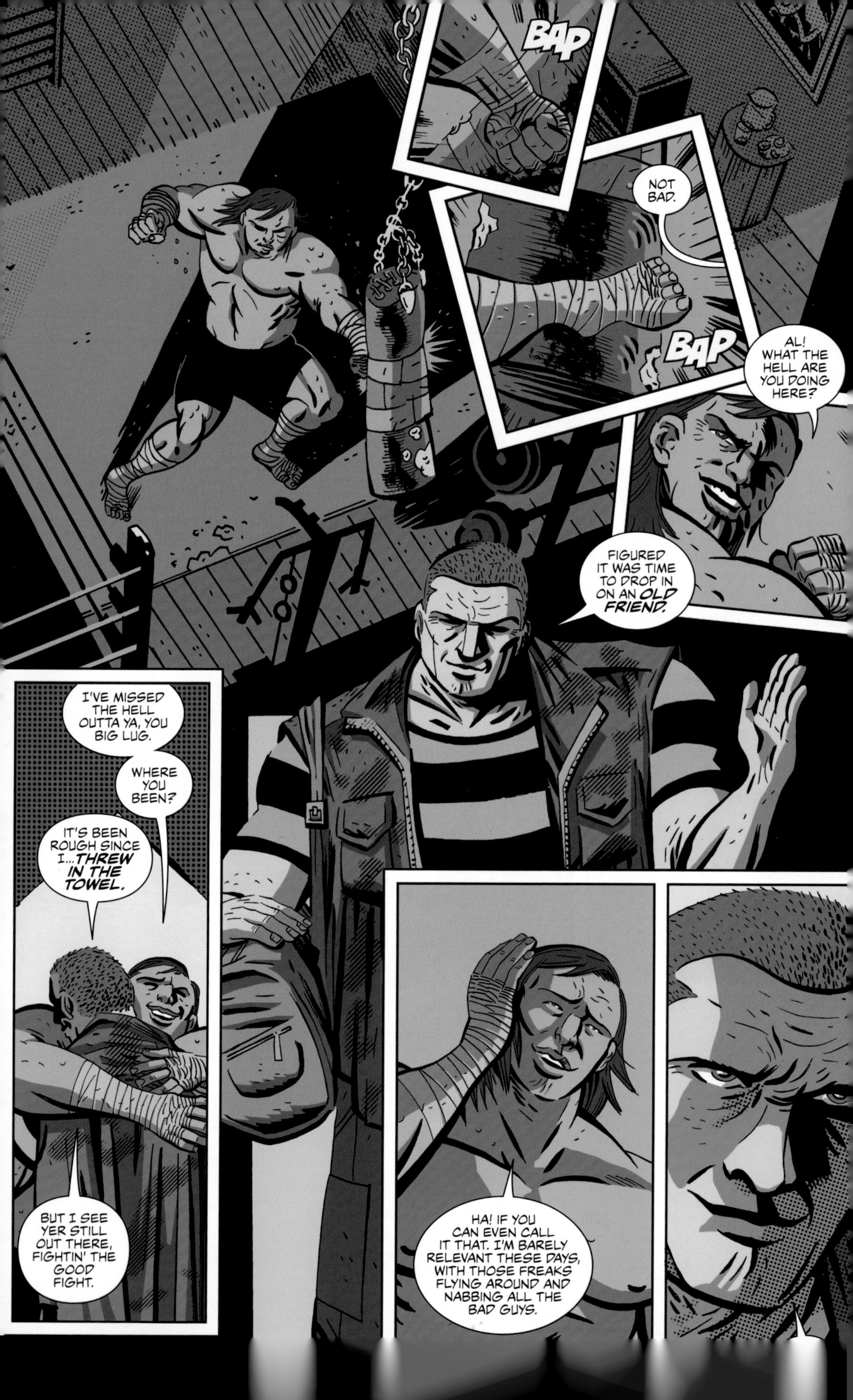
BAP
NOT BAD.
BAP
AL! WHAT THE HELL ARE YOU DOING HERE?
FIGURED IT WAS TIME TO DROP IN ON AN OLD FRIEND.
I'VE MISSED THE HELL OUTTA YA, YOU BIG LUG.
WHERE YOU BEEN?
IT'S BEEN ROUGH SINCE I...THREW IN THE TOWEL.
BUT I SEE YER STILL OUT THERE, FIGHTIN' THE GOOD FIGHT.
HA! IF YOU CAN EVEN CALL IT THAT. I'M BARELY RELEVANT THESE DAYS, WITH THOSE FREAKS FLYING AROUND AND NABBING ALL THE BAD GUYS.

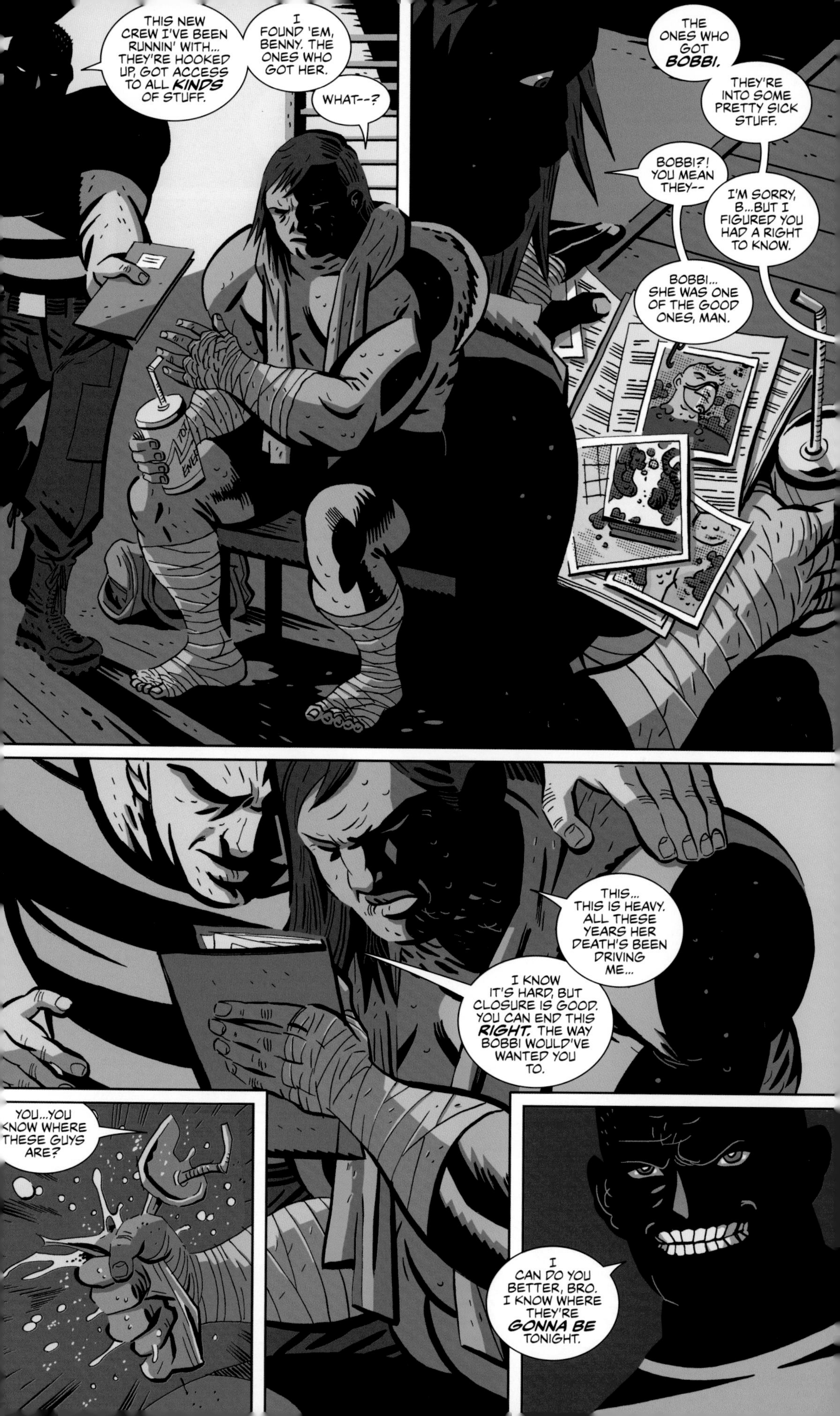
THIS NEW CREW I'VE BEEN RUNNIN' WITH... THEY'RE HOOKED UP, GOT ACCESS TO ALL KINDS OF STUFF.
I FOUND 'EM, BENNY. THE ONES WHO GOT HER.
WHAT--?
THE ONES WHO GOT BOBBI.
THEY'RE INTO SOME PRETTY SICK STUFF.
BOBBI?! YOU MEAN THEY--
I'M SORRY, B...BUT I FIGURED YOU HAD A RIGHT TO KNOW.
BOBBI... SHE WAS ONE OF THE GOOD ONES, MAN.
THIS... THIS IS HEAVY. ALL THESE YEARS HER DEATH'S BEEN DRIVING ME...
I KNOW IT'S HARD, BUT CLOSURE IS GOOD. YOU CAN END THIS RIGHT. THE WAY BOBBI WOULD'VE WANTED YOU TO.
YOU...YOU KNOW WHERE THESE GUYS ARE?
I CAN DO YOU BETTER, BRO. I KNOW WHERE THEY'RE GONNA BE TONIGHT.

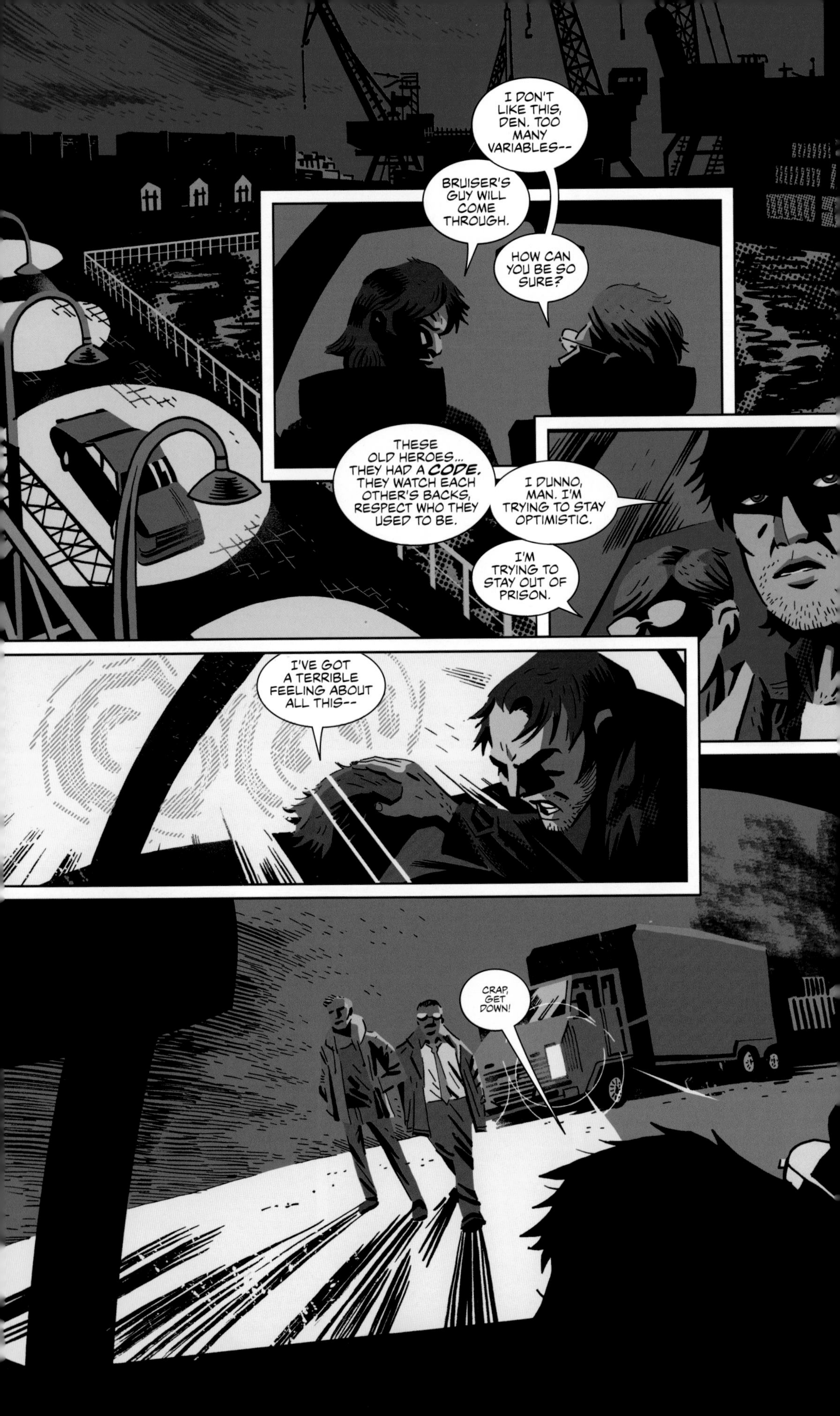
I DON'T LIKE THIS, DEN. TOO MANY VARIABLES--
BRUISER'S GUY WILL COME THROUGH.
HOW CAN YOU BE SO SURE?
THESE OLD HEROES... THEY HAD A CODE. THEY WATCH EACH OTHER'S BACKS, RESPECT WHO THEY USED TO BE.
I DUNNO, MAN. I'M TRYING TO STAY OPTIMISTIC.
I'M TRYING TO STAY OUT OF PRISON.
I'VE GOT A TERRIBLE FEELING ABOUT ALL THIS--
CRAP, GET DOWN!

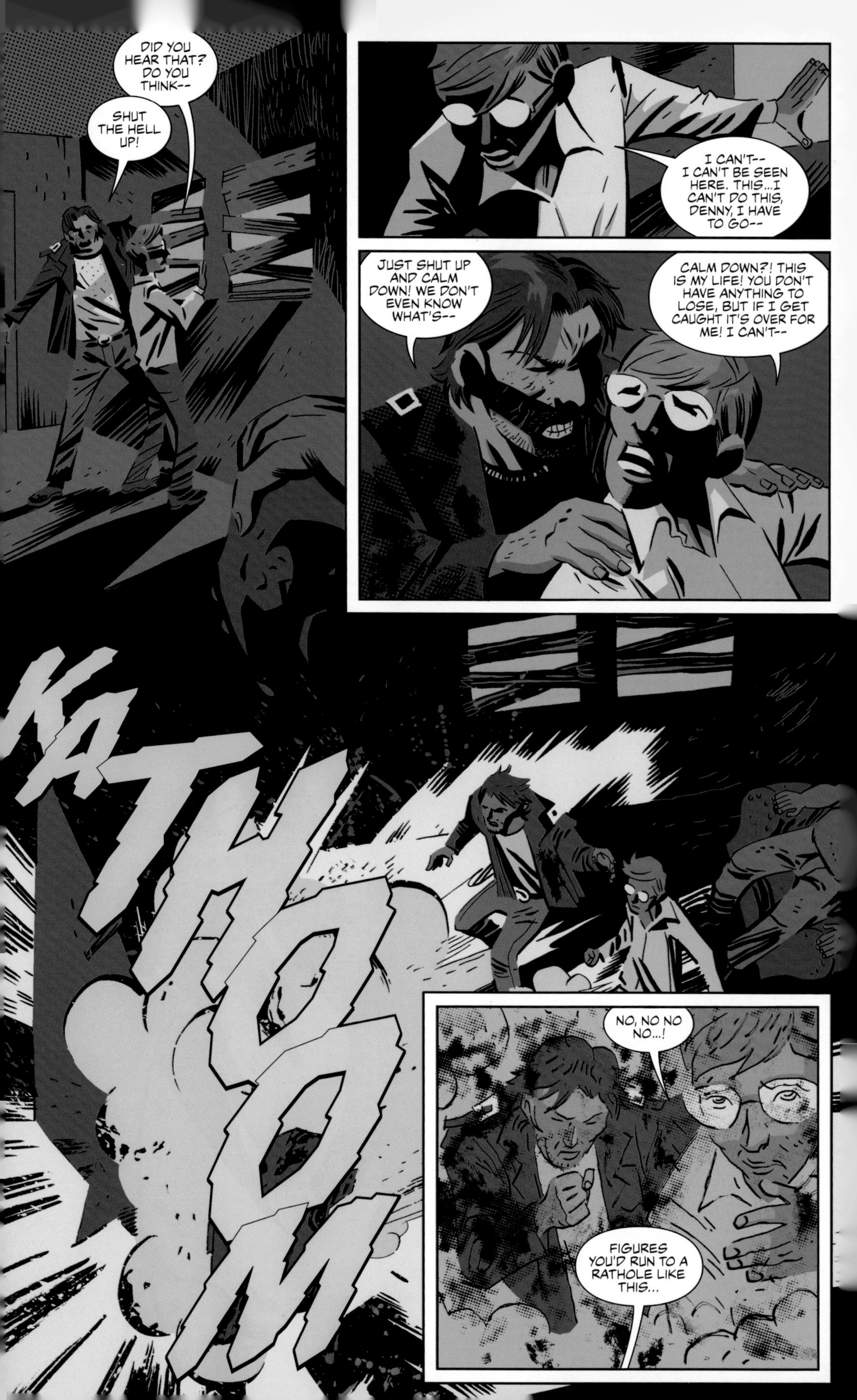
DID YOU HEAR THAT? DO YOU THINK--
SHUT THE HELL UP!
I CAN'T-- I CAN'T BE SEEN HERE. THIS...I CAN'T DO THIS, DENNY, I HAVE TO GO--
JUST SHUT UP AND CALM DOWN! WE DON'T EVEN KNOW WHAT'S--
CALM DOWN?! THIS IS MY LIFE! YOU DON'T HAVE ANYTHING TO LOSE, BUT IF I GET CAUGHT IT'S OVER FOR ME! I CAN'T--
KATHOOM
NO, NO NO NO...!
FIGURES YOU'D RUN TO A RATHOLE LIKE THIS...

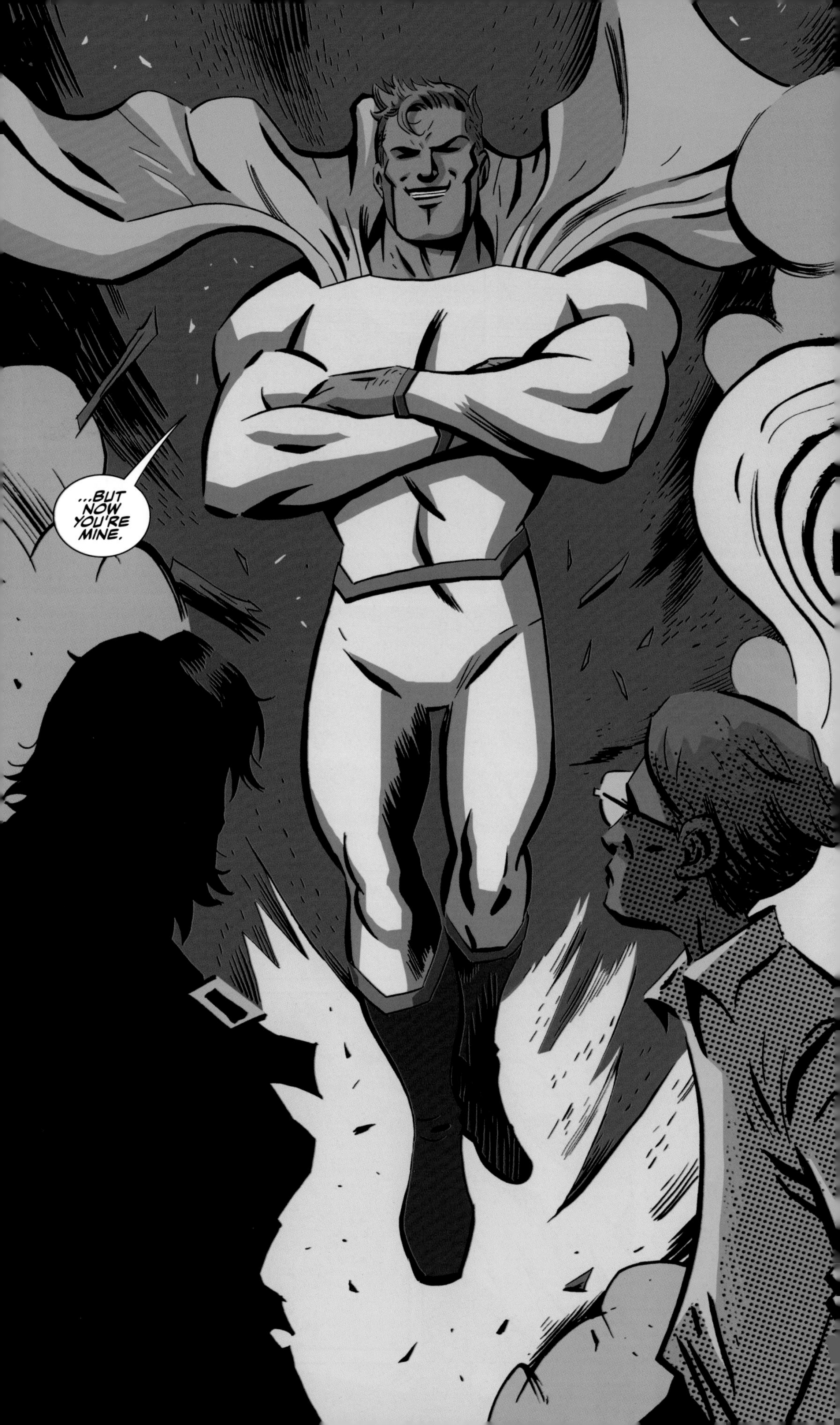
...BUT NOW YOU'RE MINE.

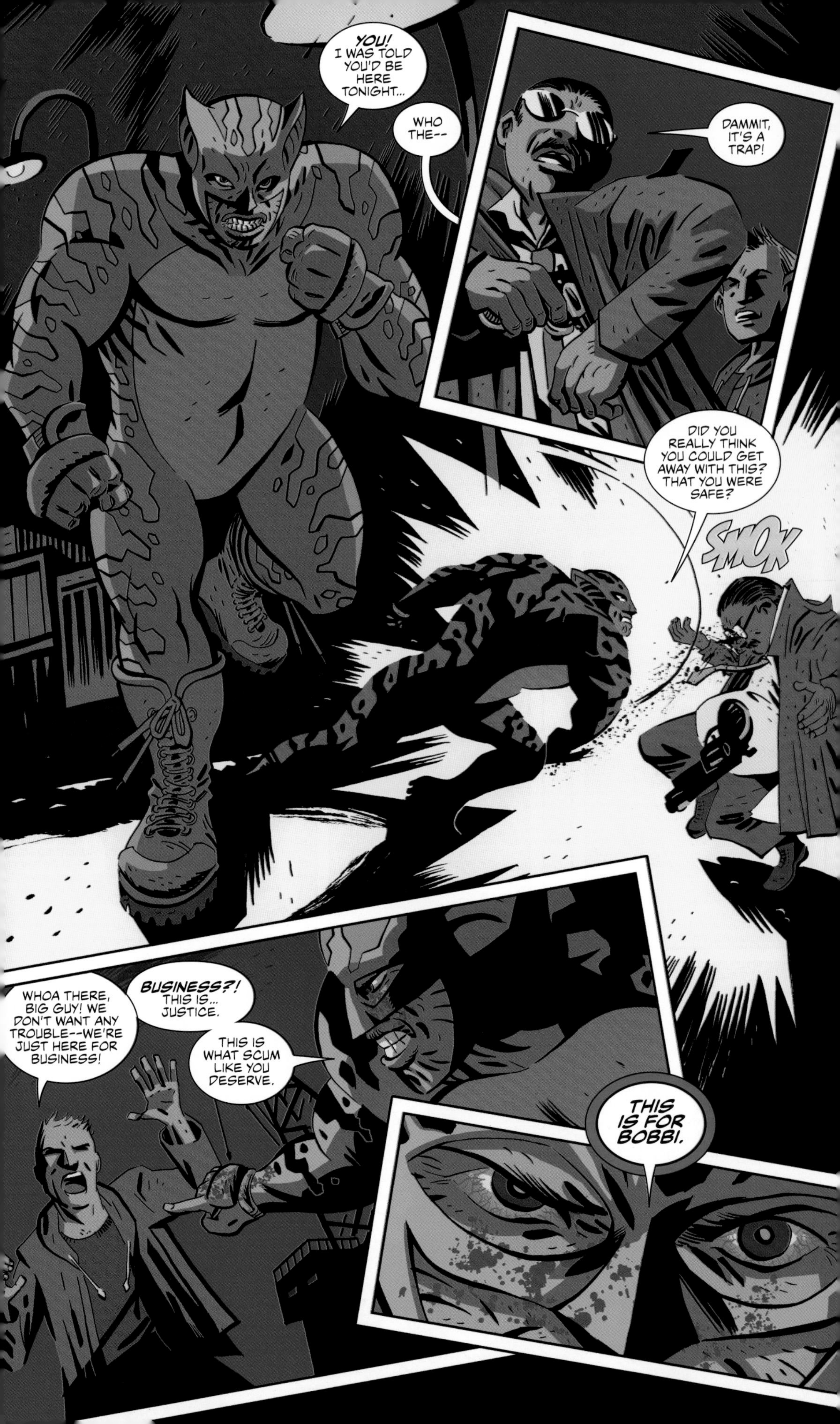
YOU! I WAS TOLD YOU'D BE HERE TONIGHT...
WHO THE--
DAMMIT, IT'S A TRAP!
DID YOU REALLY THINK YOU COULD GET AWAY WITH THIS? THAT YOU WERE SAFE?
SMOK
WHOA THERE, BIG GUY! WE DON'T WANT ANY TROUBLE--WE'RE JUST HERE FOR BUSINESS!
BUSINESS?! THIS IS... JUSTICE.
THIS IS WHAT SCUM LIKE YOU DESERVE.
THIS IS FOR BOBBI.

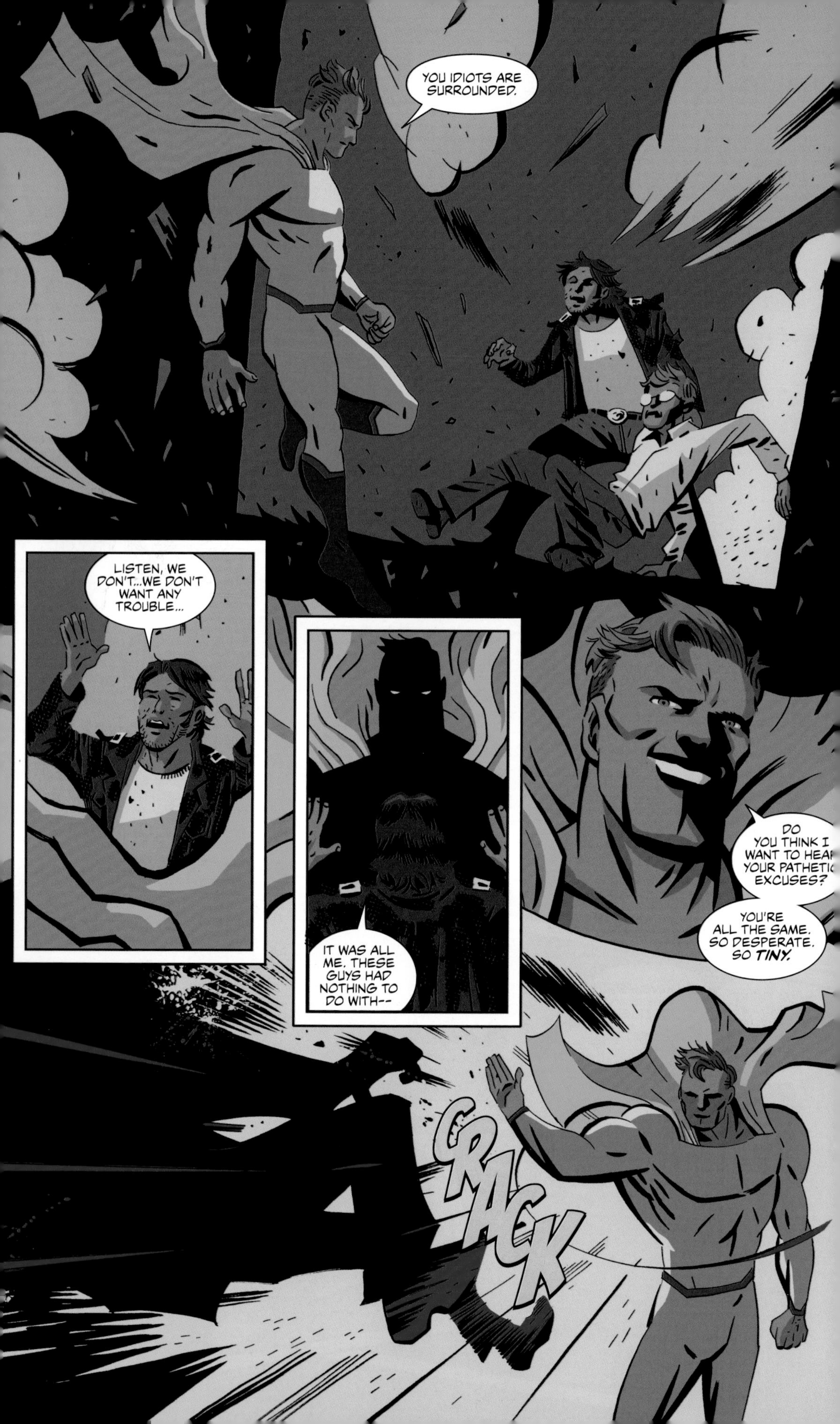
YOU IDIOTS ARE SURROUNDED.
LISTEN, WE DON'T...WE DON'T WANT ANY TROUBLE...
IT WAS ALL ME. THESE GUYS HAD NOTHING TO DO WITH--
DO YOU THINK I WANT TO HEAR YOUR PATHETIC EXCUSES?
YOU'RE ALL THE SAME. SO DESPERATE. SO TINY.
CRACK

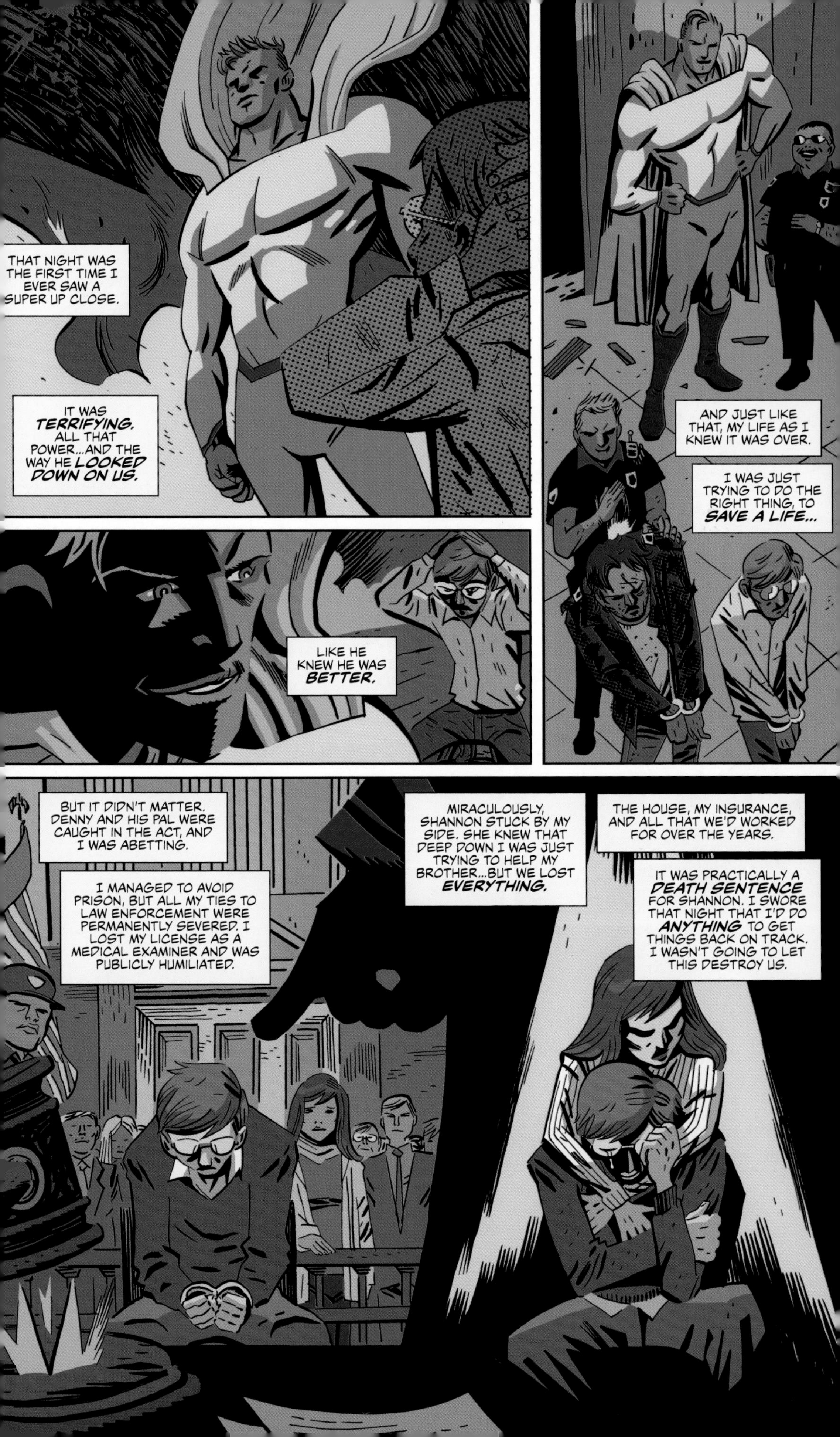

THAT NIGHT WAS THE FIRST TIME I EVER SAW A SUPER UP CLOSE.
IT WAS *TERRIFYING.* ALL THAT POWER...AND THE WAY HE *LOOKED DOWN ON US.*
LIKE HE KNEW HE WAS *BETTER.*
AND JUST LIKE THAT, MY LIFE AS I KNEW IT WAS OVER.
I WAS JUST TRYING TO DO THE RIGHT THING, TO *SAVE A LIFE...*
BUT IT DIDN'T MATTER. DENNY AND HIS PAL WERE CAUGHT IN THE ACT, AND I WAS ABETTING.
I MANAGED TO AVOID PRISON, BUT ALL MY TIES TO LAW ENFORCEMENT WERE PERMANENTLY SEVERED. I LOST MY LICENSE AS A MEDICAL EXAMINER AND WAS PUBLICLY HUMILIATED.
MIRACULOUSLY, SHANNON STUCK BY MY SIDE. SHE KNEW THAT DEEP DOWN I WAS JUST TRYING TO HELP MY BROTHER...BUT WE LOST *EVERYTHING.*
THE HOUSE, MY INSURANCE, AND ALL THAT WE'D WORKED FOR OVER THE YEARS.
IT WAS PRACTICALLY A *DEATH SENTENCE* FOR SHANNON. I SWORE THAT NIGHT THAT I'D DO *ANYTHING* TO GET THINGS BACK ON TRACK. I WASN'T GOING TO LET THIS DESTROY US.

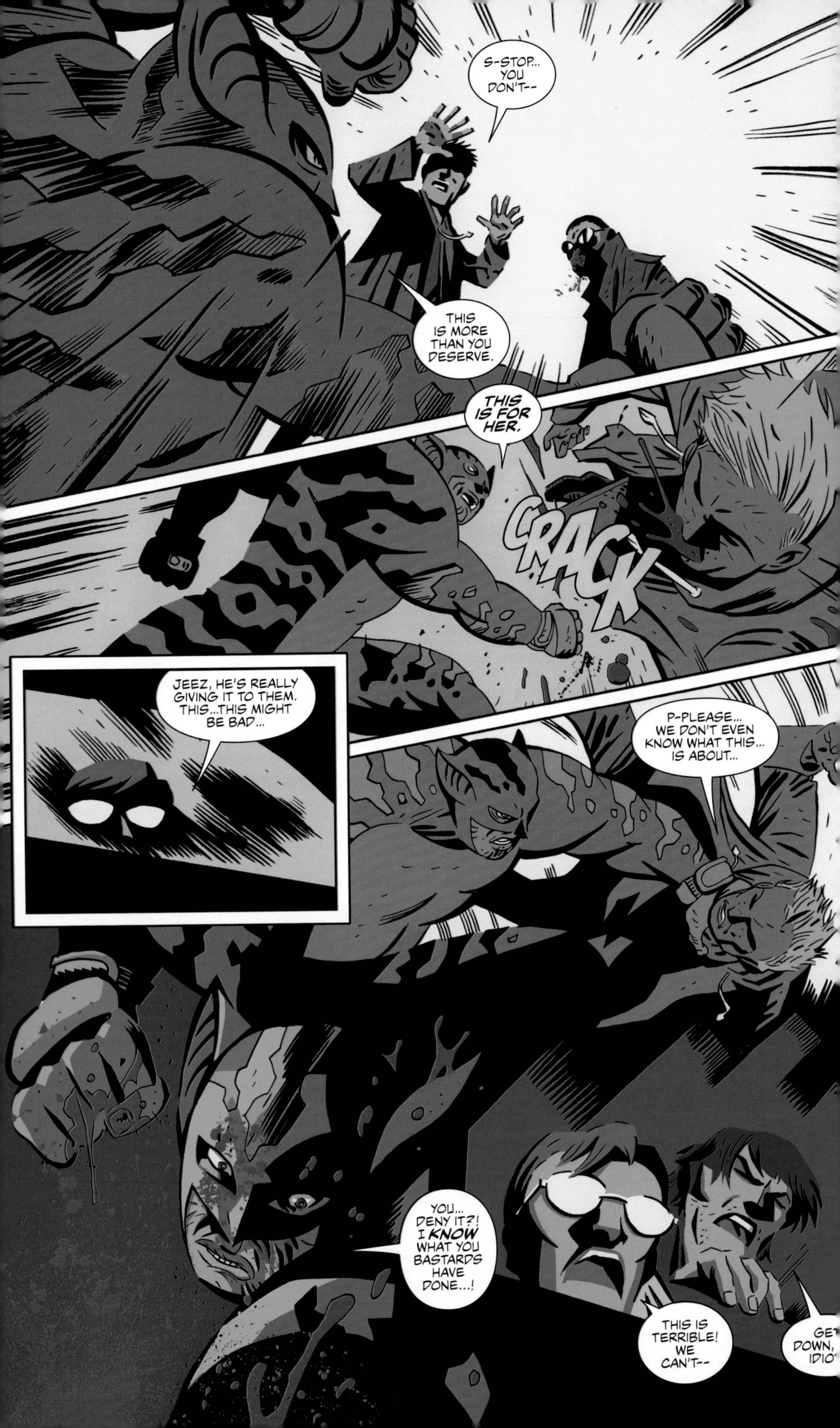
S-STOP... YOU DON'T--
THIS IS MORE THAN YOU DESERVE.
THIS IS FOR HER.
CRACK
JEEZ, HE'S REALLY GIVING IT TO THEM. THIS...THIS MIGHT BE BAD...
P-PLEASE... WE DON'T EVEN KNOW WHAT THIS... IS ABOUT...
YOU... DENY IT?! I KNOW WHAT YOU BASTARDS HAVE DONE...!
THIS IS TERRIBLE! WE CAN'T--
GET DOWN, IDIO

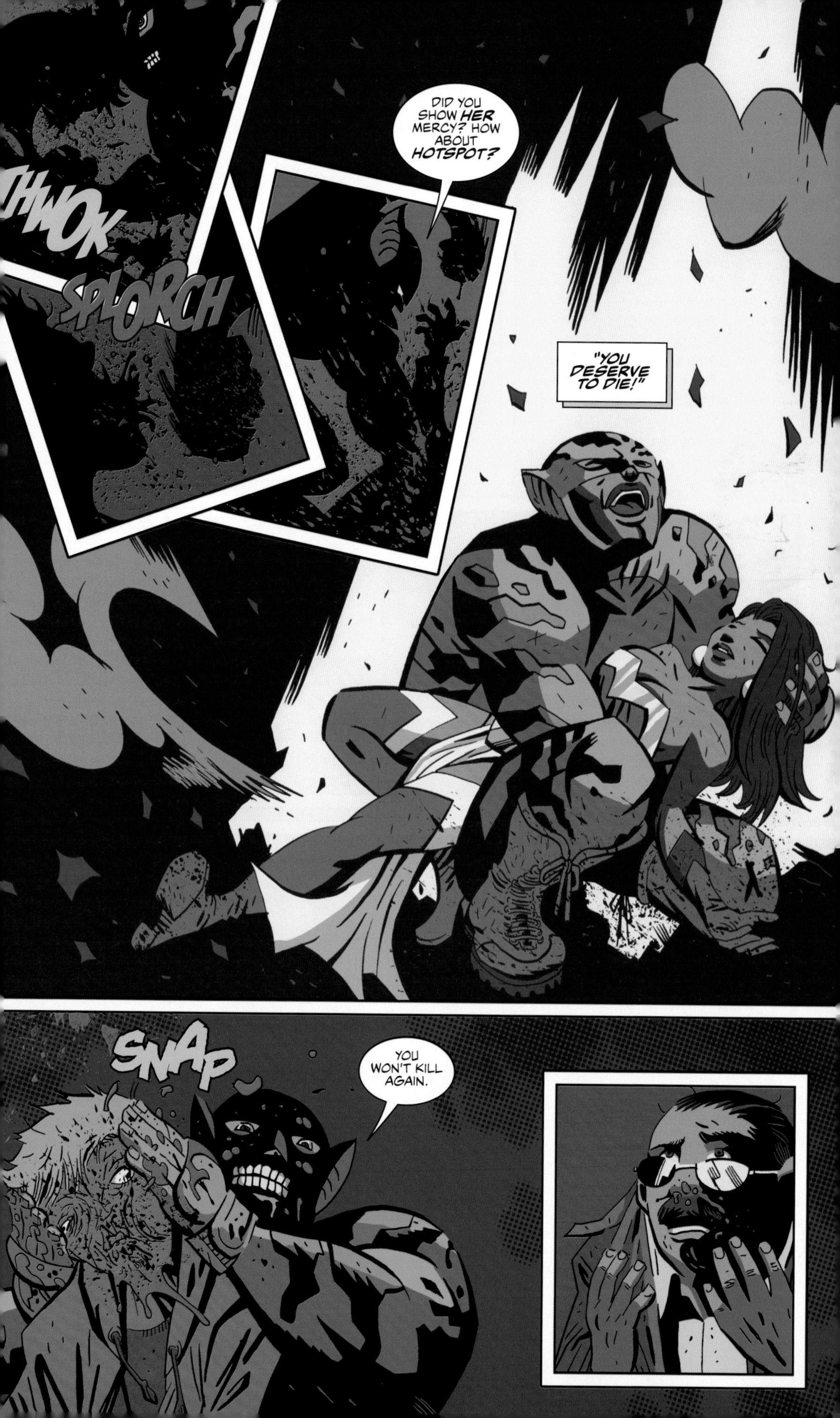
THWOK
SPLORCH
DID YOU SHOW HER MERCY? HOW ABOUT HOTSPOT?
"YOU DESERVE TO DIE!"
SNAP
YOU WON'T KILL AGAIN.

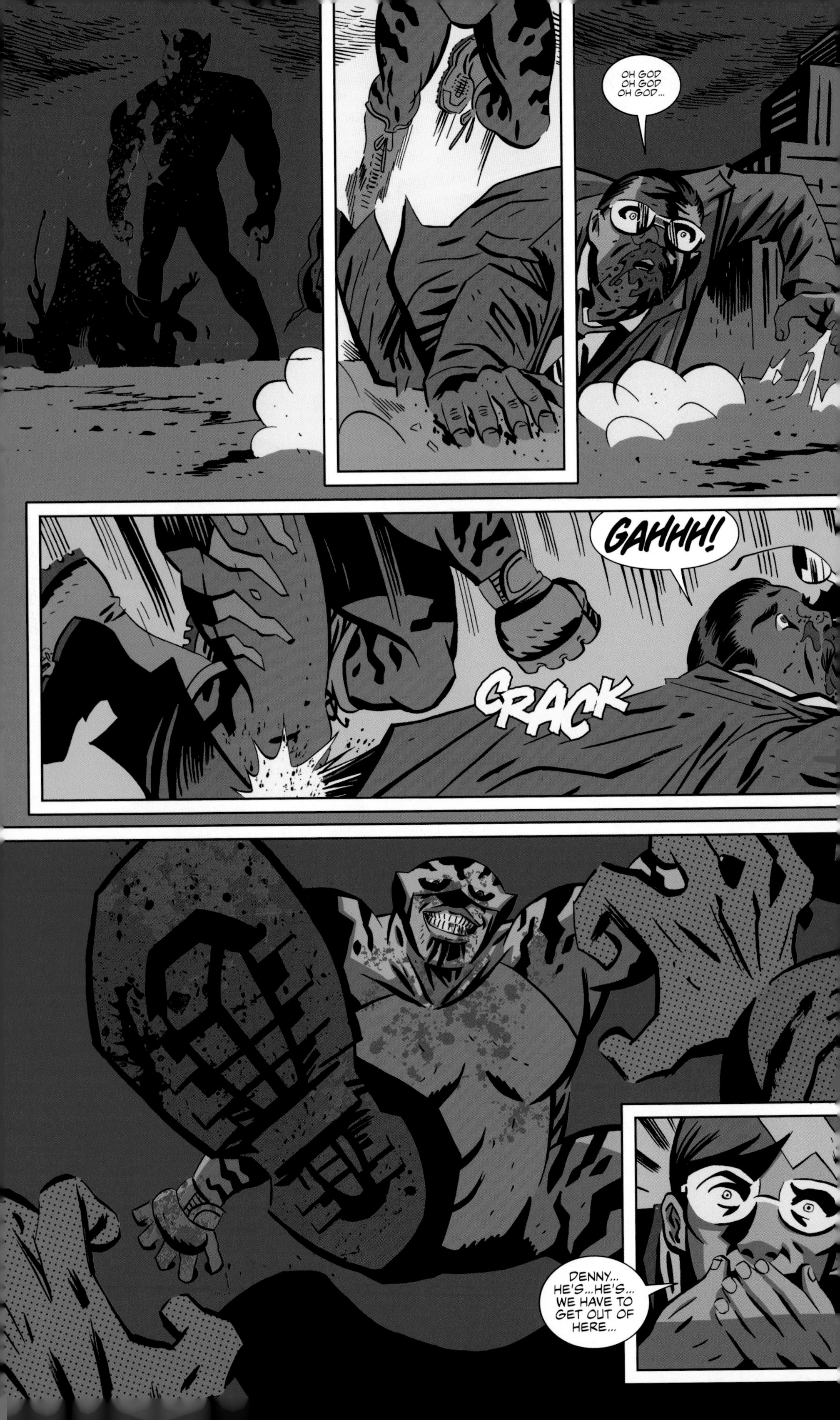
OH GOD
OH GOD
OH GOD...
GAHHH!
CRACK
DENNY... HE'S...HE'S... WE HAVE TO GET OUT OF HERE...

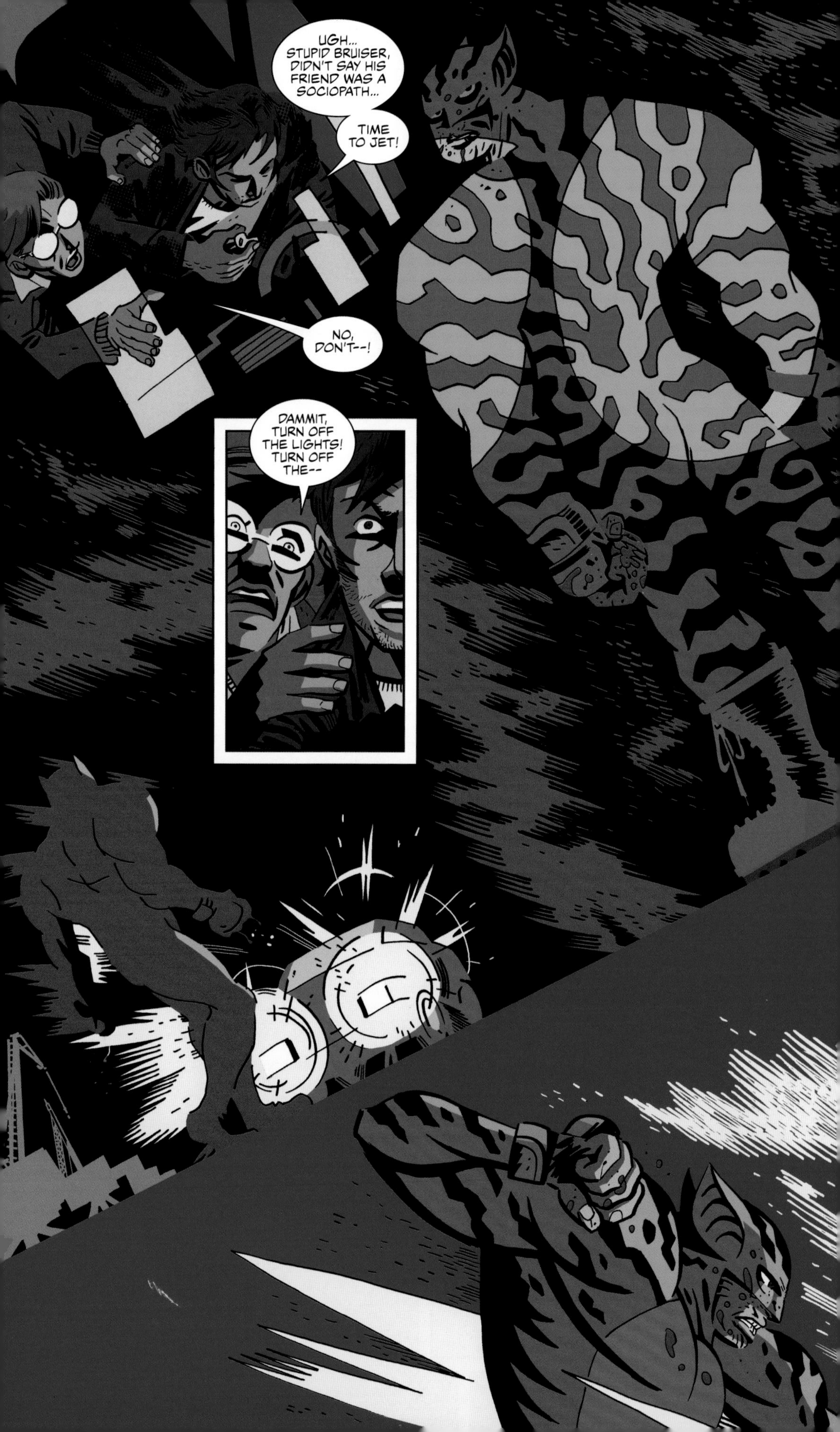
UGH... STUPID BRUISER, DIDN'T SAY HIS FRIEND WAS A SOCIOPATH...
TIME TO JET!
NO, DON'T--!
DAMMIT, TURN OFF THE LIGHTS! TURN OFF THE--

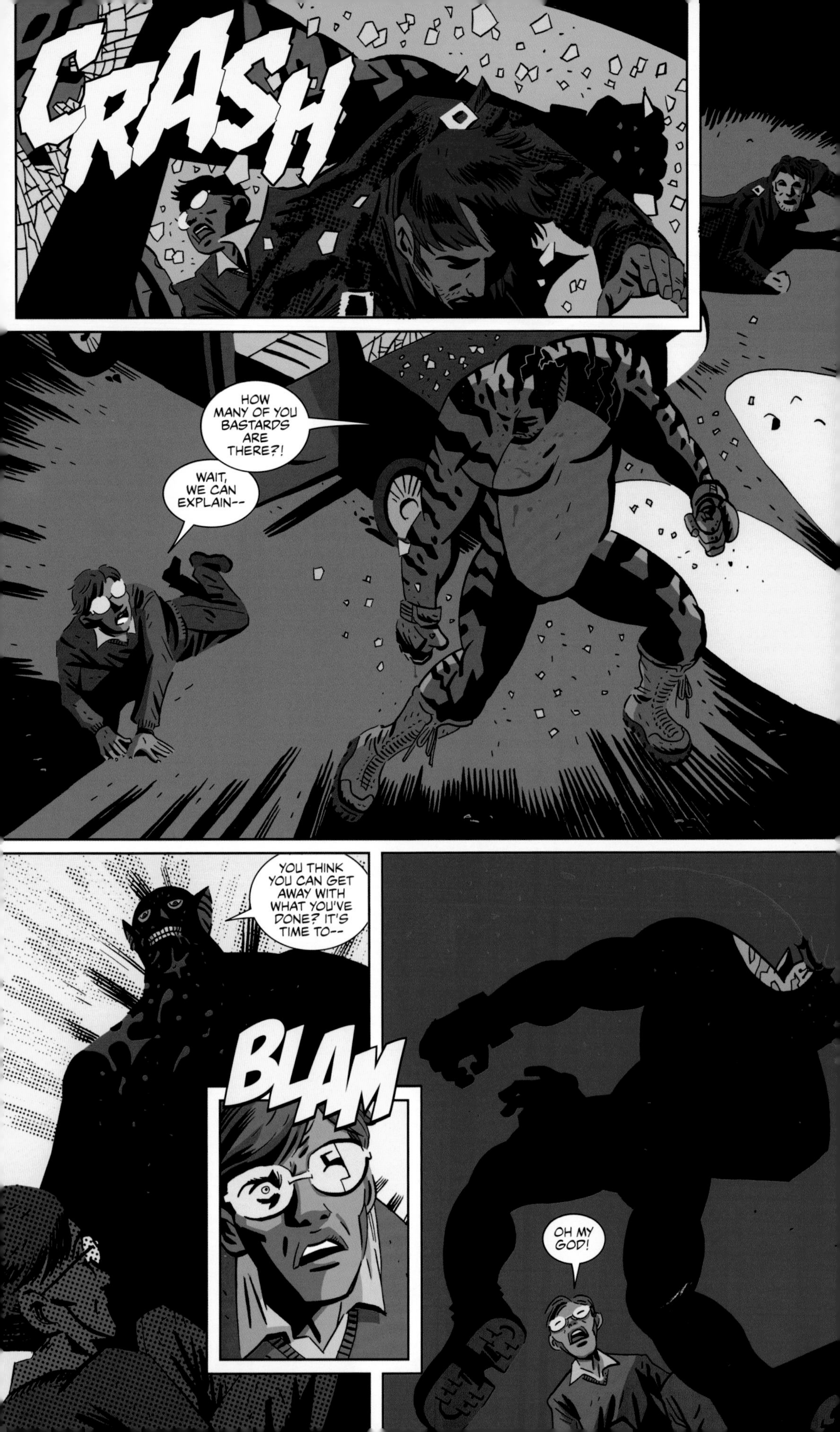
CRASH
HOW MANY OF YOU BASTARDS ARE THERE?!
WAIT, WE CAN EXPLAIN--
YOU THINK YOU CAN GET AWAY WITH WHAT YOU'VE DONE? IT'S TIME TO--
BLAM
OH MY GOD!

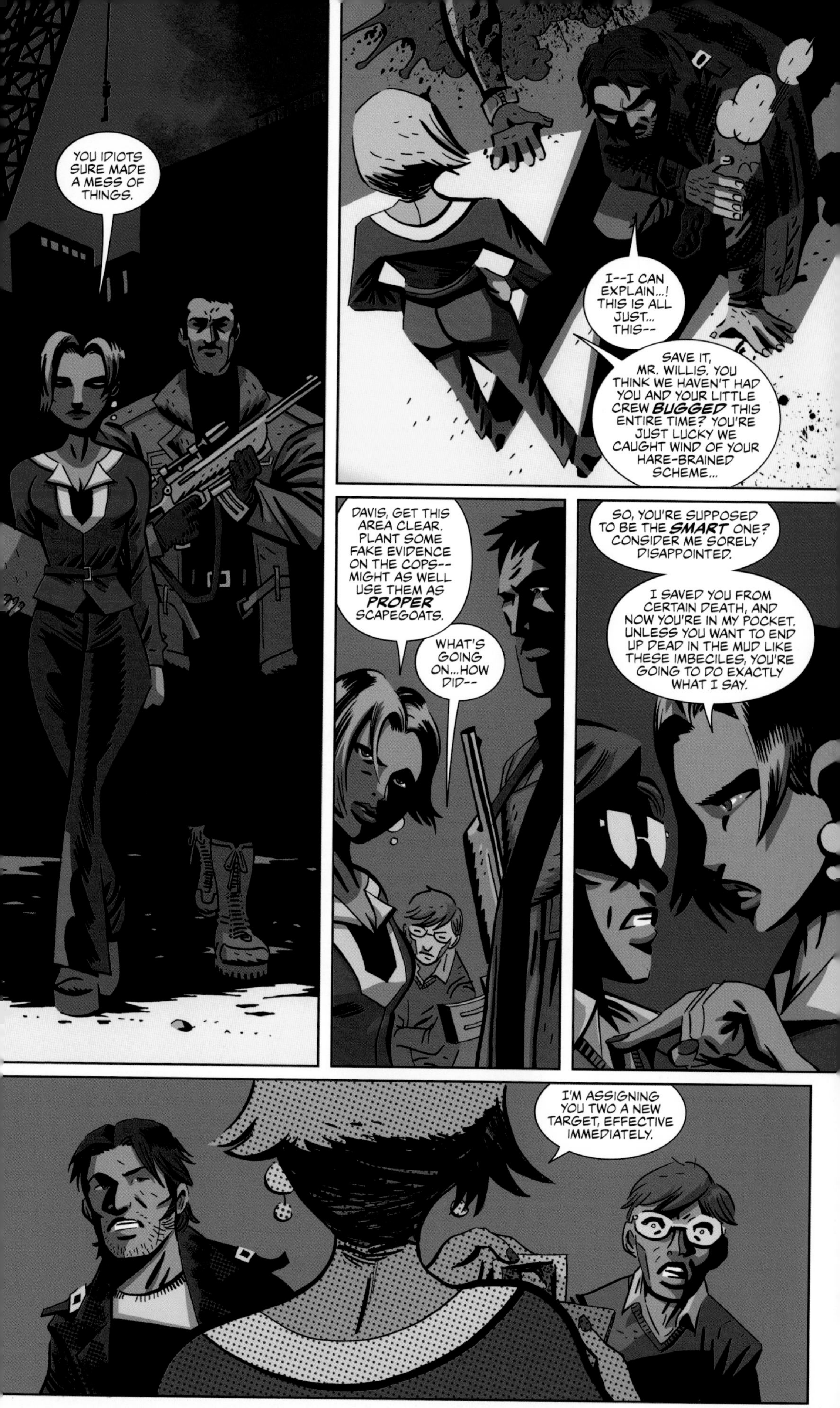
YOU IDIOTS SURE MADE A MESS OF THINGS.
I--I CAN EXPLAIN...! THIS IS ALL JUST... THIS--
SAVE IT, MR. WILLIS. YOU THINK WE HAVEN'T HAD YOU AND YOUR LITTLE CREW BUGGED THIS ENTIRE TIME? YOU'RE JUST LUCKY WE CAUGHT WIND OF YOUR HARE-BRAINED SCHEME...
DAVIS, GET THIS AREA CLEAR. PLANT SOME FAKE EVIDENCE ON THE COPS-- MIGHT AS WELL USE THEM AS PROPER SCAPEGOATS.
WHAT'S GOING ON...HOW DID--
SO, YOU'RE SUPPOSED TO BE THE SMART ONE? CONSIDER ME SORELY DISAPPOINTED.
I SAVED YOU FROM CERTAIN DEATH, AND NOW YOU'RE IN MY POCKET. UNLESS YOU WANT TO END UP DEAD IN THE MUD LIKE THESE IMBECILES, YOU'RE GOING TO DO EXACTLY WHAT I SAY.
I'M ASSIGNING YOU TWO A NEW TARGET, EFFECTIVE IMMEDIATELY.

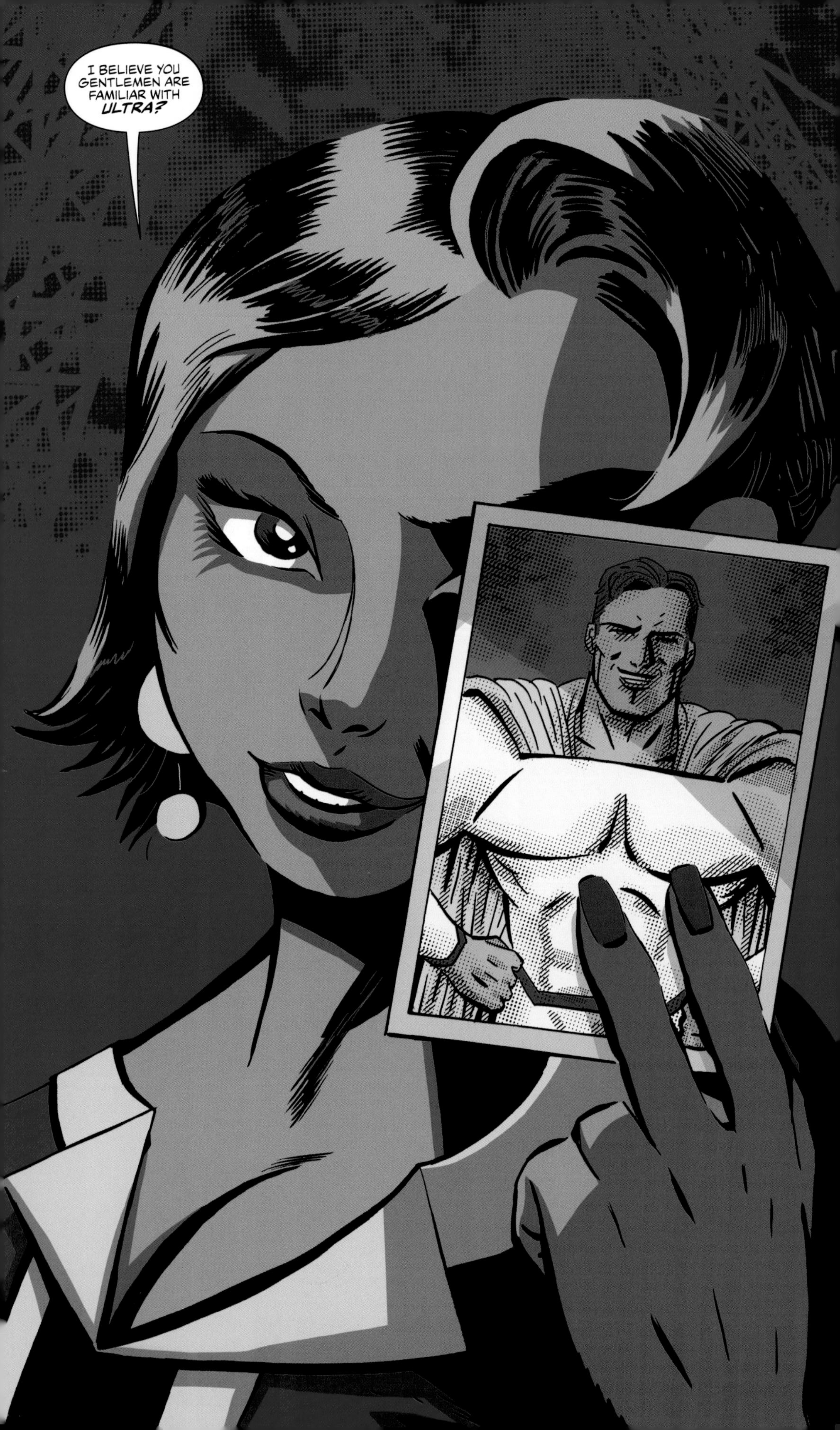
I BELIEVE YOU GENTLEMEN ARE FAMILIAR WITH *ULTRA?*

chapter four

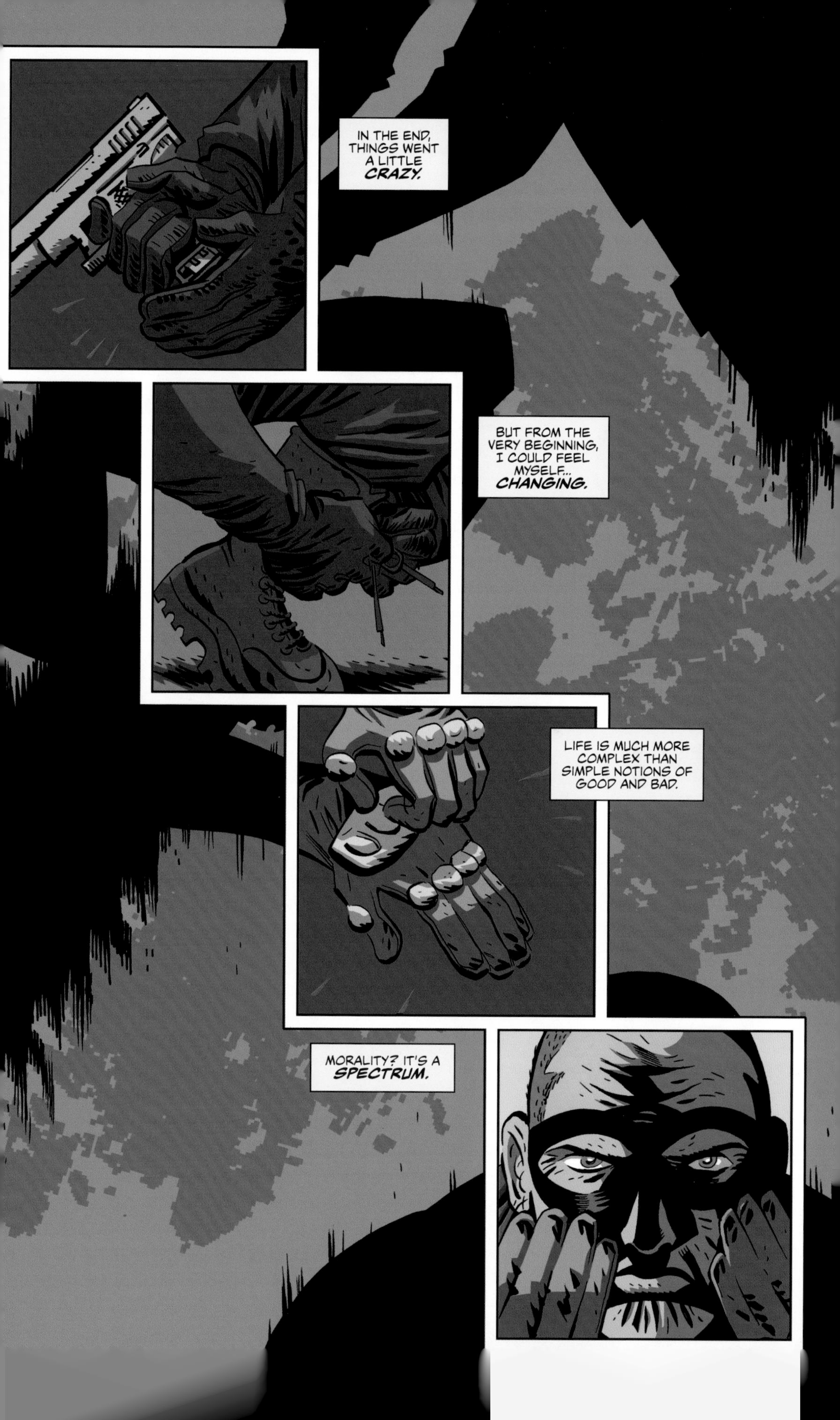
IN THE END, THINGS WENT A LITTLE *CRAZY.*
BUT FROM THE VERY BEGINNING, I COULD FEEL MYSELF... *CHANGING.*
LIFE IS MUCH MORE COMPLEX THAN SIMPLE NOTIONS OF GOOD AND BAD.
MORALITY? IT'S A *SPECTRUM.*

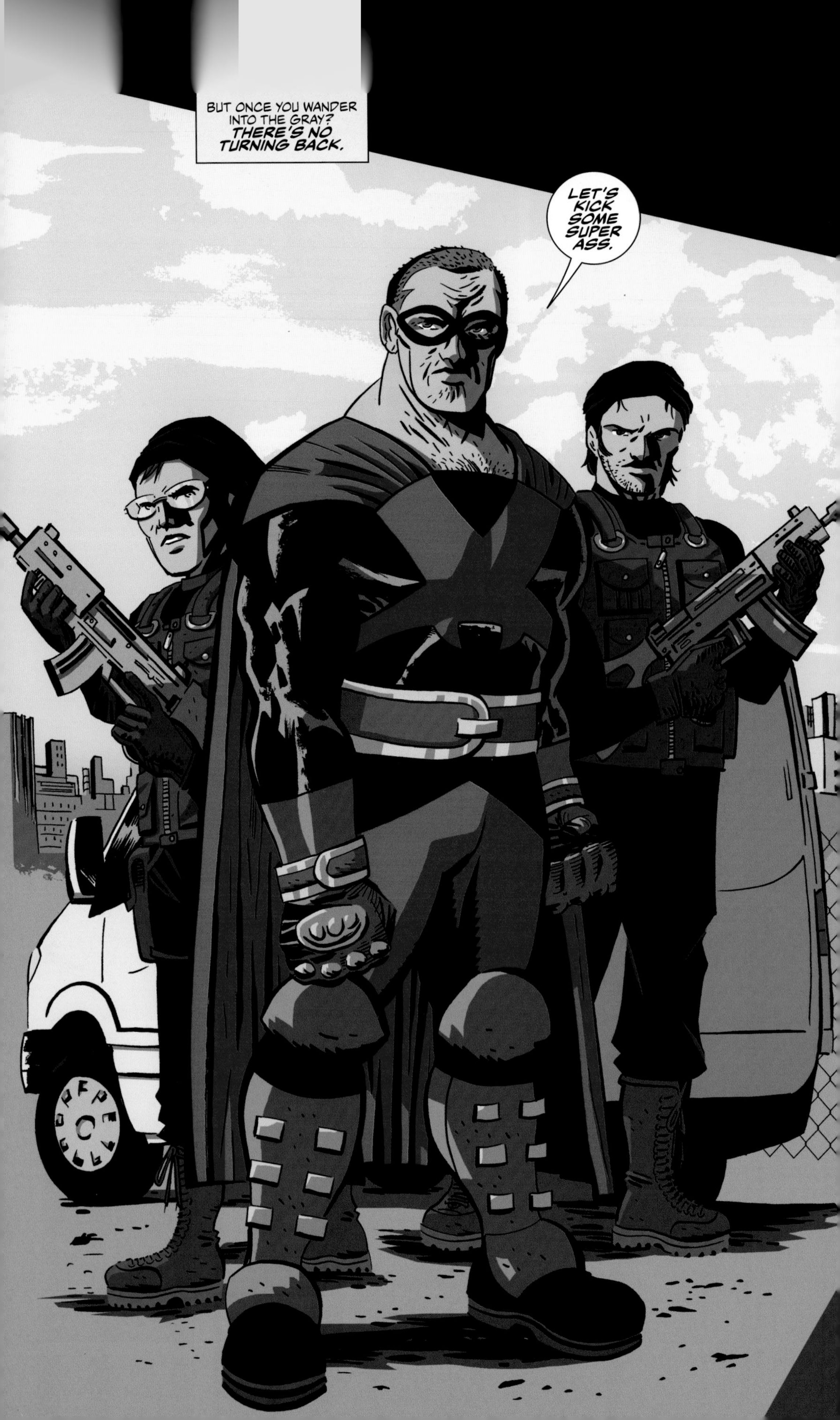
BUT ONCE YOU WANDER INTO THE GRAY? *THERE'S NO TURNING BACK.*
LET'S KICK SOME SUPER ASS.

NOVEMBER 8TH, 2012.

IT ALL STARTED THAT DAY IN THE LAB.

I COULD NEVER HAVE KNOWN, BUT LOOKING AT THAT SLIDE... THAT *SUPER DNA*...

WOULD YOU LOOK AT THAT...

THE CELLS ARE... DIVIDING.

OH MY GOD.

IT'S... *HEALING!*

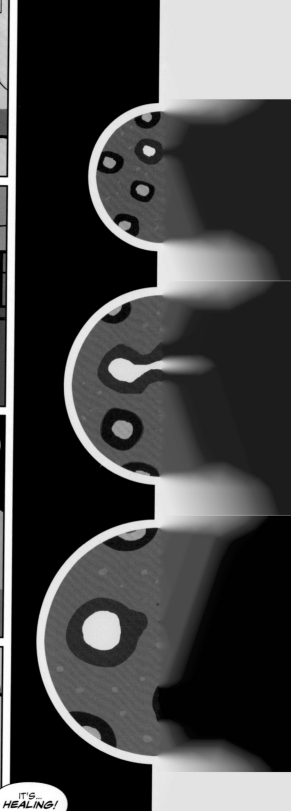

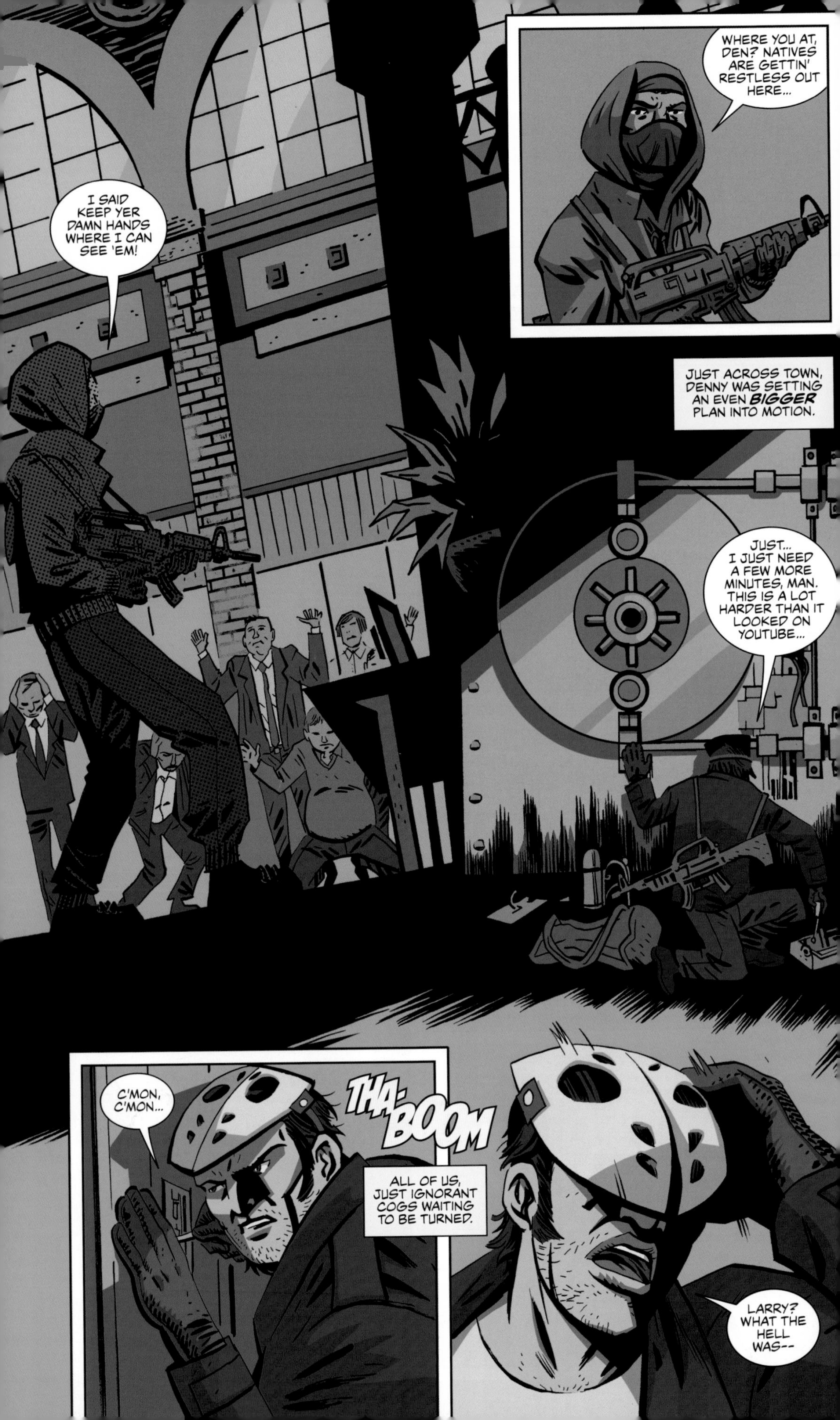
I SAID KEEP YER DAMN HANDS WHERE I CAN SEE 'EM!
WHERE YOU AT, DEN? NATIVES ARE GETTIN' RESTLESS OUT HERE...
JUST ACROSS TOWN, DENNY WAS SETTING AN EVEN BIGGER PLAN INTO MOTION.
JUST... I JUST NEED A FEW MORE MINUTES, MAN. THIS IS A LOT HARDER THAN IT LOOKED ON YOUTUBE...
C'MON, C'MON...
THA-BOOM
ALL OF US, JUST IGNORANT COGS WAITING TO BE TURNED.
LARRY? WHAT THE HELL WAS--

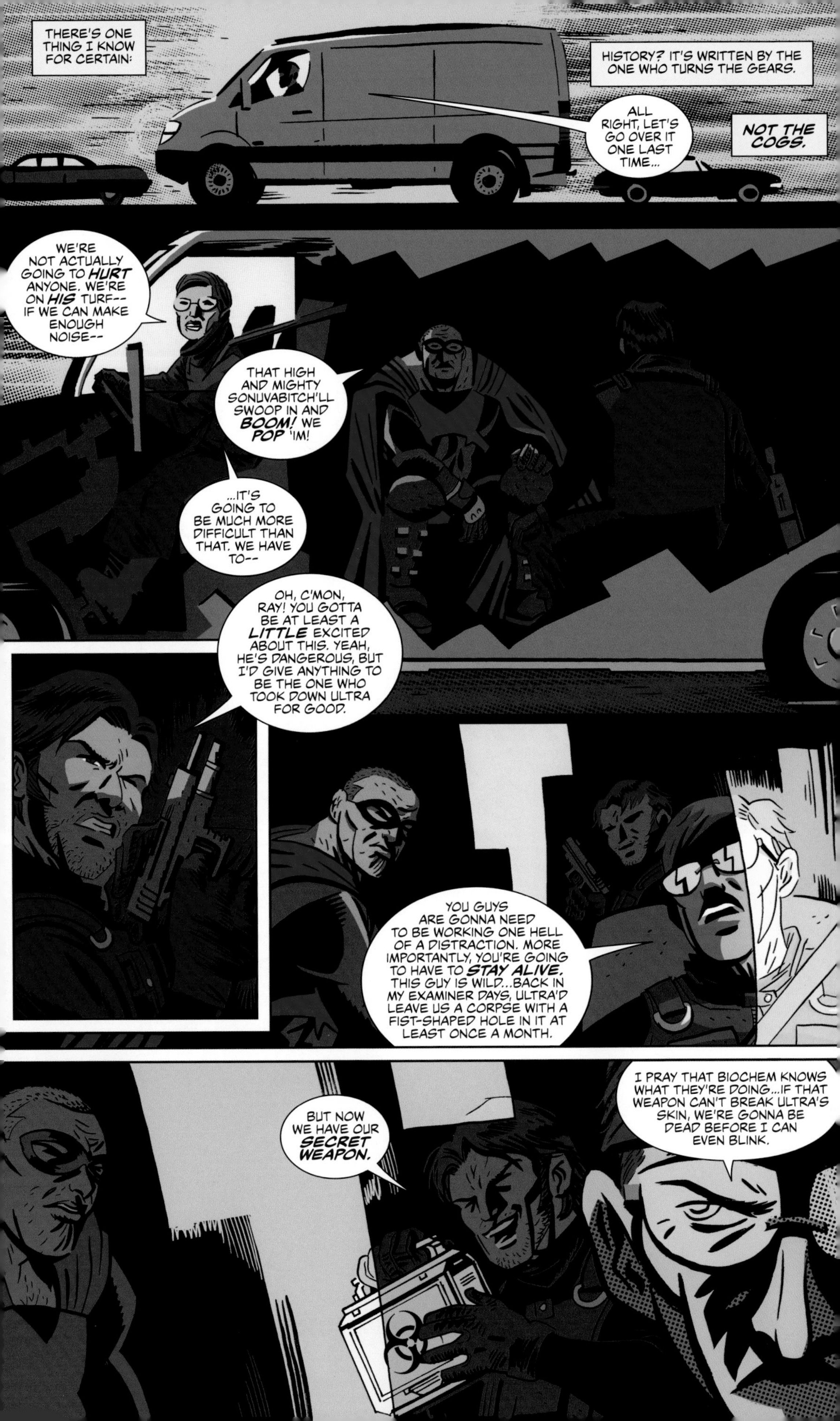
THERE'S ONE THING I KNOW FOR CERTAIN:
HISTORY? IT'S WRITTEN BY THE ONE WHO TURNS THE GEARS.
ALL RIGHT, LET'S GO OVER IT ONE LAST TIME...
NOT THE COGS.
WE'RE NOT ACTUALLY GOING TO HURT ANYONE. WE'RE ON HIS TURF-- IF WE CAN MAKE ENOUGH NOISE--
THAT HIGH AND MIGHTY SONUVABITCH'LL SWOOP IN AND BOOM! WE POP 'IM!
...IT'S GOING TO BE MUCH MORE DIFFICULT THAN THAT. WE HAVE TO--
OH, C'MON, RAY! YOU GOTTA BE AT LEAST A LITTLE EXCITED ABOUT THIS. YEAH, HE'S DANGEROUS, BUT I'D GIVE ANYTHING TO BE THE ONE WHO TOOK DOWN ULTRA FOR GOOD.
YOU GUYS ARE GONNA NEED TO BE WORKING ONE HELL OF A DISTRACTION. MORE IMPORTANTLY, YOU'RE GOING TO HAVE TO STAY ALIVE. THIS GUY IS WILD...BACK IN MY EXAMINER DAYS, ULTRA'D LEAVE US A CORPSE WITH A FIST-SHAPED HOLE IN IT AT LEAST ONCE A MONTH.
BUT NOW WE HAVE OUR SECRET WEAPON.
I PRAY THAT BIOCHEM KNOWS WHAT THEY'RE DOING...IF THAT WEAPON CAN'T BREAK ULTRA'S SKIN, WE'RE GONNA BE DEAD BEFORE I CAN EVEN BLINK.

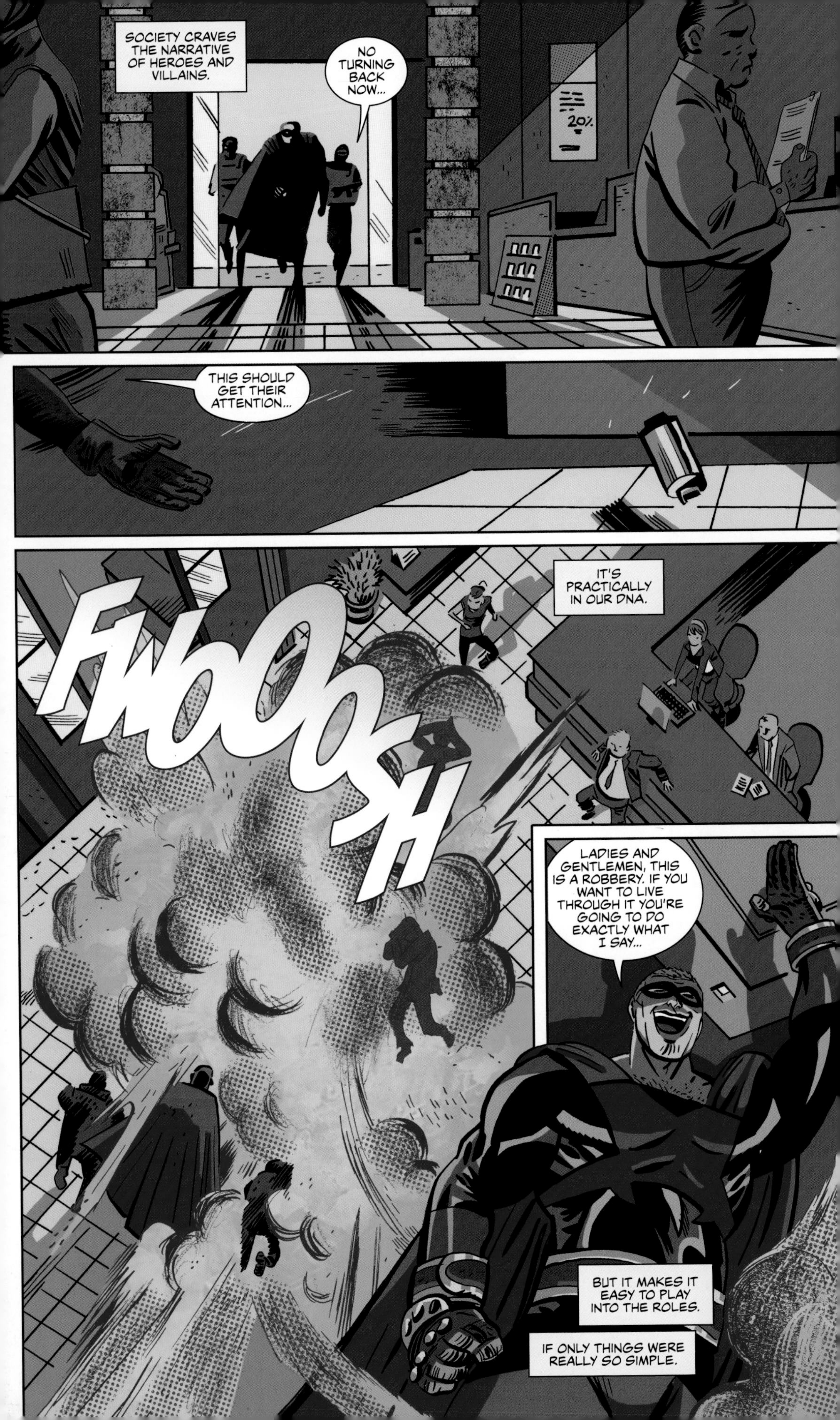
SOCIETY CRAVES THE NARRATIVE OF HEROES AND VILLAINS.
NO TURNING BACK NOW...
20%
THIS SHOULD GET THEIR ATTENTION...
FWOOOSH
IT'S PRACTICALLY IN OUR DNA.
LADIES AND GENTLEMEN, THIS IS A ROBBERY. IF YOU WANT TO LIVE THROUGH IT YOU'RE GOING TO DO EXACTLY WHAT I SAY...
BUT IT MAKES IT EASY TO PLAY INTO THE ROLES.
IF ONLY THINGS WERE REALLY SO SIMPLE.

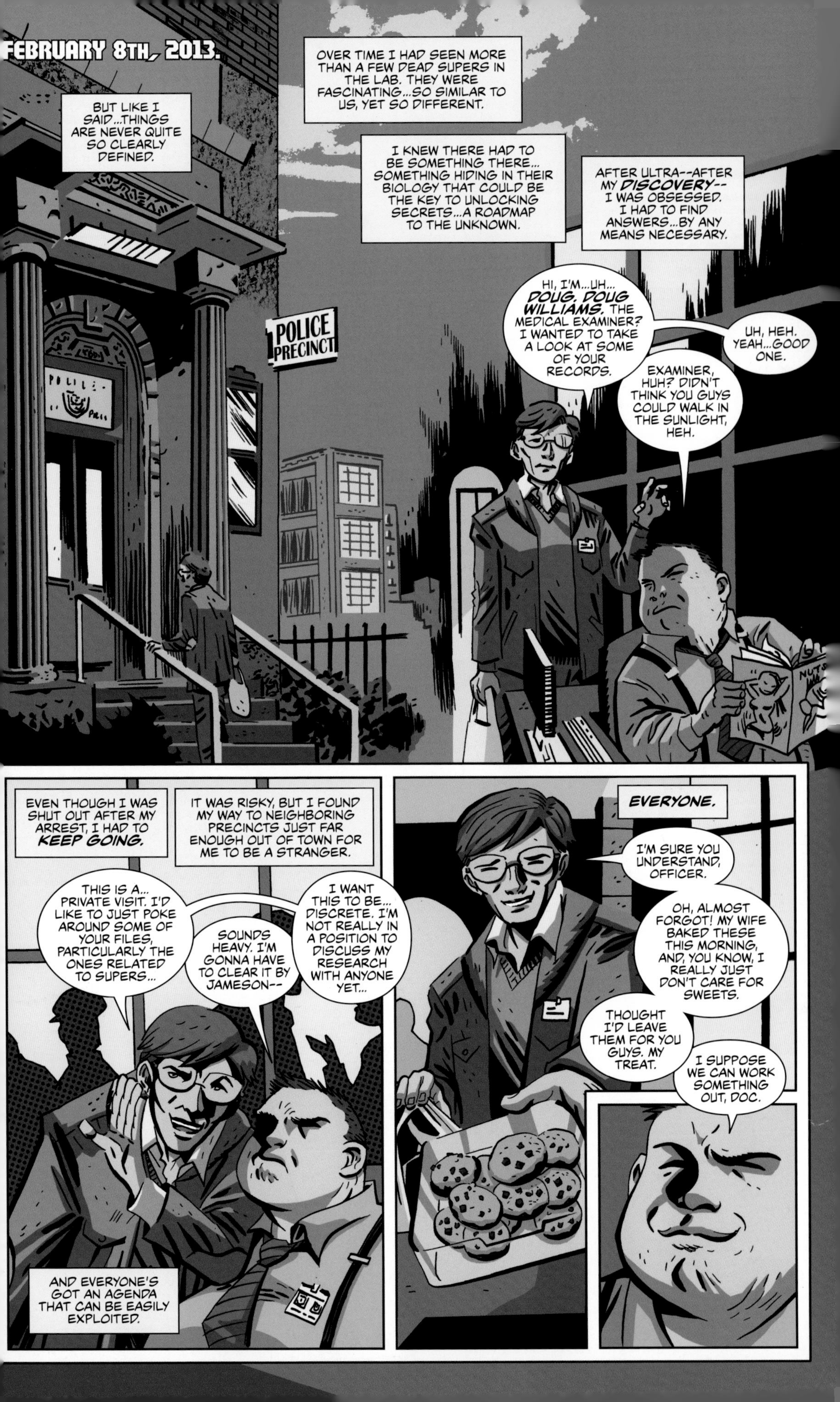

FEBRUARY 8TH, 2013.
BUT LIKE I SAID...THINGS ARE NEVER QUITE SO CLEARLY DEFINED.
OVER TIME I HAD SEEN MORE THAN A FEW DEAD SUPERS IN THE LAB. THEY WERE FASCINATING...SO SIMILAR TO US, YET SO DIFFERENT.
I KNEW THERE HAD TO BE SOMETHING THERE... SOMETHING HIDING IN THEIR BIOLOGY THAT COULD BE THE KEY TO UNLOCKING SECRETS...A ROADMAP TO THE UNKNOWN.
AFTER ULTRA--AFTER MY DISCOVERY-- I WAS OBSESSED. I HAD TO FIND ANSWERS...BY ANY MEANS NECESSARY.
POLICE PRECINCT
HI, I'M...UH... DOUG. DOUG WILLIAMS. THE MEDICAL EXAMINER? I WANTED TO TAKE A LOOK AT SOME OF YOUR RECORDS.
EXAMINER, HUH? DIDN'T THINK YOU GUYS COULD WALK IN THE SUNLIGHT, HEH.
UH, HEH. YEAH...GOOD ONE.
EVEN THOUGH I WAS SHUT OUT AFTER MY ARREST, I HAD TO KEEP GOING.
IT WAS RISKY, BUT I FOUND MY WAY TO NEIGHBORING PRECINCTS JUST FAR ENOUGH OUT OF TOWN FOR ME TO BE A STRANGER.
THIS IS A... PRIVATE VISIT. I'D LIKE TO JUST POKE AROUND SOME OF YOUR FILES, PARTICULARLY THE ONES RELATED TO SUPERS...
SOUNDS HEAVY. I'M GONNA HAVE TO CLEAR IT BY JAMESON--
I WANT THIS TO BE... DISCRETE. I'M NOT REALLY IN A POSITION TO DISCUSS MY RESEARCH WITH ANYONE YET...
AND EVERYONE'S GOT AN AGENDA THAT CAN BE EASILY EXPLOITED.
EVERYONE.
I'M SURE YOU UNDERSTAND, OFFICER.
OH, ALMOST FORGOT! MY WIFE BAKED THESE THIS MORNING, AND, YOU KNOW, I REALLY JUST DON'T CARE FOR SWEETS.
THOUGHT I'D LEAVE THEM FOR YOU GUYS. MY TREAT.
I SUPPOSE WE CAN WORK SOMETHING OUT, DOC.

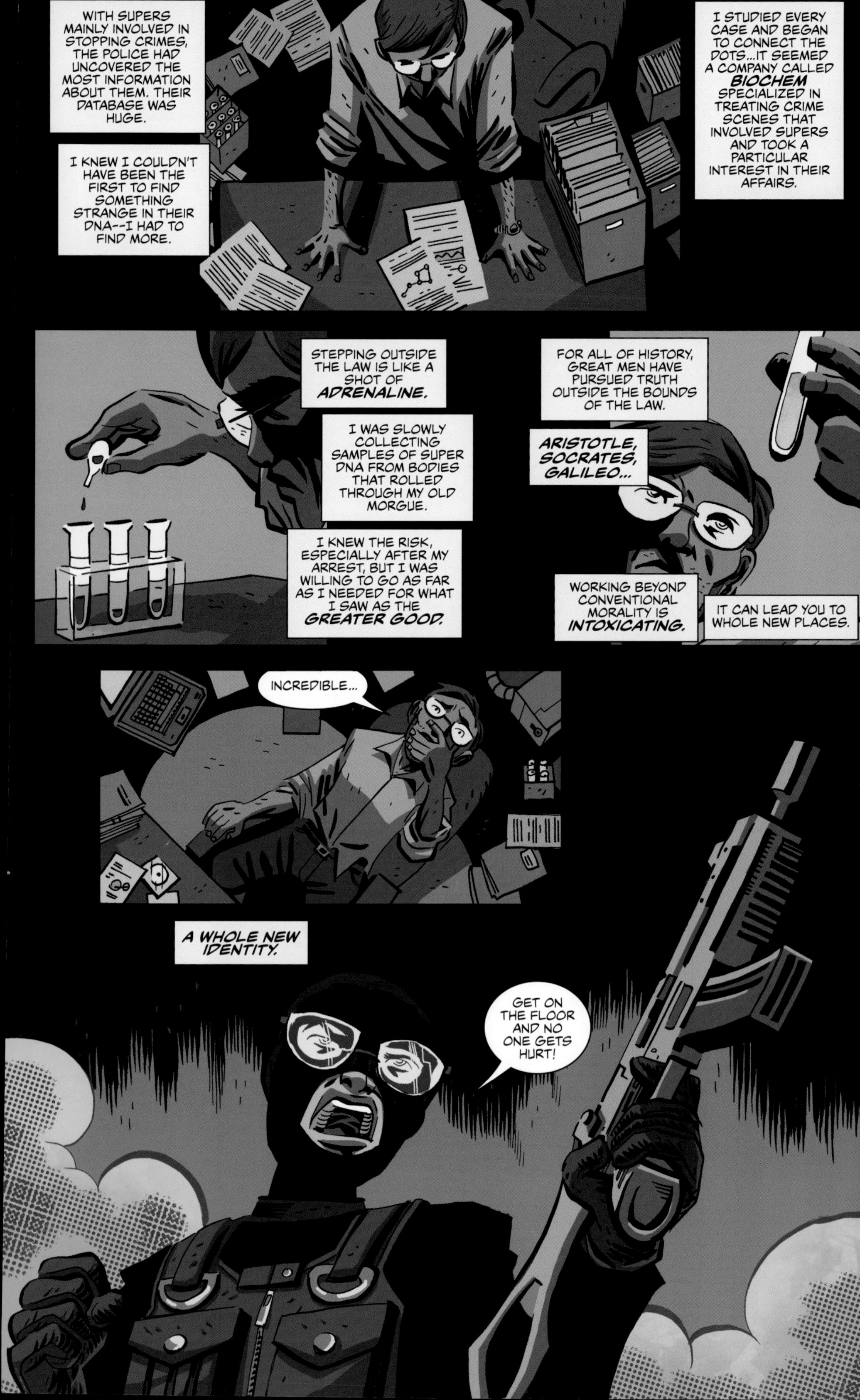
WITH SUPERS MAINLY INVOLVED IN STOPPING CRIMES, THE POLICE HAD UNCOVERED THE MOST INFORMATION ABOUT THEM. THEIR DATABASE WAS HUGE.
I KNEW I COULDN'T HAVE BEEN THE FIRST TO FIND SOMETHING STRANGE IN THEIR DNA--I HAD TO FIND MORE.
I STUDIED EVERY CASE AND BEGAN TO CONNECT THE DOTS...IT SEEMED A COMPANY CALLED BIOCHEM SPECIALIZED IN TREATING CRIME SCENES THAT INVOLVED SUPERS AND TOOK A PARTICULAR INTEREST IN THEIR AFFAIRS.
STEPPING OUTSIDE THE LAW IS LIKE A SHOT OF ADRENALINE.
I WAS SLOWLY COLLECTING SAMPLES OF SUPER DNA FROM BODIES THAT ROLLED THROUGH MY OLD MORGUE.
I KNEW THE RISK, ESPECIALLY AFTER MY ARREST, BUT I WAS WILLING TO GO AS FAR AS I NEEDED FOR WHAT I SAW AS THE GREATER GOOD.
FOR ALL OF HISTORY, GREAT MEN HAVE PURSUED TRUTH OUTSIDE THE BOUNDS OF THE LAW.
ARISTOTLE, SOCRATES, GALILEO...
WORKING BEYOND CONVENTIONAL MORALITY IS INTOXICATING.
IT CAN LEAD YOU TO WHOLE NEW PLACES.
INCREDIBLE...
A WHOLE NEW IDENTITY.
GET ON THE FLOOR AND NO ONE GETS HURT!

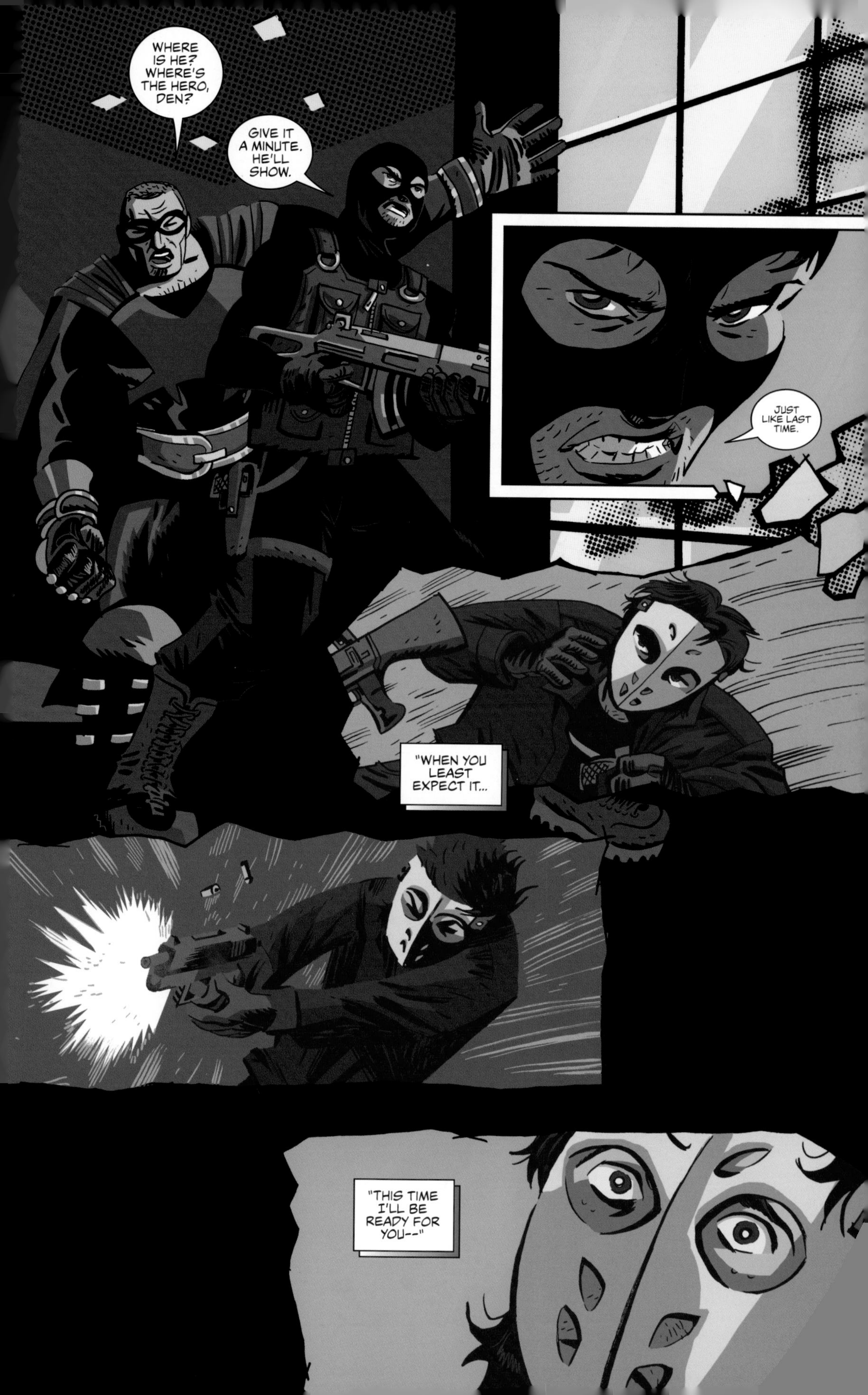
WHERE IS HE? WHERE'S THE HERO, DEN?
GIVE IT A MINUTE. HE'LL SHOW.
JUST LIKE LAST TIME.
"WHEN YOU LEAST EXPECT IT...
"THIS TIME I'LL BE READY FOR YOU--"

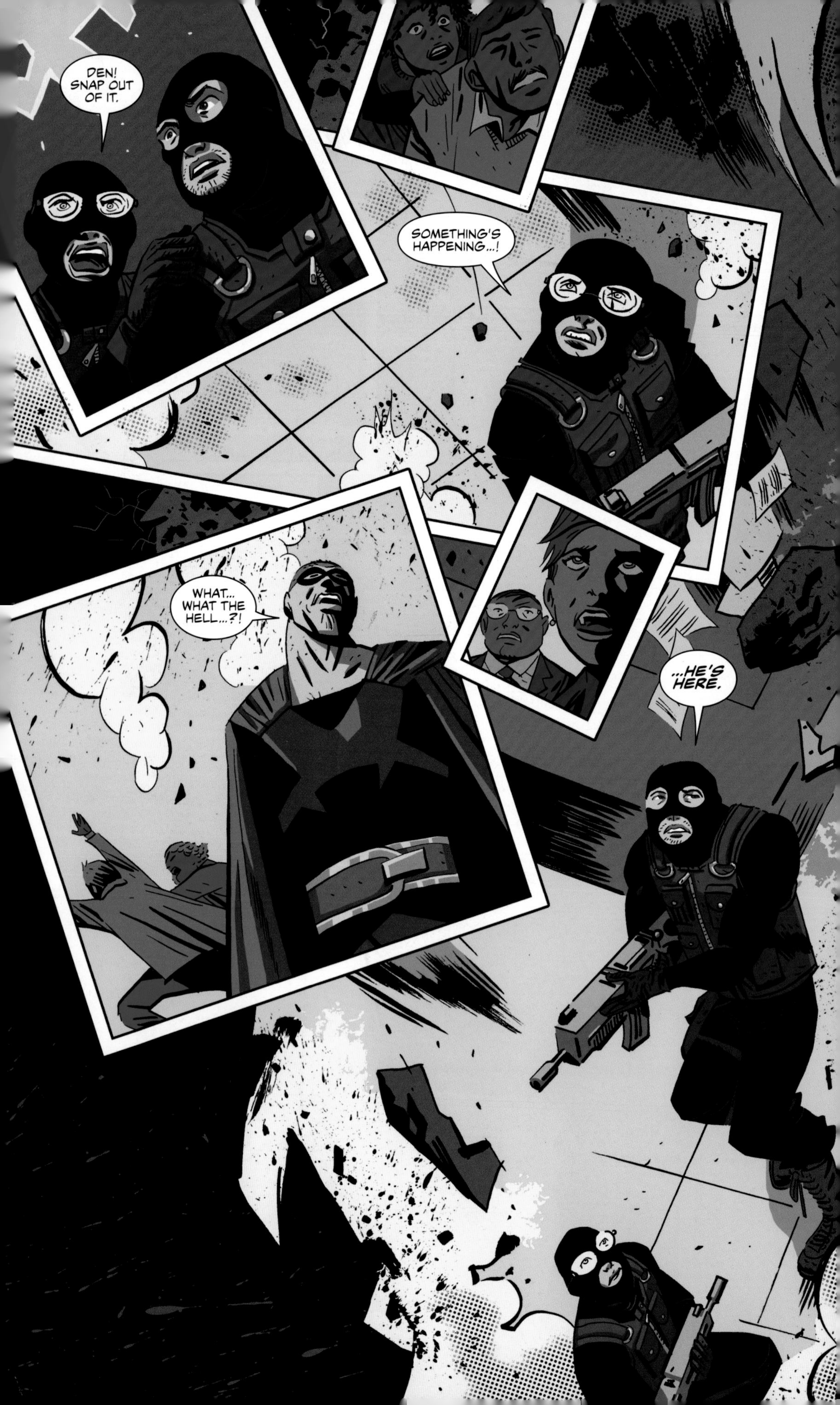
DEN! SNAP OUT OF IT.
SOMETHING'S HAPPENING...!
WHAT... WHAT THE HELL...?!
...HE'S HERE.

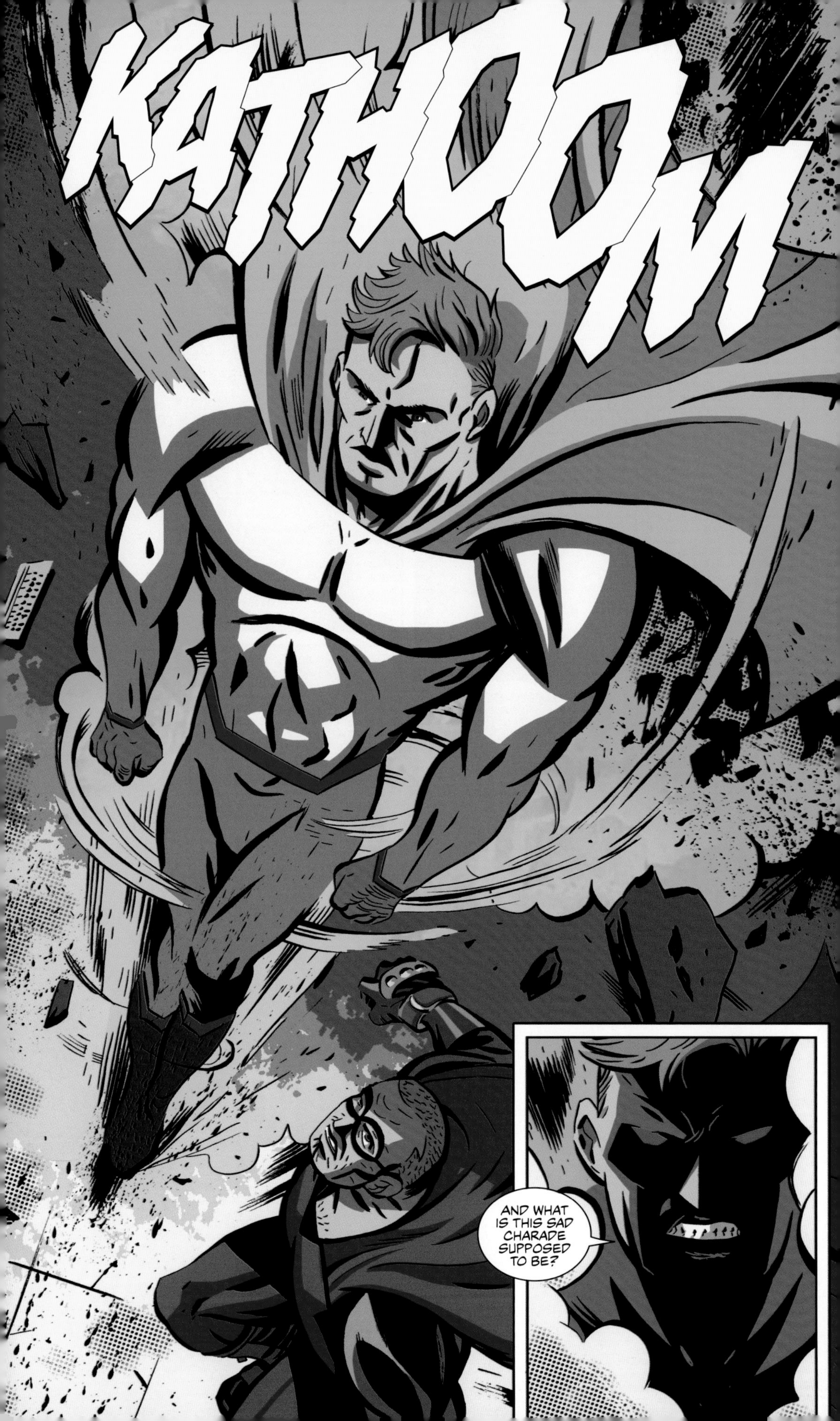
KATHOOM
AND WHAT IS THIS SAD CHARADE SUPPOSED TO BE?

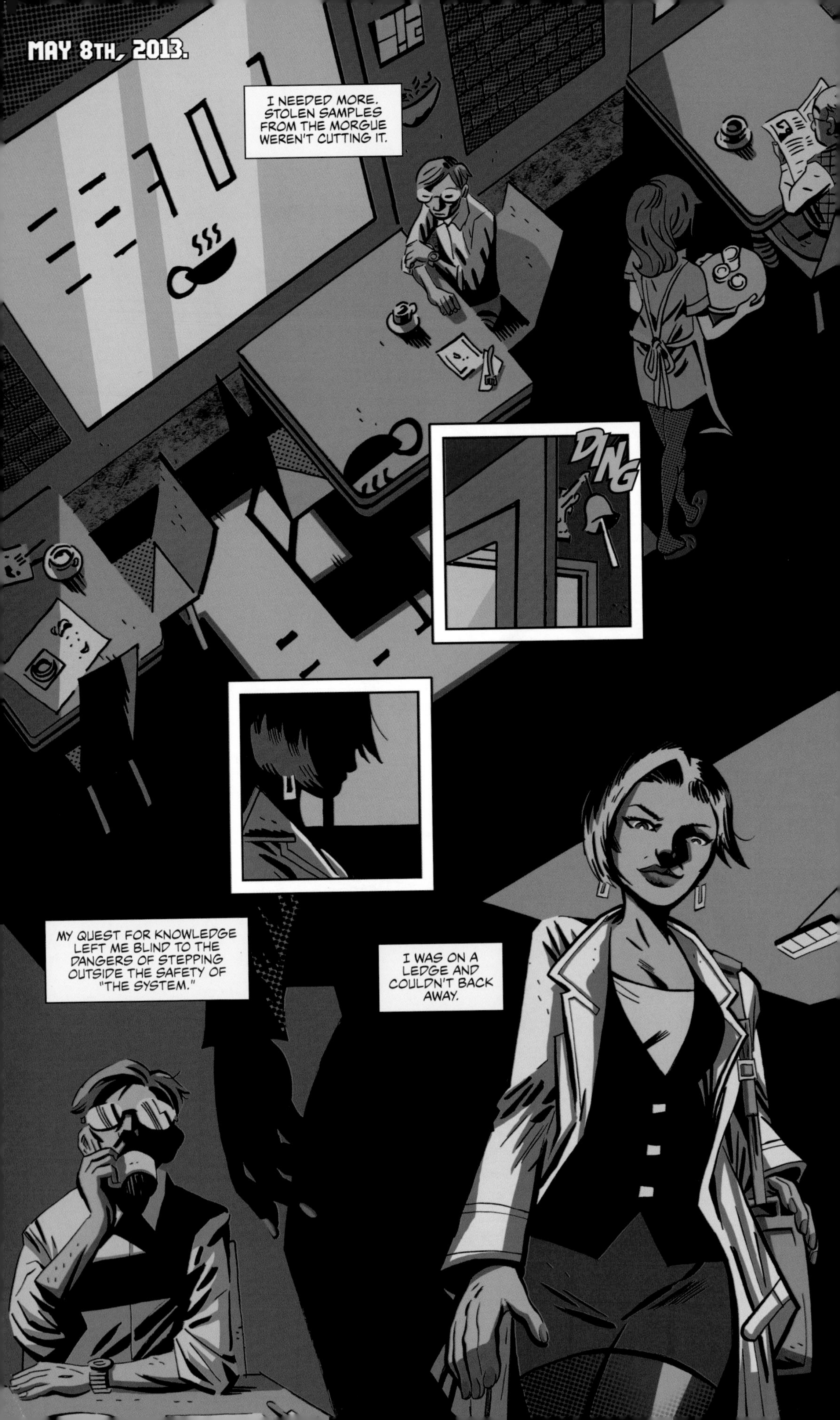
MAY 8TH, 2013.
I NEEDED MORE. STOLEN SAMPLES FROM THE MORGUE WEREN'T CUTTING IT.
DING
MY QUEST FOR KNOWLEDGE LEFT ME BLIND TO THE DANGERS OF STEPPING OUTSIDE THE SAFETY OF "THE SYSTEM."
I WAS ON A LEDGE AND COULDN'T BACK AWAY.

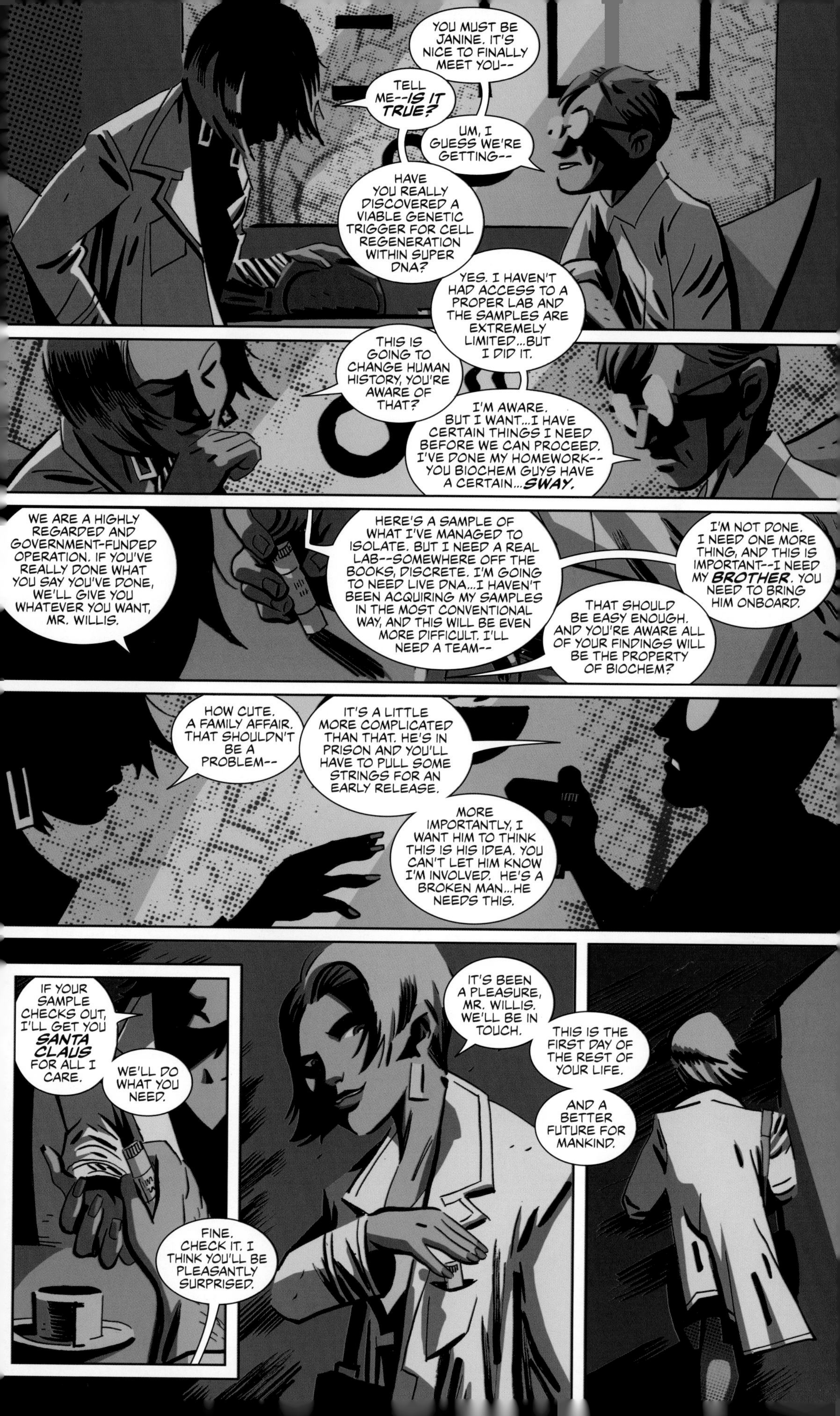

YOU MUST BE JANINE. IT'S NICE TO FINALLY MEET YOU--
TELL ME--*IS IT TRUE?*
UM, I GUESS WE'RE GETTING--
HAVE YOU REALLY DISCOVERED A VIABLE GENETIC TRIGGER FOR CELL REGENERATION WITHIN SUPER DNA?
YES. I HAVEN'T HAD ACCESS TO A PROPER LAB AND THE SAMPLES ARE EXTREMELY LIMITED...BUT I DID IT.
THIS IS GOING TO CHANGE HUMAN HISTORY, YOU'RE AWARE OF THAT?
I'M AWARE. BUT I WANT...I HAVE CERTAIN THINGS I NEED BEFORE WE CAN PROCEED. I'VE DONE MY HOMEWORK--YOU BIOCHEM GUYS HAVE A CERTAIN...*SWAY.*
WE ARE A HIGHLY REGARDED AND GOVERNMENT-FUNDED OPERATION. IF YOU'VE REALLY DONE WHAT YOU SAY YOU'VE DONE, WE'LL GIVE YOU WHATEVER YOU WANT, MR. WILLIS.
HERE'S A SAMPLE OF WHAT I'VE MANAGED TO ISOLATE. BUT I NEED A REAL LAB--SOMEWHERE OFF THE BOOKS, DISCRETE. I'M GOING TO NEED LIVE DNA...I HAVEN'T BEEN ACQUIRING MY SAMPLES IN THE MOST CONVENTIONAL WAY, AND THIS WILL BE EVEN MORE DIFFICULT. I'LL NEED A TEAM--
THAT SHOULD BE EASY ENOUGH. AND YOU'RE AWARE ALL OF YOUR FINDINGS WILL BE THE PROPERTY OF BIOCHEM?
I'M NOT DONE. I NEED ONE MORE THING, AND THIS IS IMPORTANT--I NEED MY **BROTHER**. YOU NEED TO BRING HIM ONBOARD.
HOW CUTE. A FAMILY AFFAIR. THAT SHOULDN'T BE A PROBLEM--
IT'S A LITTLE MORE COMPLICATED THAN THAT. HE'S IN PRISON AND YOU'LL HAVE TO PULL SOME STRINGS FOR AN EARLY RELEASE.
MORE IMPORTANTLY, I WANT HIM TO THINK THIS IS HIS IDEA. YOU CAN'T LET HIM KNOW I'M INVOLVED. HE'S A BROKEN MAN...HE NEEDS THIS.
IF YOUR SAMPLE CHECKS OUT, I'LL GET YOU **SANTA CLAUS** FOR ALL I CARE.
WE'LL DO WHAT YOU NEED.
FINE. CHECK IT. I THINK YOU'LL BE PLEASANTLY SURPRISED.
IT'S BEEN A PLEASURE, MR. WILLIS. WE'LL BE IN TOUCH.
THIS IS THE FIRST DAY OF THE REST OF YOUR LIFE.
AND A BETTER FUTURE FOR MANKIND.

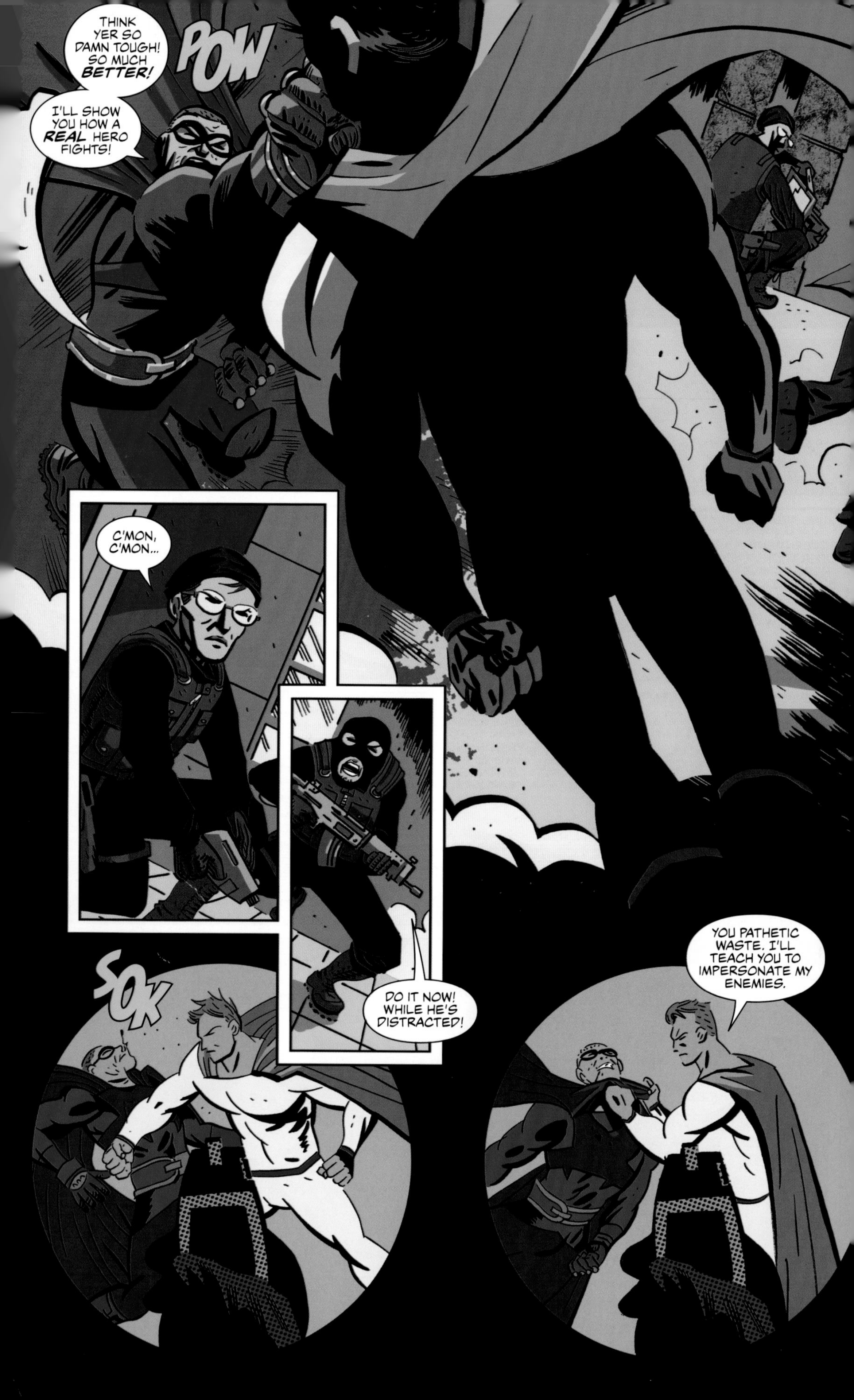
THINK YER SO DAMN TOUGH! SO MUCH BETTER!
POW
I'LL SHOW YOU HOW A REAL HERO FIGHTS!
C'MON, C'MON...
DO IT NOW! WHILE HE'S DISTRACTED!
SOK
YOU PATHETIC WASTE. I'LL TEACH YOU TO IMPERSONATE MY ENEMIES.

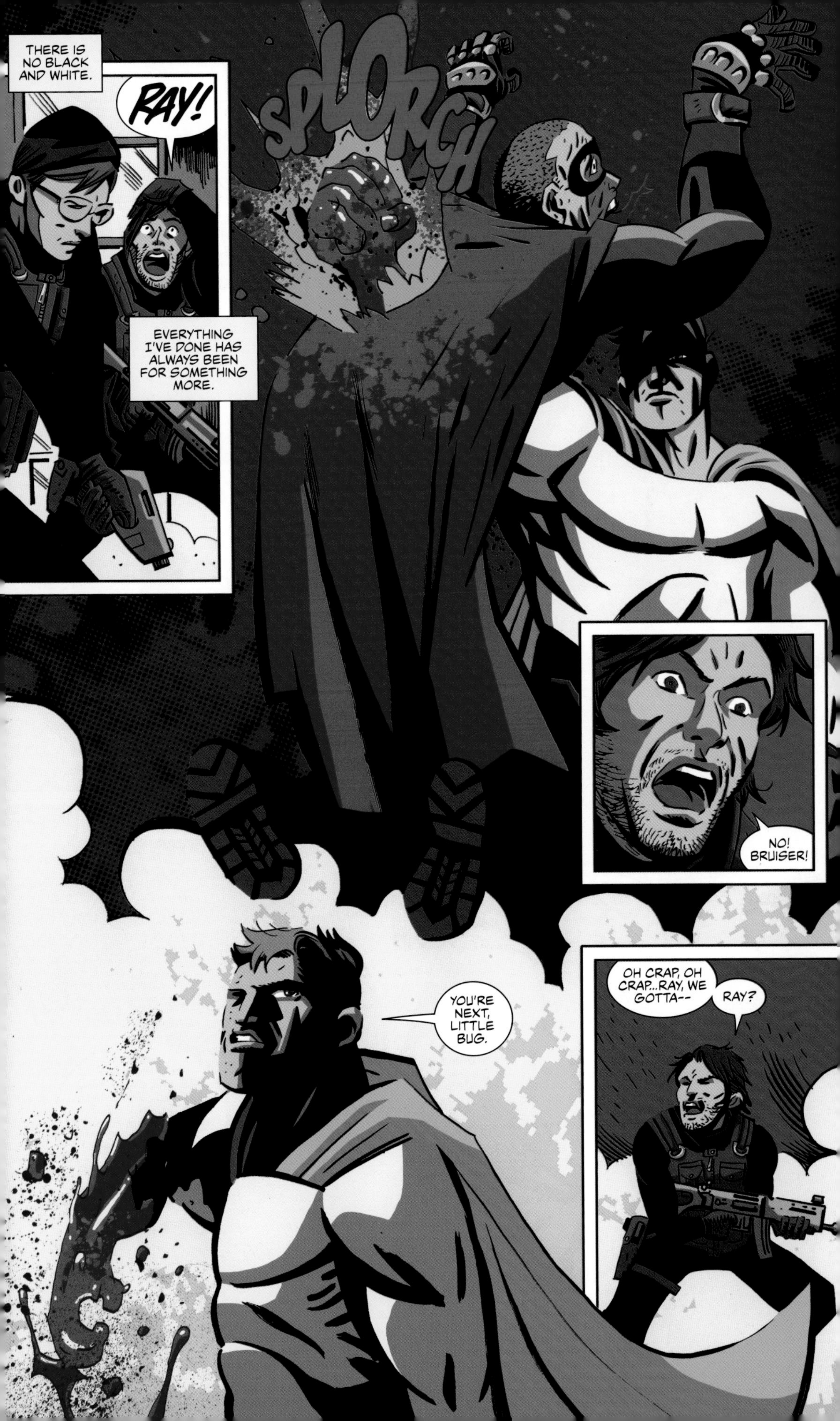
THERE IS NO BLACK AND WHITE.
RAY!
SPLORCH
EVERYTHING I'VE DONE HAS ALWAYS BEEN FOR SOMETHING MORE.
NO! BRUISER!
YOU'RE NEXT, LITTLE BUG.
OH CRAP, OH CRAP...RAY, WE GOTTA--
RAY?

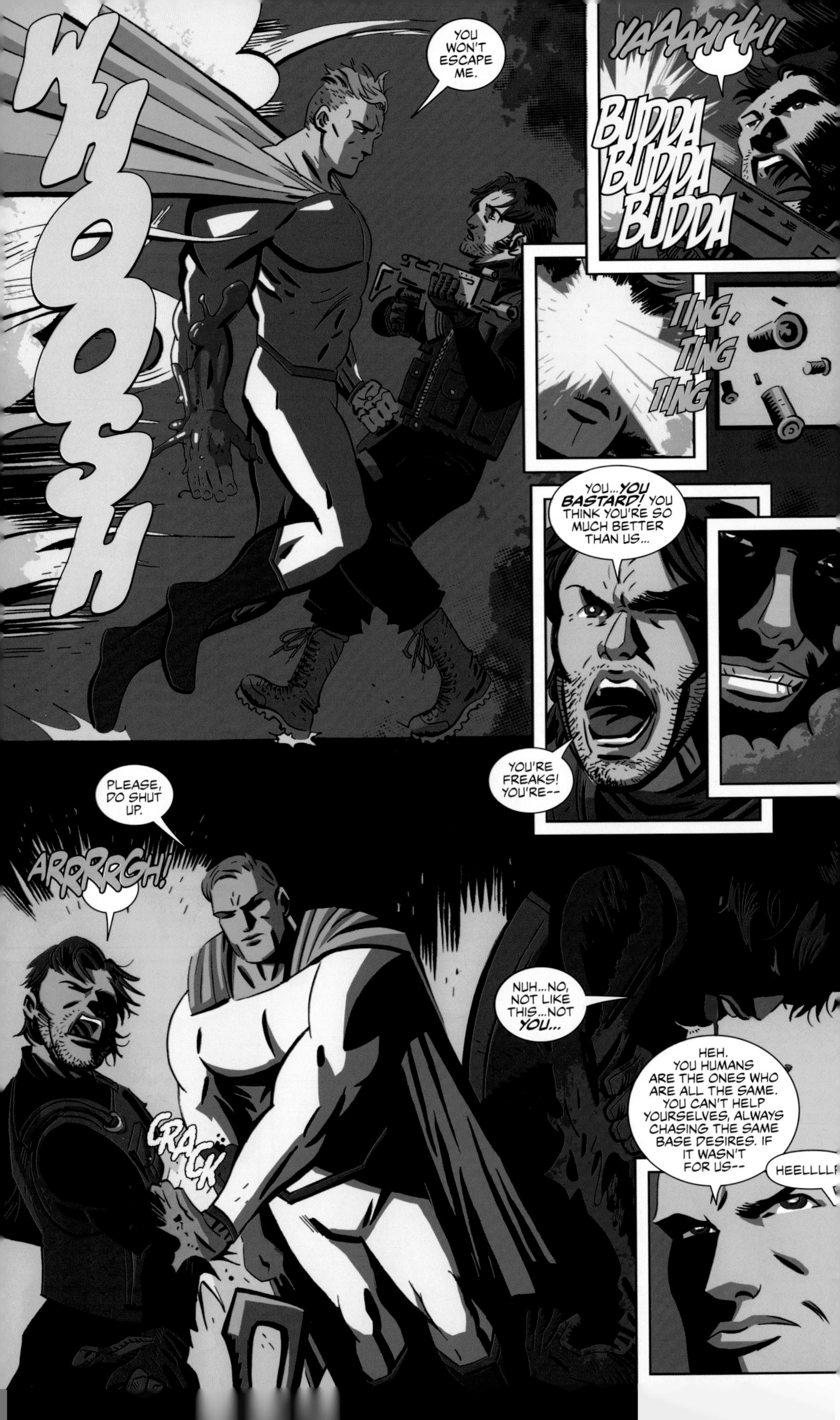
WHOOSH
YOU WON'T ESCAPE ME.
YAAAHHH!
BUDDA BUDDA BUDDA
TING, TING TING TING
YOU...YOU BASTARD! YOU THINK YOU'RE SO MUCH BETTER THAN US...
YOU'RE FREAKS! YOU'RE--
PLEASE, DO SHUT UP.
ARRRRGH!
CRACK
NUH...NO, NOT LIKE THIS...NOT YOU...
HEH. YOU HUMANS ARE THE ONES WHO ARE ALL THE SAME. YOU CAN'T HELP YOURSELVES, ALWAYS CHASING THE SAME BASE DESIRES. IF IT WASN'T FOR US--
HEELLLLP

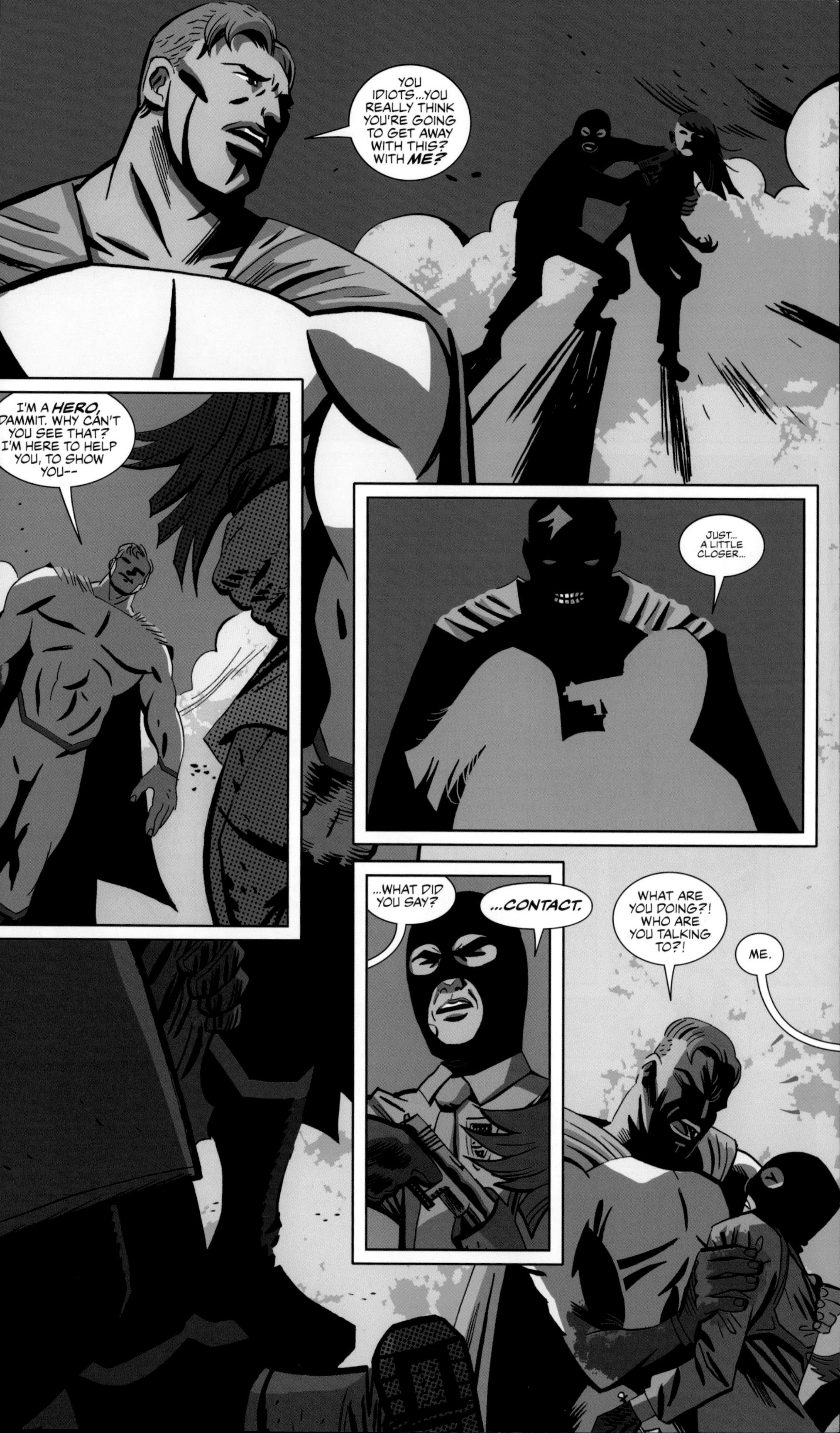
YOU IDIOTS...YOU REALLY THINK YOU'RE GOING TO GET AWAY WITH THIS? WITH ME?
I'M A HERO, DAMMIT. WHY CAN'T YOU SEE THAT? I'M HERE TO HELP YOU, TO SHOW YOU--
JUST... A LITTLE CLOSER...
...WHAT DID YOU SAY?
...CONTACT.
WHAT ARE YOU DOING?! WHO ARE YOU TALKING TO?!
ME.

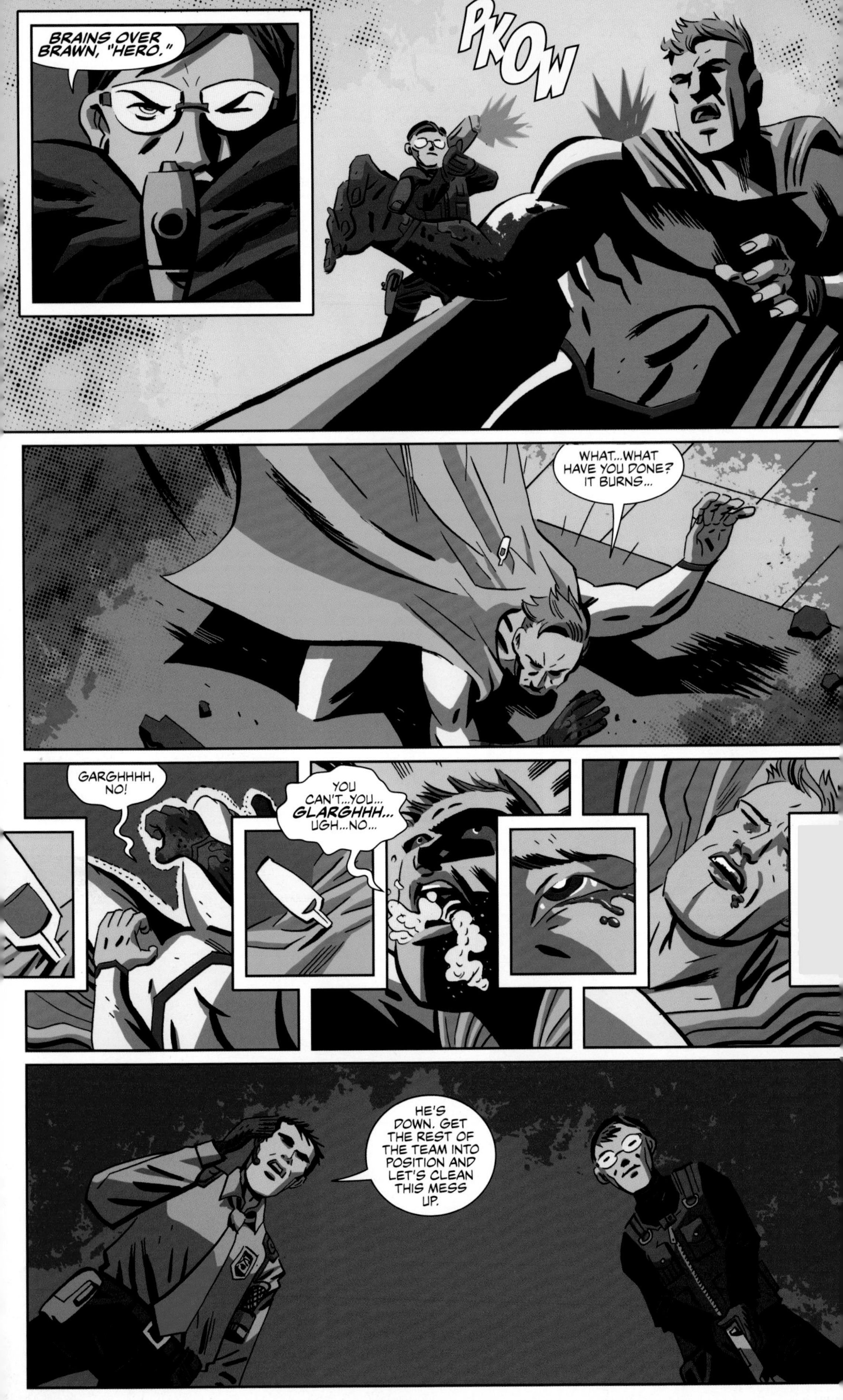
BRAINS OVER BRAWN, "HERO."
PKOW
WHAT...WHAT HAVE YOU DONE? IT BURNS...
GARGHHHH, NO!
YOU CAN'T...YOU... GLARGHHH... UGH...NO...
HE'S DOWN. GET THE REST OF THE TEAM INTO POSITION AND LET'S CLEAN THIS MESS UP.

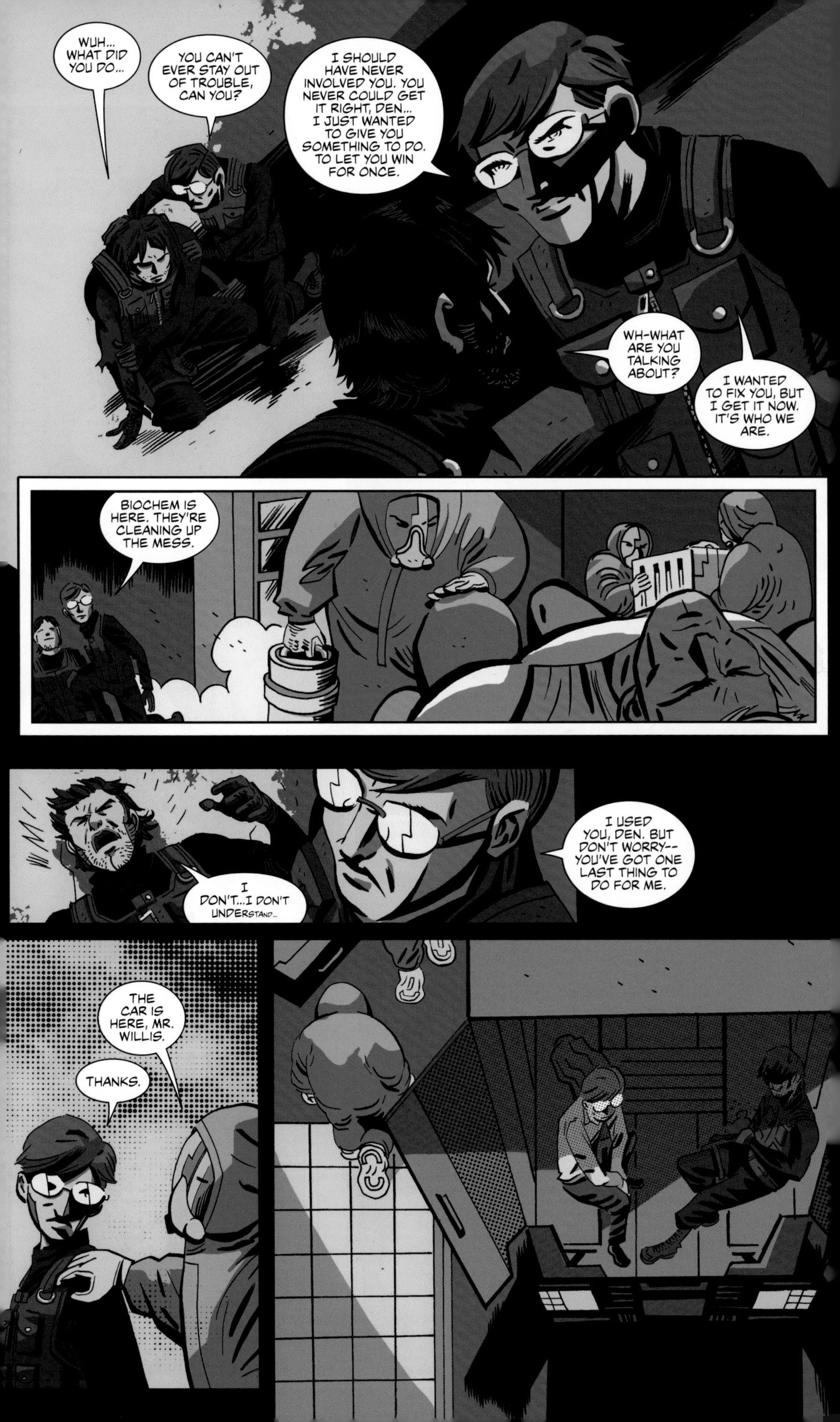
WUH... WHAT DID YOU DO...
YOU CAN'T EVER STAY OUT OF TROUBLE, CAN YOU?
I SHOULD HAVE NEVER INVOLVED YOU. YOU NEVER COULD GET IT RIGHT, DEN... I JUST WANTED TO GIVE YOU SOMETHING TO DO. TO LET YOU WIN FOR ONCE.
WH-WHAT ARE YOU TALKING ABOUT?
I WANTED TO FIX YOU, BUT I GET IT NOW. IT'S WHO WE ARE.
BIOCHEM IS HERE. THEY'RE CLEANING UP THE MESS.
I DON'T...I DON'T UNDERSTAND...
I USED YOU, DEN. BUT DON'T WORRY-- YOU'VE GOT ONE LAST THING TO DO FOR ME.
THE CAR IS HERE, MR. WILLIS.
THANKS.

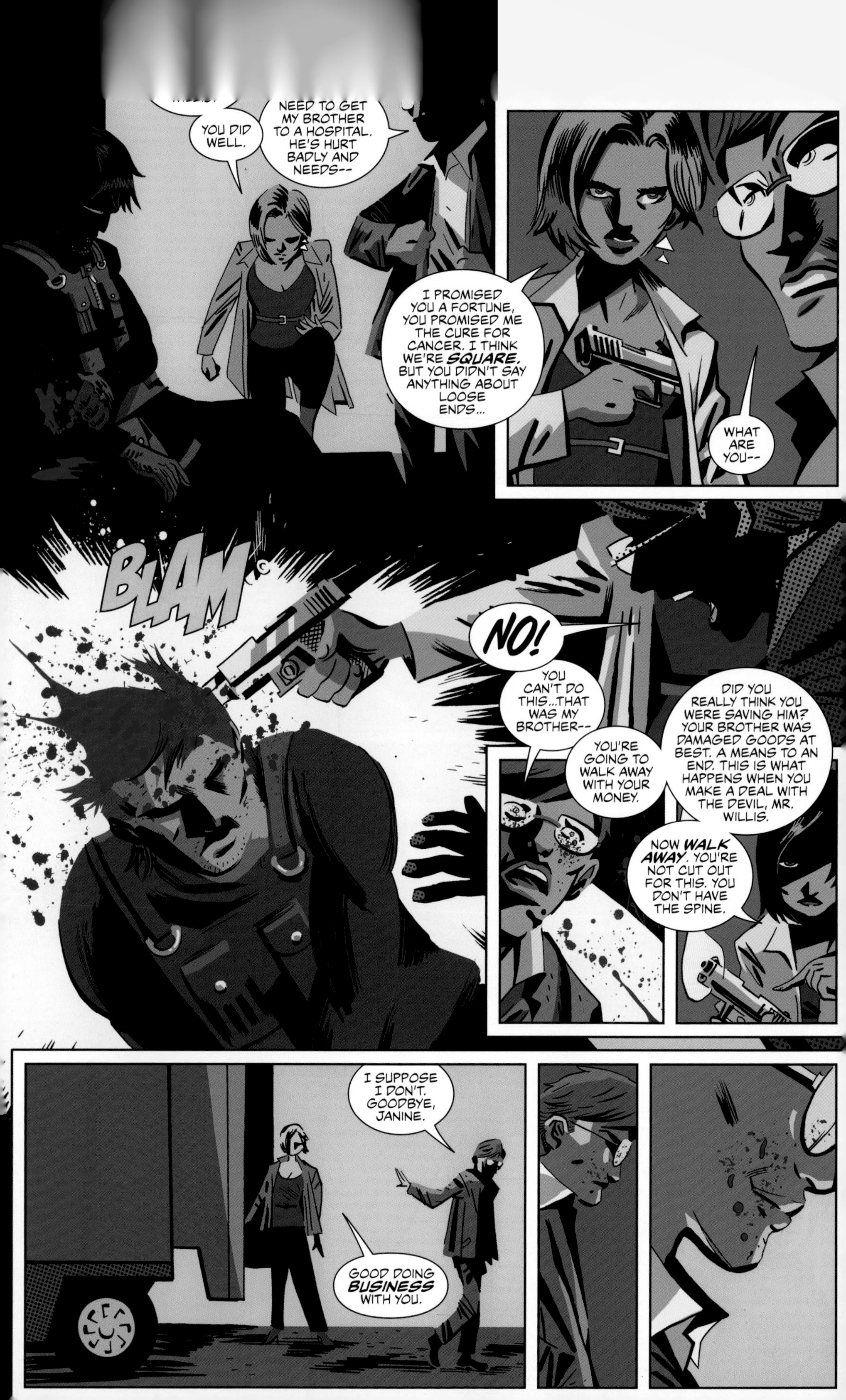
YOU DID WELL.
NEED TO GET MY BROTHER TO A HOSPITAL. HE'S HURT BADLY AND NEEDS--
I PROMISED YOU A FORTUNE, YOU PROMISED ME THE CURE FOR CANCER. I THINK WE'RE SQUARE. BUT YOU DIDN'T SAY ANYTHING ABOUT LOOSE ENDS...
WHAT ARE YOU--
BLAM
NO!
YOU CAN'T DO THIS...THAT WAS MY BROTHER--
DID YOU REALLY THINK YOU WERE SAVING HIM? YOUR BROTHER WAS DAMAGED GOODS AT BEST. A MEANS TO AN END. THIS IS WHAT HAPPENS WHEN YOU MAKE A DEAL WITH THE DEVIL, MR. WILLIS.
YOU'RE GOING TO WALK AWAY WITH YOUR MONEY.
NOW WALK AWAY. YOU'RE NOT CUT OUT FOR THIS. YOU DON'T HAVE THE SPINE.
I SUPPOSE I DON'T. GOODBYE, JANINE.
GOOD DOING BUSINESS WITH YOU.

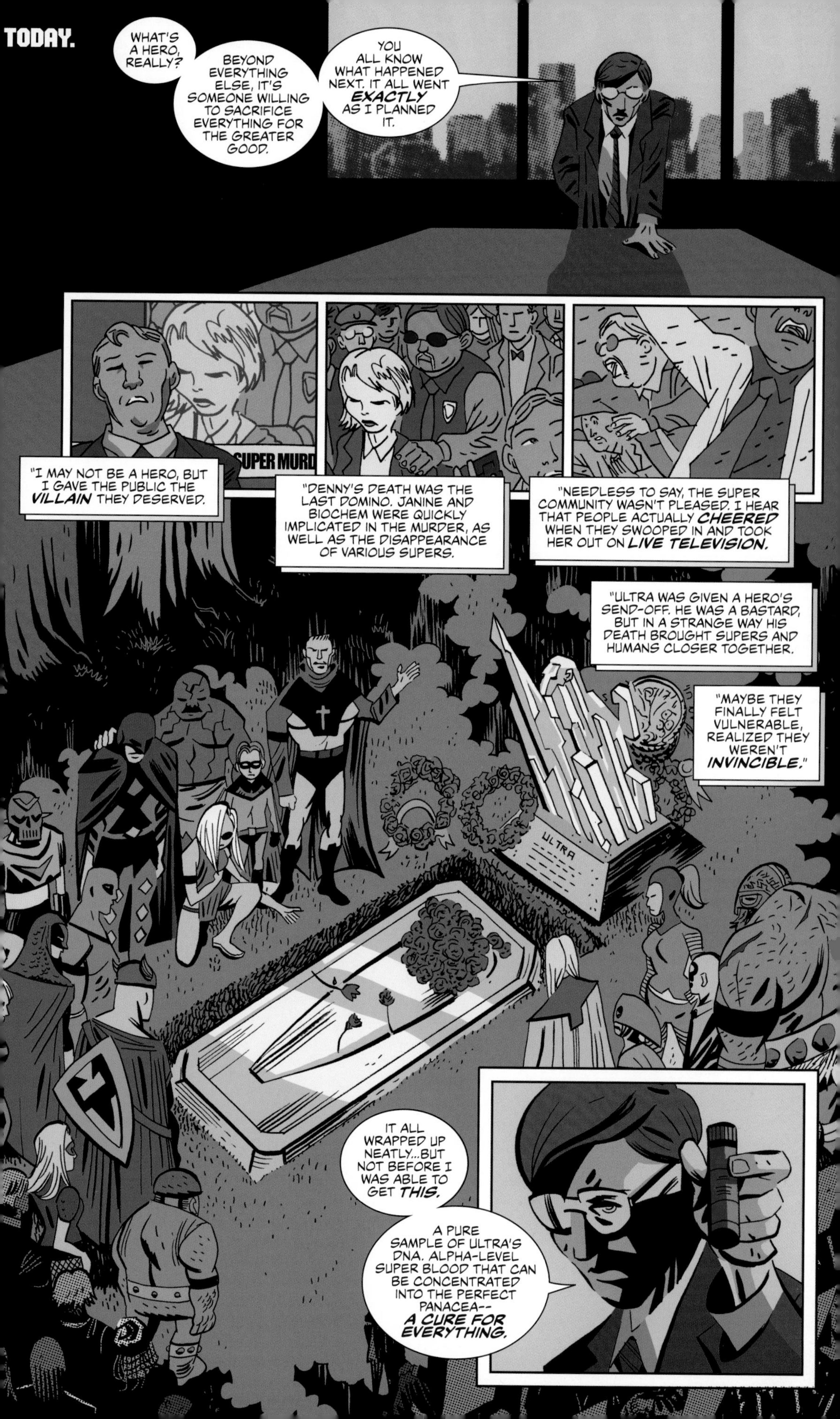
TODAY.
WHAT'S A HERO, REALLY?
BEYOND EVERYTHING ELSE, IT'S SOMEONE WILLING TO SACRIFICE EVERYTHING FOR THE GREATER GOOD.
YOU ALL KNOW WHAT HAPPENED NEXT. IT ALL WENT EXACTLY AS I PLANNED IT.
SUPER MURD
"I MAY NOT BE A HERO, BUT I GAVE THE PUBLIC THE VILLAIN THEY DESERVED.
"DENNY'S DEATH WAS THE LAST DOMINO. JANINE AND BIOCHEM WERE QUICKLY IMPLICATED IN THE MURDER, AS WELL AS THE DISAPPEARANCE OF VARIOUS SUPERS.
"NEEDLESS TO SAY, THE SUPER COMMUNITY WASN'T PLEASED. I HEAR THAT PEOPLE ACTUALLY CHEERED WHEN THEY SWOOPED IN AND TOOK HER OUT ON LIVE TELEVISION.
"ULTRA WAS GIVEN A HERO'S SEND-OFF. HE WAS A BASTARD, BUT IN A STRANGE WAY HIS DEATH BROUGHT SUPERS AND HUMANS CLOSER TOGETHER.
"MAYBE THEY FINALLY FELT VULNERABLE, REALIZED THEY WEREN'T INVINCIBLE."
ULTRA
IT ALL WRAPPED UP NEATLY...BUT NOT BEFORE I WAS ABLE TO GET THIS.
A PURE SAMPLE OF ULTRA'S DNA. ALPHA-LEVEL SUPER BLOOD THAT CAN BE CONCENTRATED INTO THE PERFECT PANACEA-- A CURE FOR EVERYTHING.

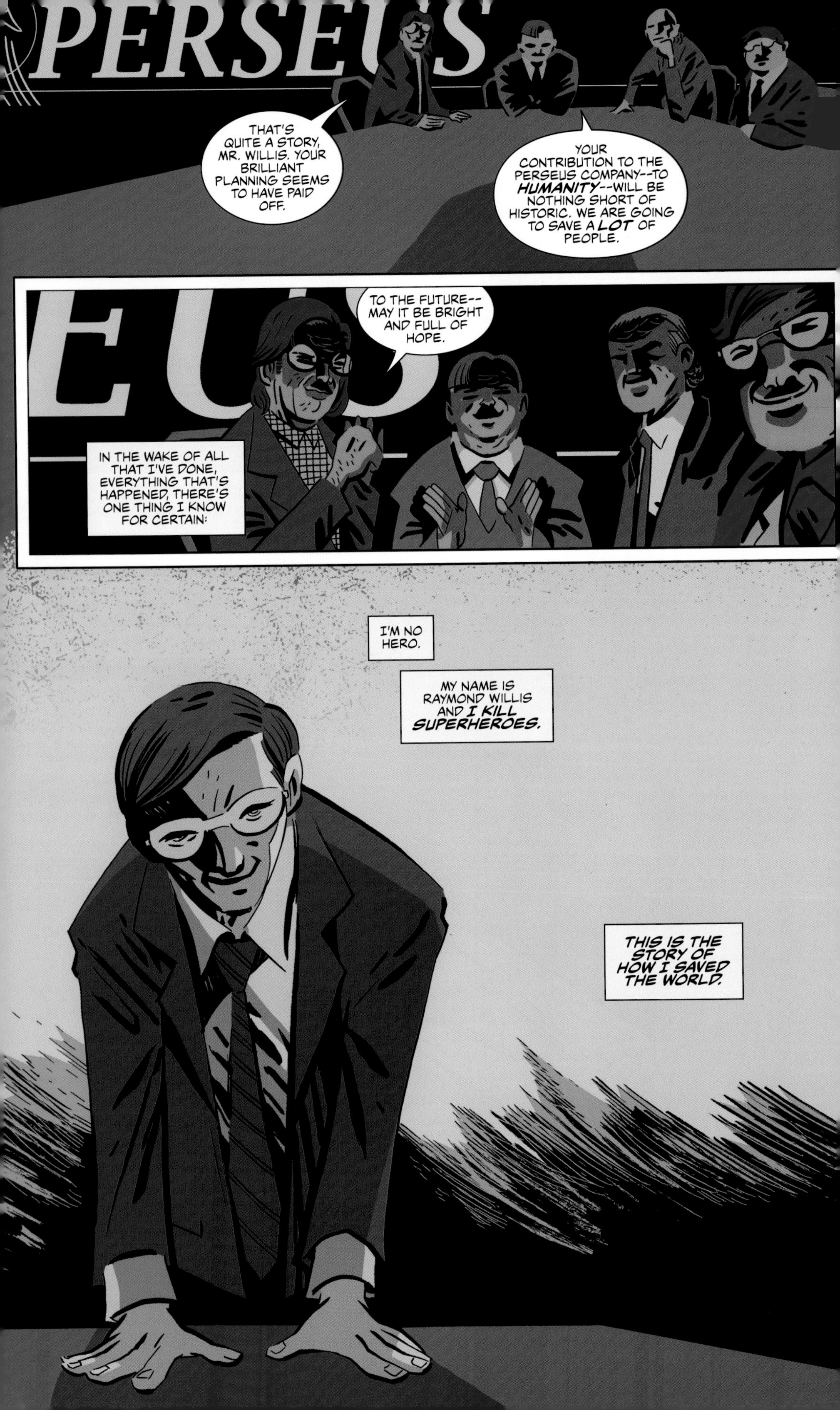
PERSEUS
THAT'S QUITE A STORY, MR. WILLIS. YOUR BRILLIANT PLANNING SEEMS TO HAVE PAID OFF.
YOUR CONTRIBUTION TO THE PERSEUS COMPANY--TO HUMANITY--WILL BE NOTHING SHORT OF HISTORIC. WE ARE GOING TO SAVE A LOT OF PEOPLE.
TO THE FUTURE--MAY IT BE BRIGHT AND FULL OF HOPE.
IN THE WAKE OF ALL THAT I'VE DONE, EVERYTHING THAT'S HAPPENED, THERE'S ONE THING I KNOW FOR CERTAIN:
I'M NO HERO.
MY NAME IS RAYMOND WILLIS AND I KILL SUPERHEROES.
THIS IS THE STORY OF HOW I SAVED THE WORLD.

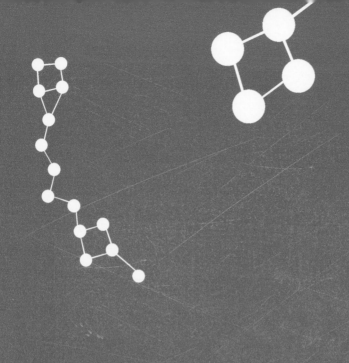
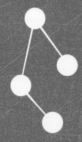

Cover Gallery

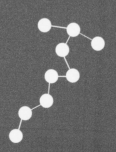

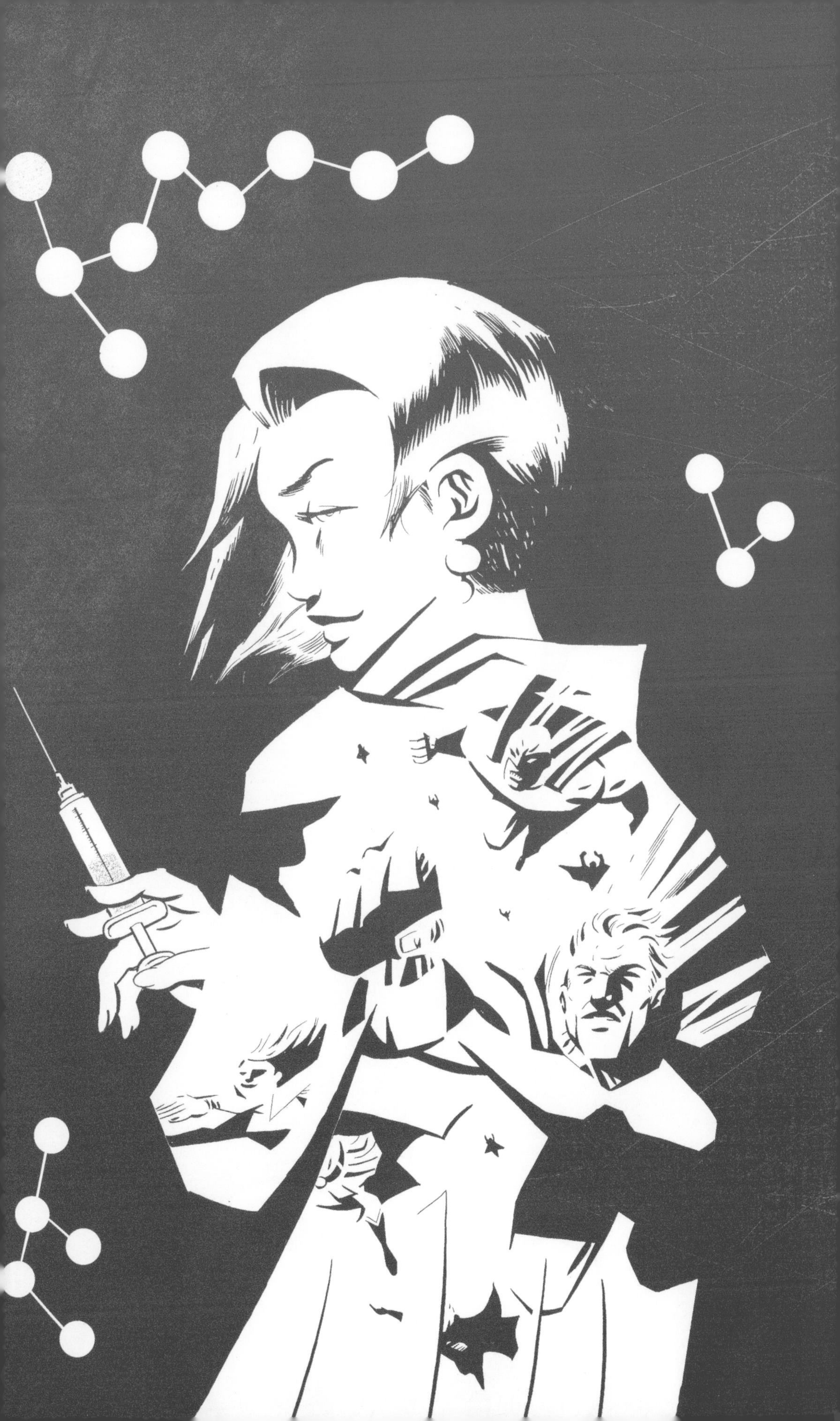

Issue One Cover
Victor Santos

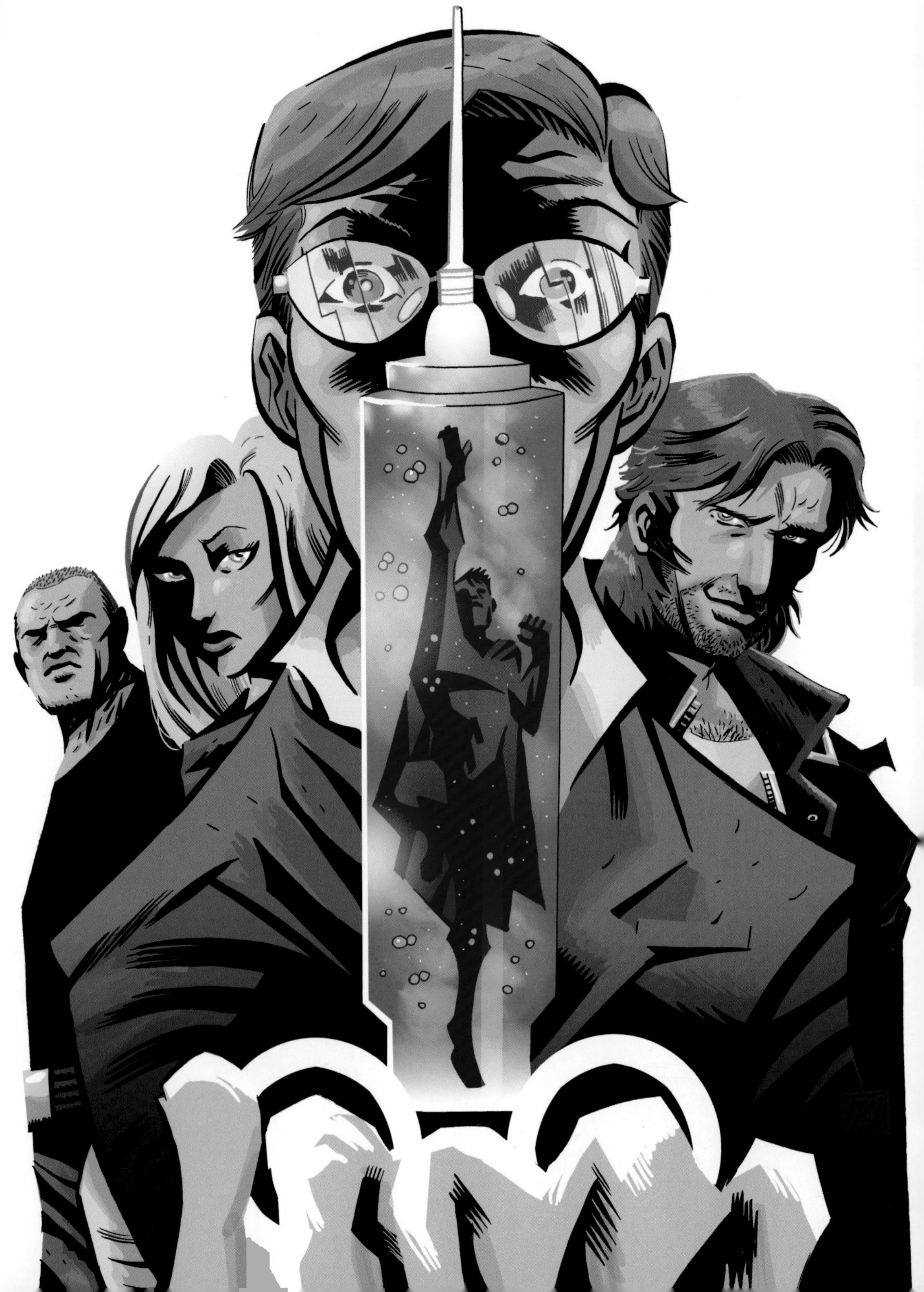

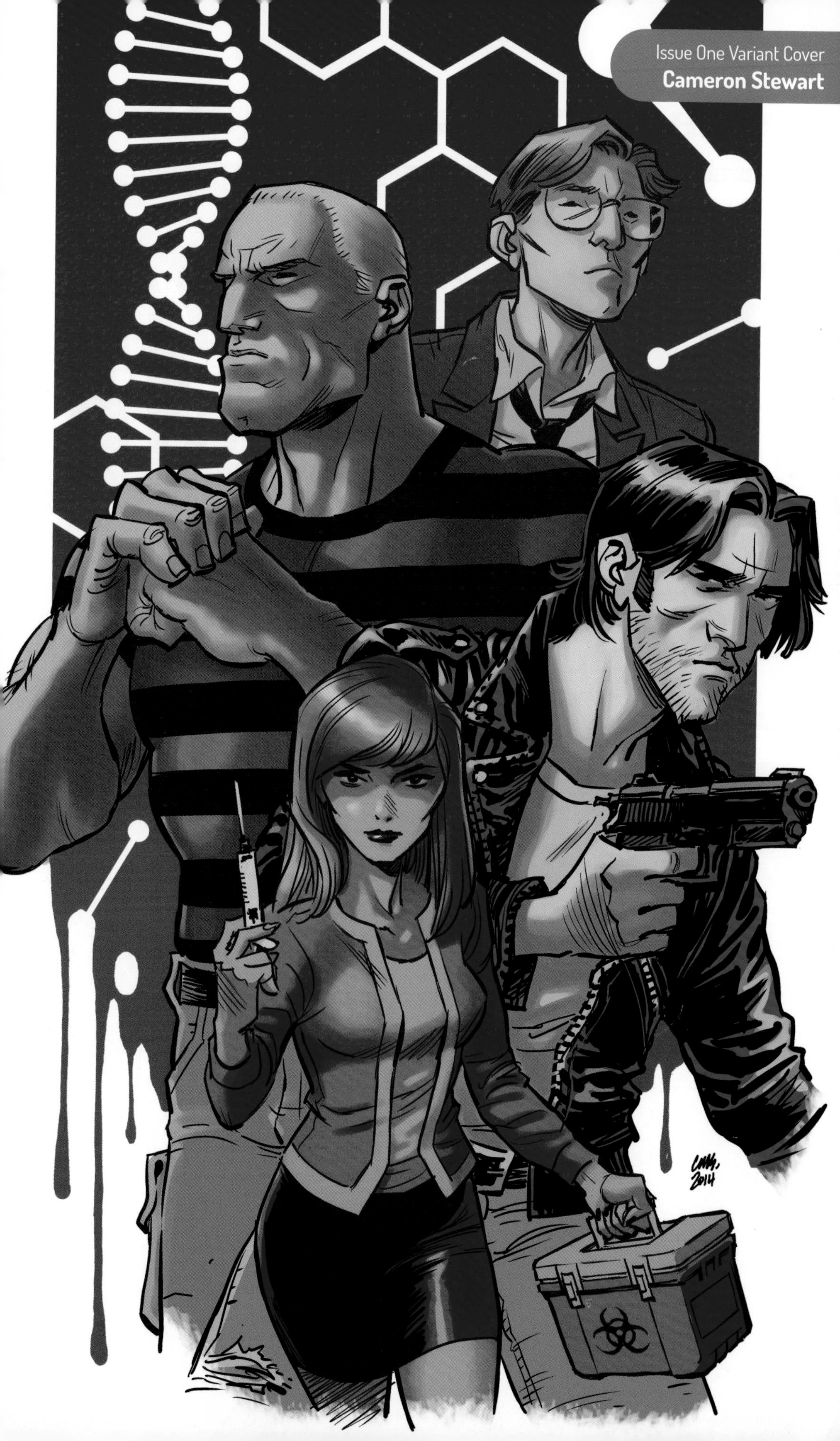

Issue One Variant Cover
Cameron Stewart

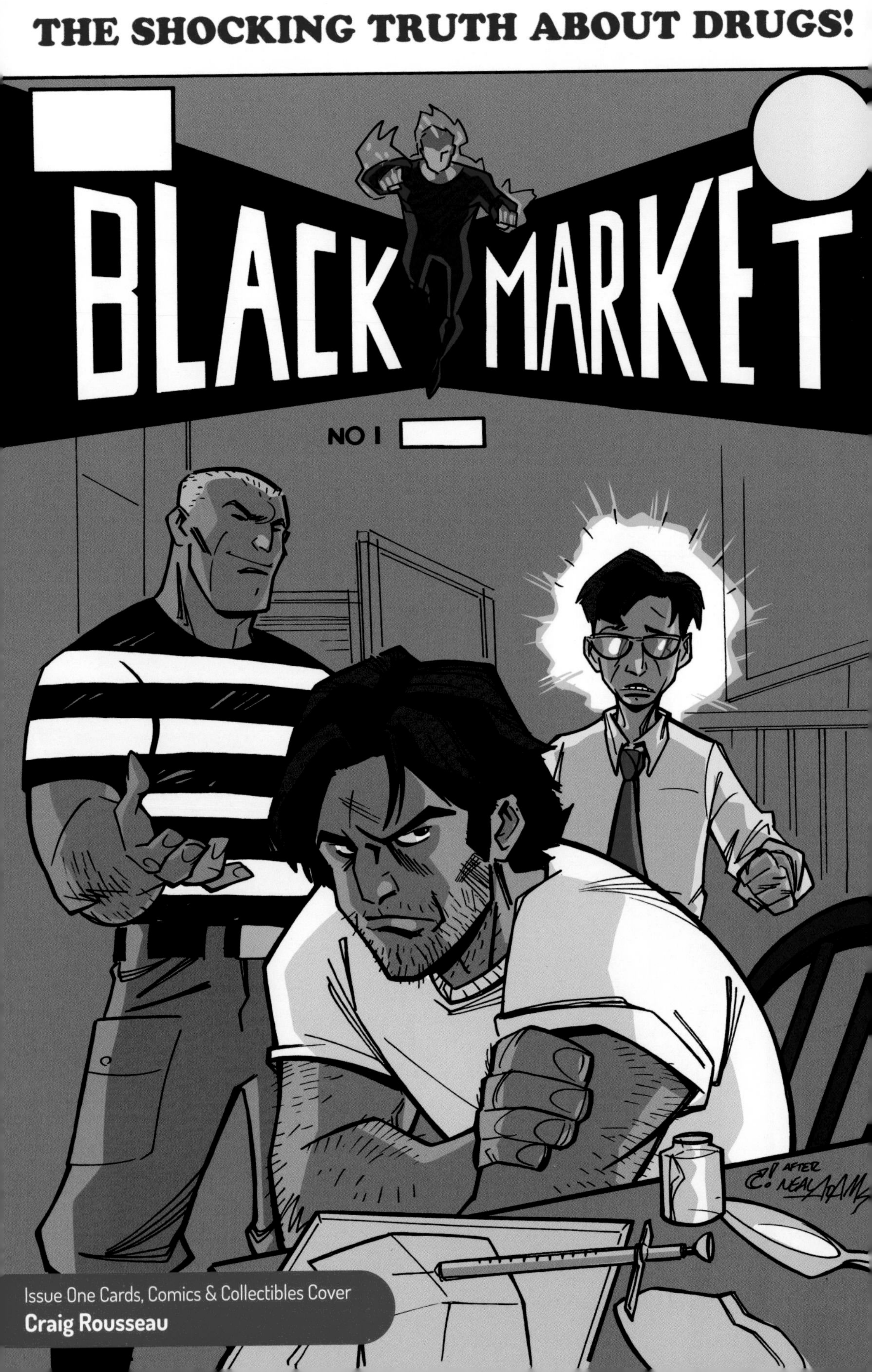
THE SHOCKING TRUTH ABOUT DRUGS!
BLACK MARKET
NO 1

Issue One Cards, Comics & Collectibles Cover
Craig Rousseau

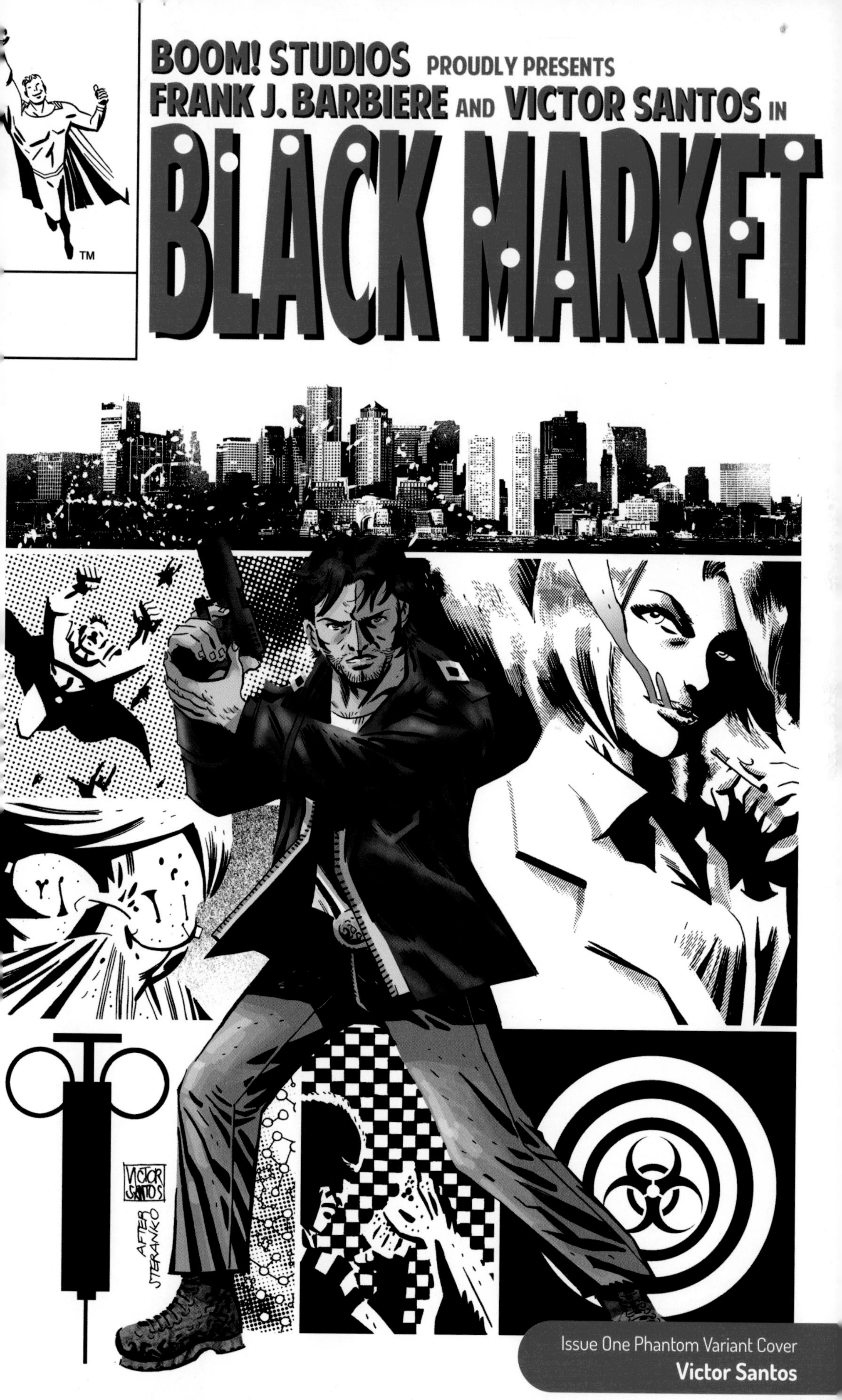
BOOM! STUDIOS PROUDLY PRESENTS
FRANK J. BARBIERE AND VICTOR SANTOS IN
BLACK MARKET
TM
VICTOR SANTOS
AFTER STERANKO

Issue One Phantom Variant Cover
Victor Santos

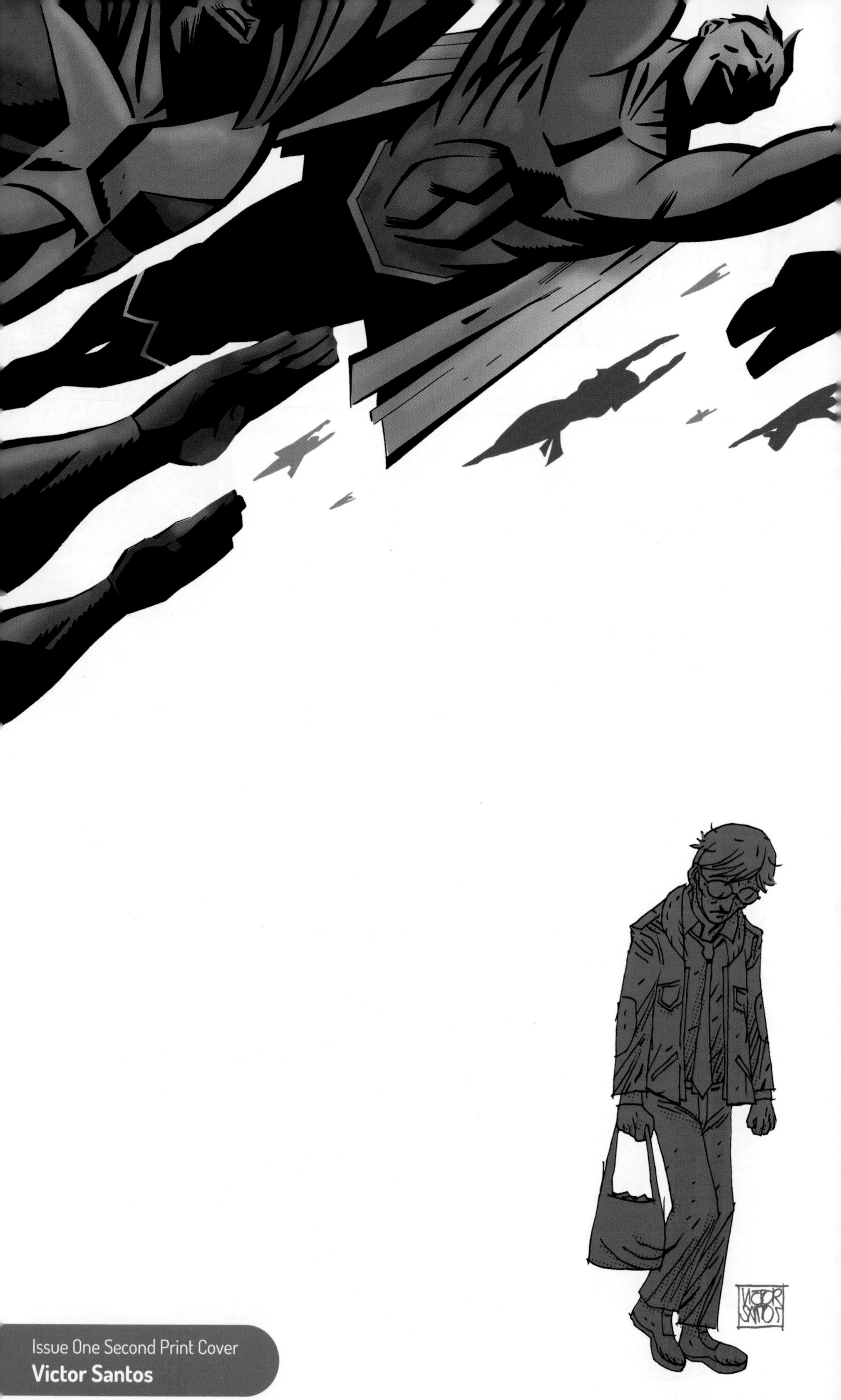
VICTOR SANTOS

Issue One Second Print Cover
Victor Santos

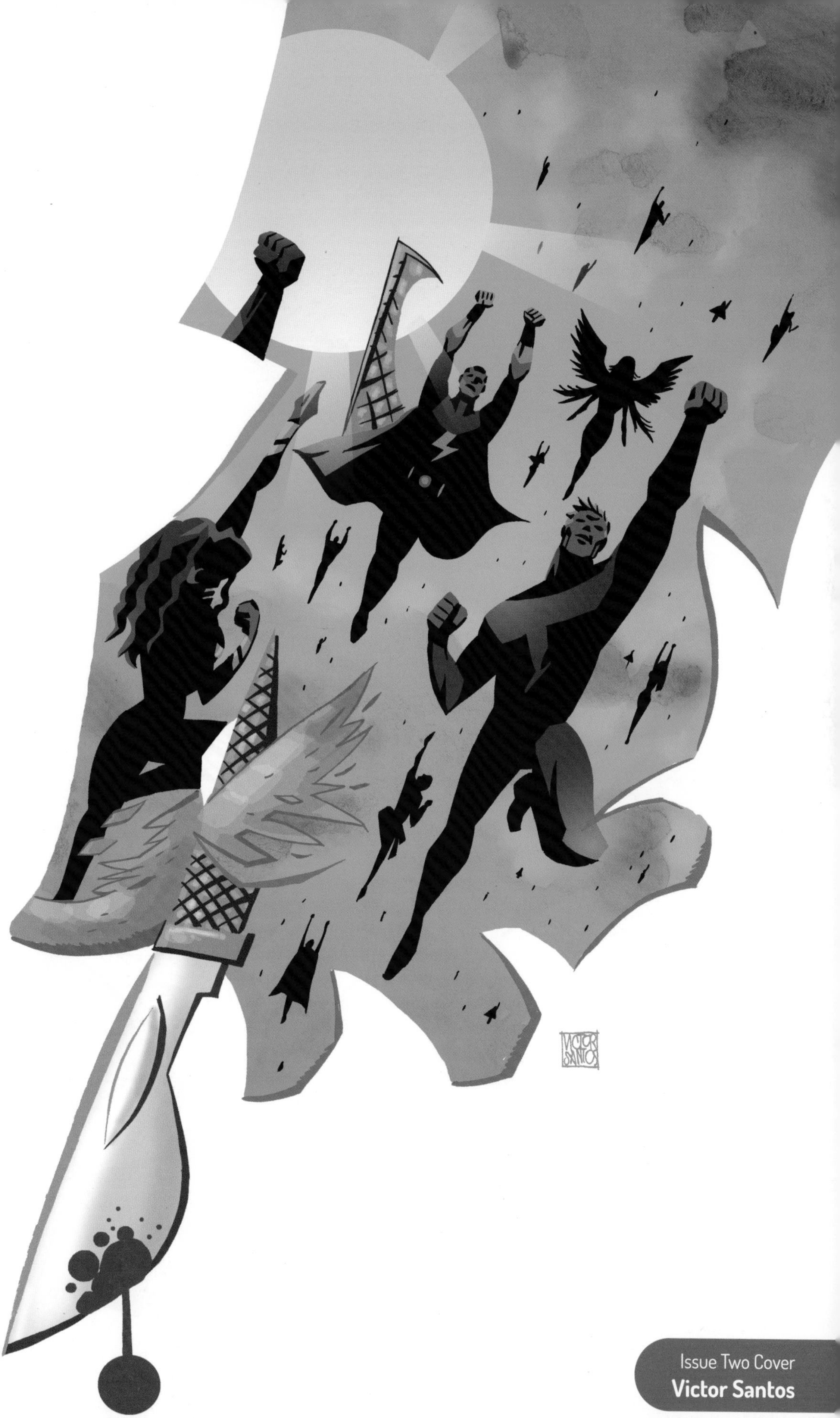
VICTOR SANTOS

Issue Two Cover
Victor Santos

Issue Three Cover
Victor Santos

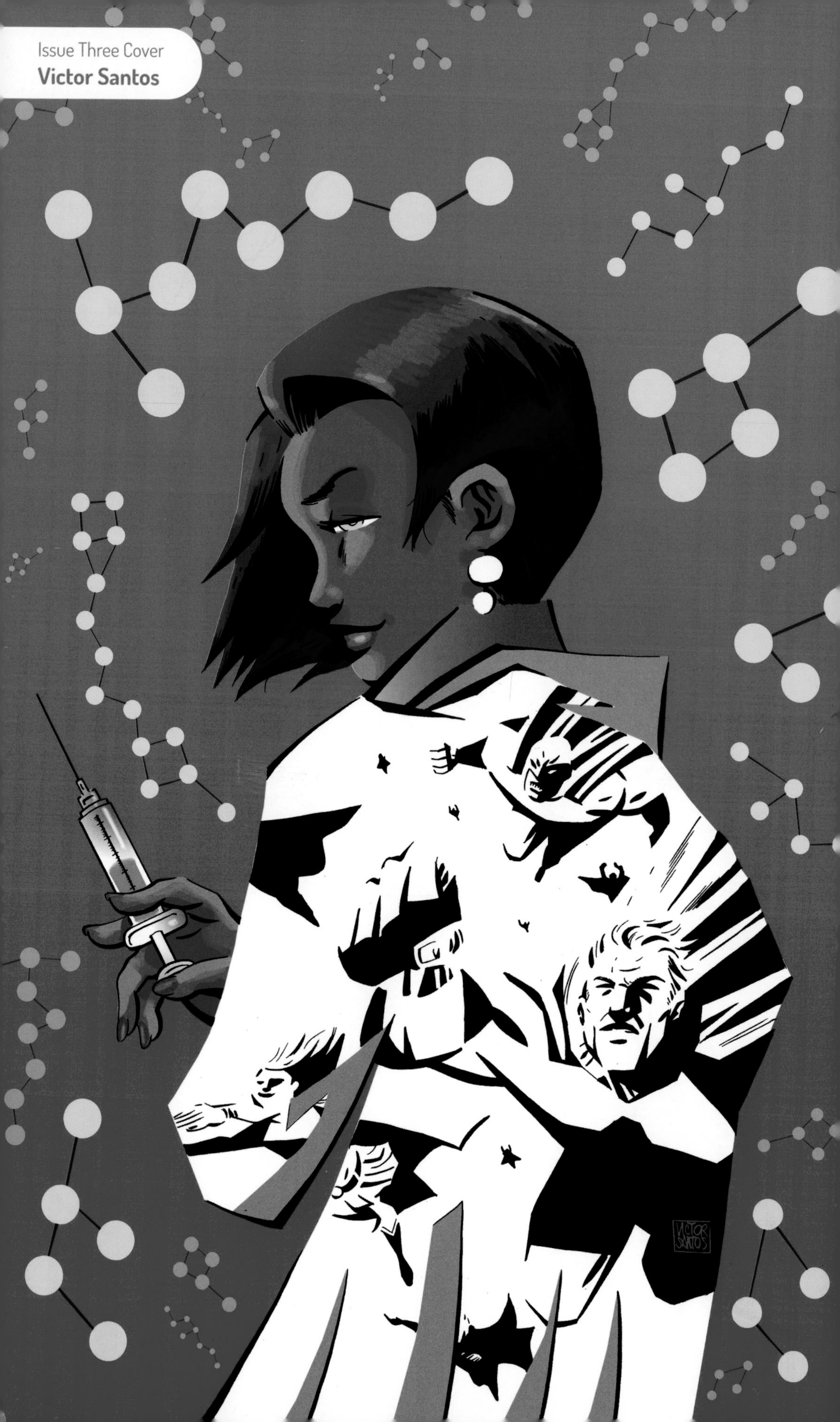
VICTOR SANTOS

Issue Four Cover
Victor Santos

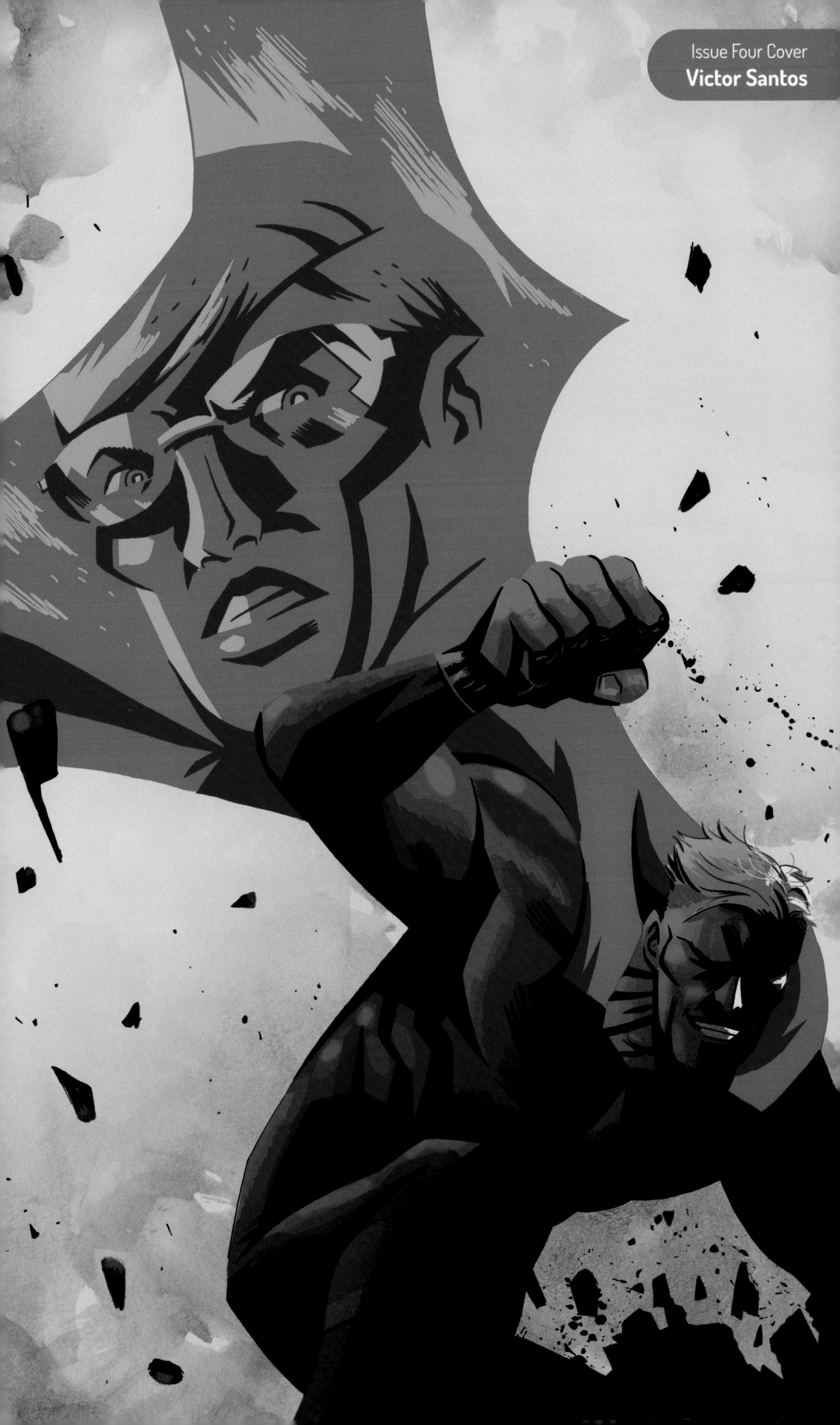

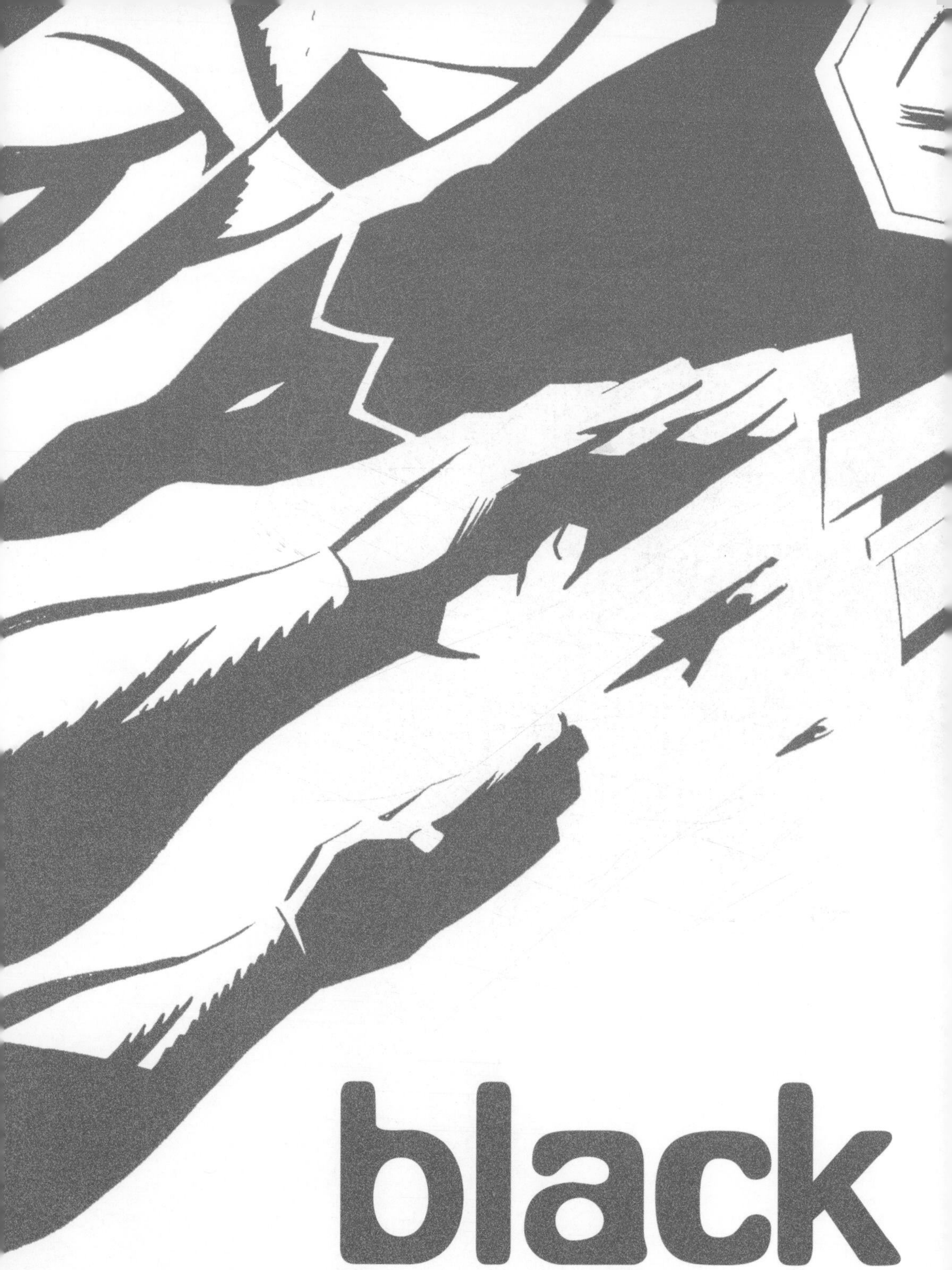

black

market™

Behind the Scenes

Script to Page

The evolution of *Black Market*, from original script to final illustration

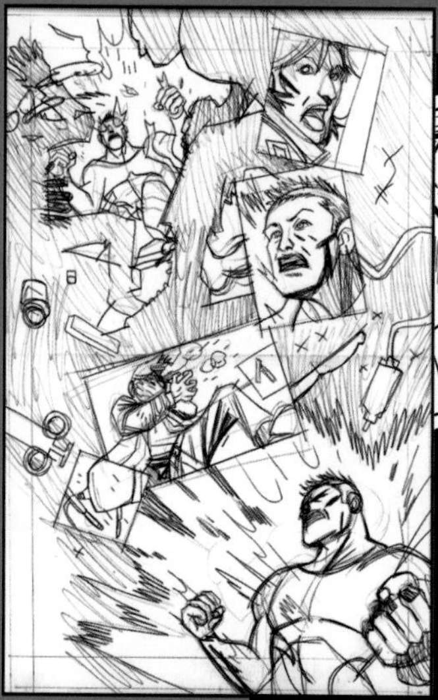

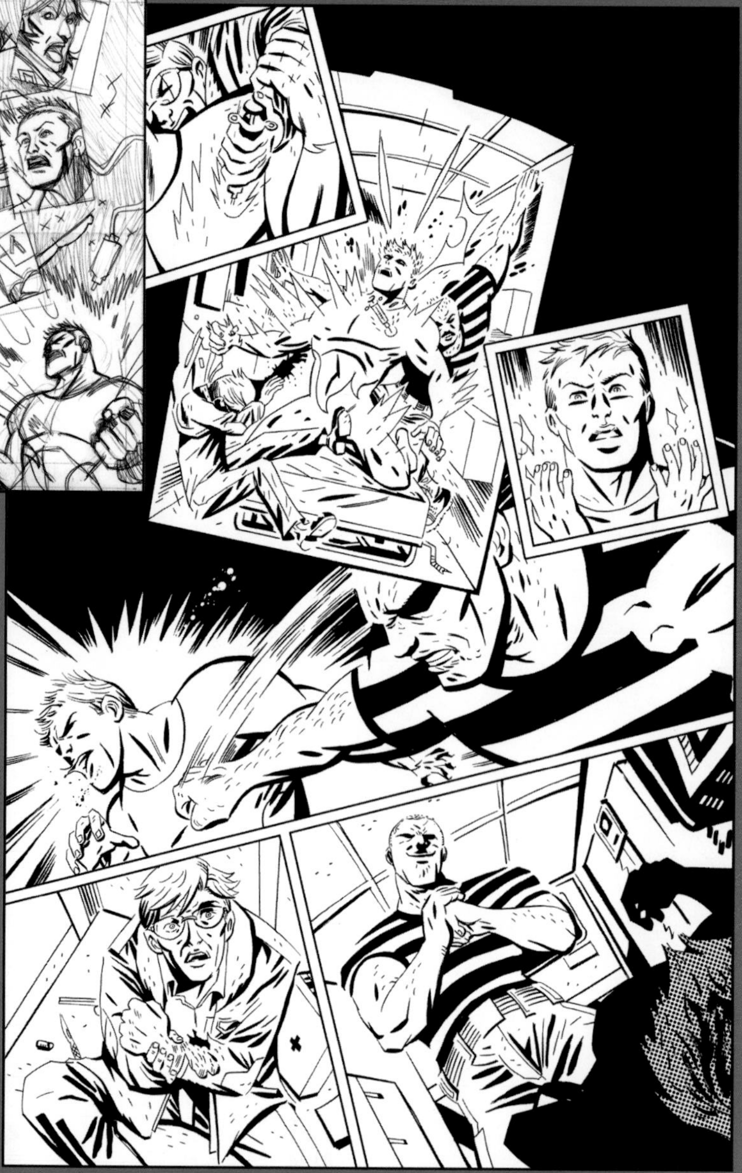

Issue One, Page Seventeen

Panel 1: Ray springs up from behind Hotspot, jamming a needle into his heart. Hotspot grabs Ray's wrist which BURNS.

Panel 2: Ray falls, clenching his burnt wrist as Bruiser watches.

Panel 3: Hotspot is startled as his flame power is snuffed out...he looks at his hands in shock.

HOTSPOT: You bastard! What...what have you done—

Panel 4: Bruiser PUNCHES THE HERO IN THE FACE.

Panel 5: Ray clutches his wrist, looking up and yelling to Denny.

RAY: Get us home, Denny. NOW.

Panel 6: Bruiser cracks his knuckles over the unconscious hero.

BRUISER: Still got it! Not so high and mighty now, eh, firebug?

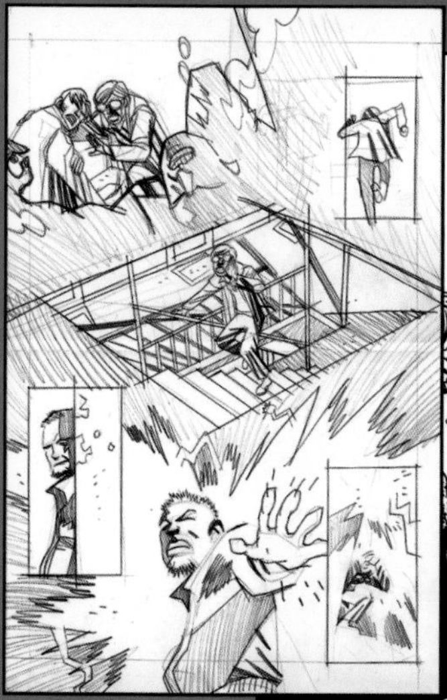

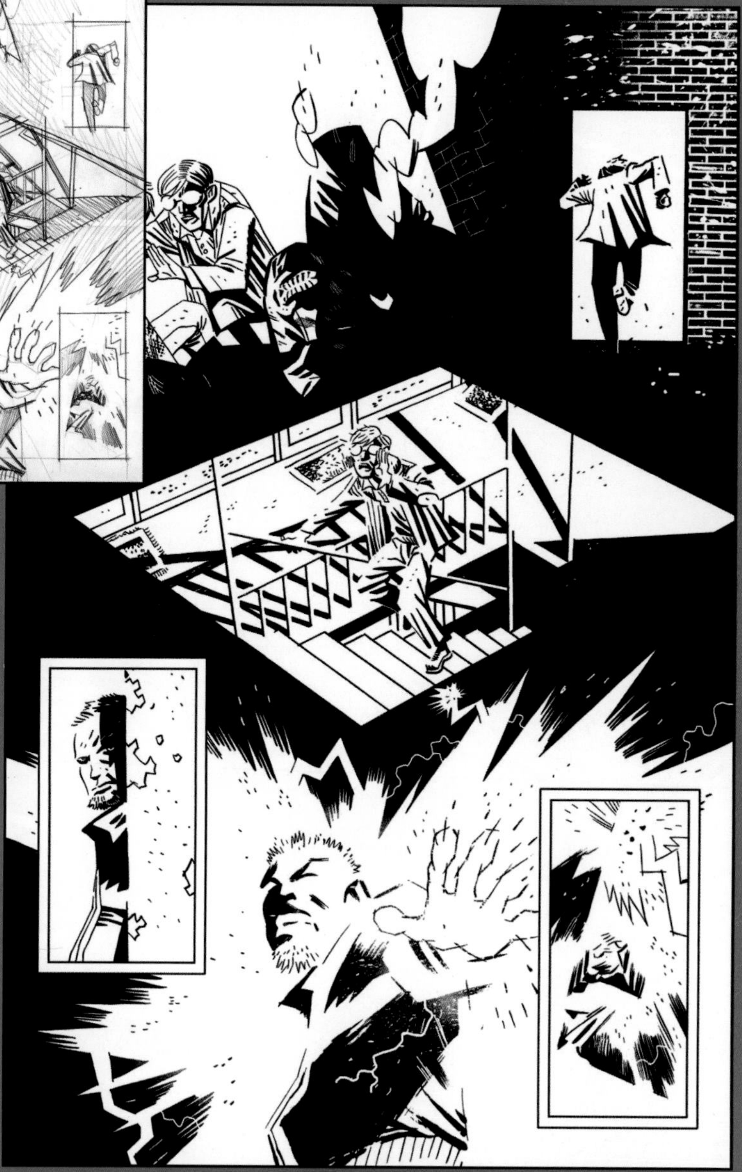

Issue Two, Page Eighteen

Panel 1: Ray bends down to talk to Denny, who is a little burnt from being shocked.

RAY: Jeez, Denny, you gotta get to a hospital—

DENNY: Ray, I'm fine! You gotta get him! Go!

Panel 2: Ray apprehensively enters the door the Super opened, hugging the frame.

RAY (small): What am I doing...I can't believe this...

Panel 3: Ray is in a hallway. It's a run-down apartment building. He calls out.

RAY: Leonard! We just want to talk! We're...um...*scientists*, and we didn't know how else to get in touch...

Panel 4: Leonard turns the corner, where he was hiding, shocking and looking furious.

LEONARD: You...you people...you're not worth my time, I don't want to play into your tricks...

Panel 5: Leonard starts to spark and release electricity violently at the end of the hall, screaming out. Ray shields his face, cowering a bit.

LEONARD: YOU HEAR ME?!

Panel 6: Ray cowers behind his corner of the hallway, ducking for cover.

RAY: Idiot's...gonna destroy this whole building...

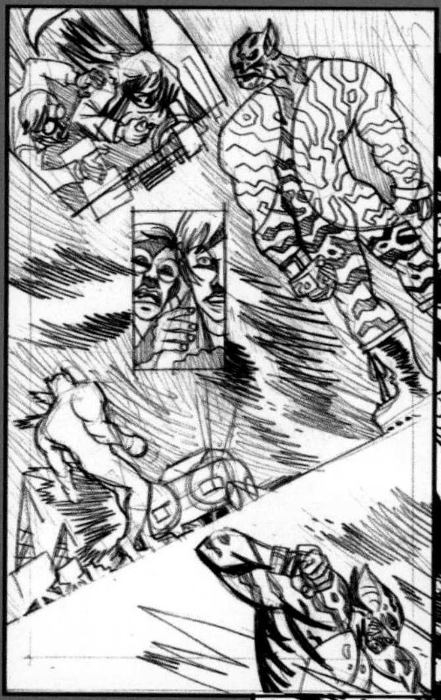

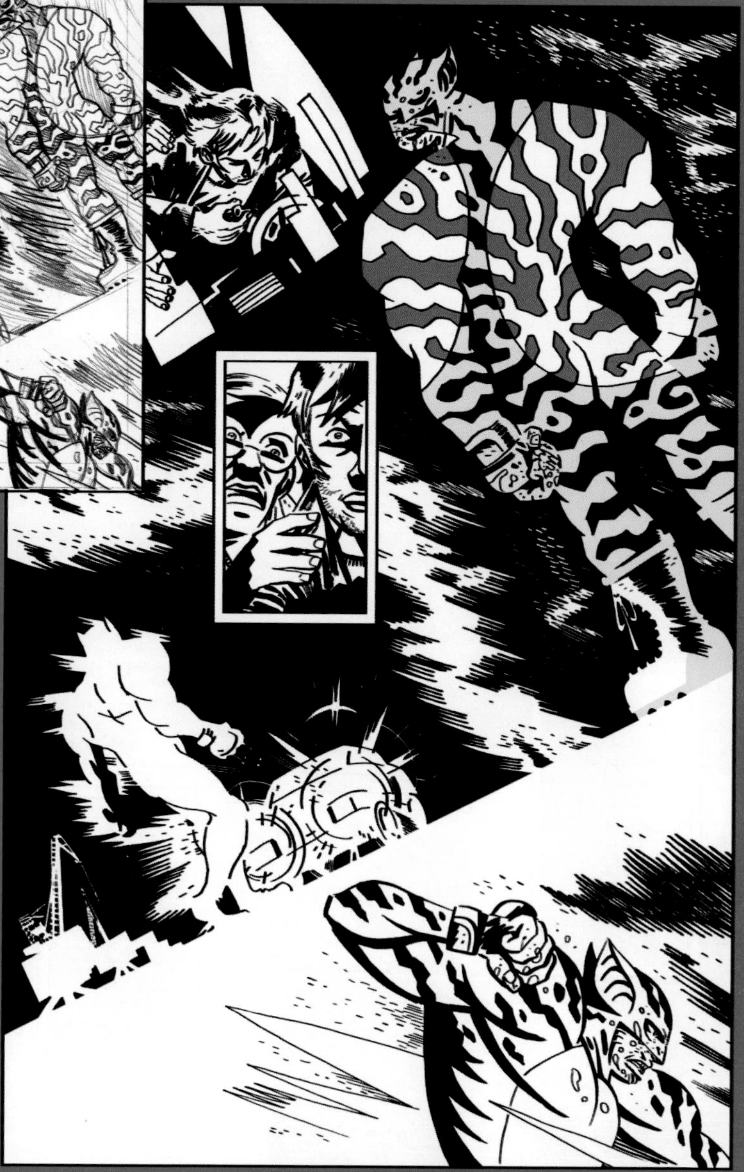

Issue Three, Page Nineteen

Panel 1: Denny scurries into the car and tries to put his keys in the ignition.

DENNY: Ugh...stupid Bruiser, didn't say his friend was a sociopath...

Panel 2: Tiger Bomb stands, bloody, over the body of the cop and in the background we see THE LIGHTS from Denny's car come on. Tiger Bomb looks over his shoulder, noticing the lights.

Panel 3: Ray turns to Denny, yelling.

RAY: Dammit, turn off the lights! Turn off the—

Panel 4: A big panel from behind Ray and Denny as they look up and see TIGER BOMB STANDING IN FRONT OF THE CAR. They are horrified and he looks ominous as all hell, blood on him.

Panel 5: Small panel as Tiger Bomb winds back his arm for a punch.

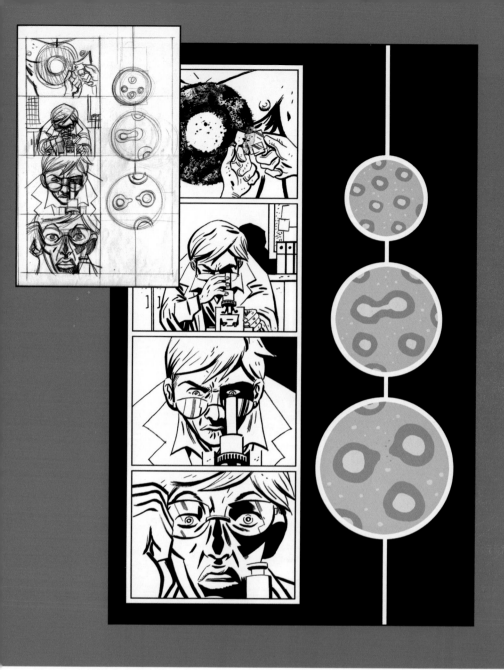

Issue Four, Page Three

Panel 1: Let's see a shot from overhead as Ray continues to examine the body from Issue #2 (with the huge hole in it). Ray is scraping some of the wound off onto a slide.

    TIMESTAMP: NOVEMBER 8TH, 2012.

    CAP RAY: Looking at that corpse, the final pieces began to snap together.

    CAP RAY: I didn't know it yet, but I was about to change the course of history.

Panel 2: Ray sits at a desk and looks into a microscope.

    RAY: Would you look at that...

Panel 3: Let's see what Ray is seeing—close on the slide and we see the cells DIVIDING. The idea is that the wound is actually healing.

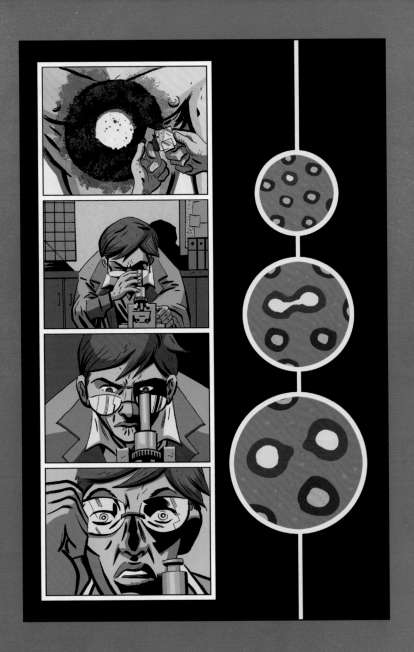

RAY: It's...*healing*.

Panel 4: Ray looks shocked as he looks through the microscope.

RAY: I can't...this is...this is it. This is...*everything*.

Panel 5: Pull out, and have Ray looking up at the camera. He looks shocked and almost a little worried—the gears are turning in his head that he can use this to make a cure. He's still over his microscope.

RAY: I was *right*.

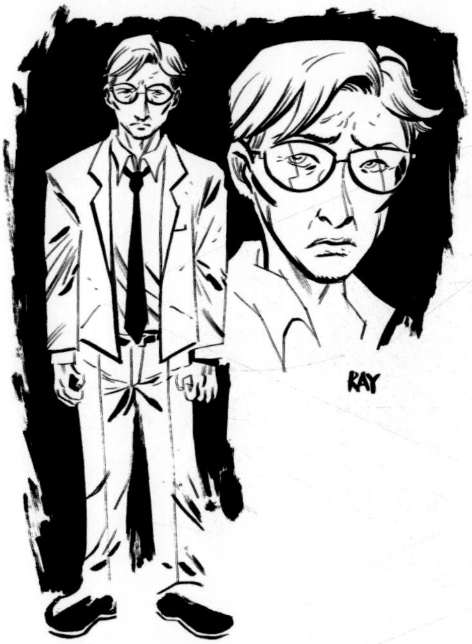
RAY

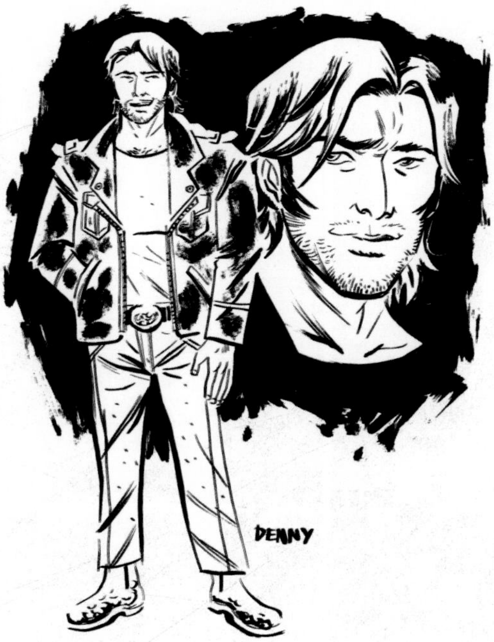
DENNY

Issue One Layouts, Pages 1-11

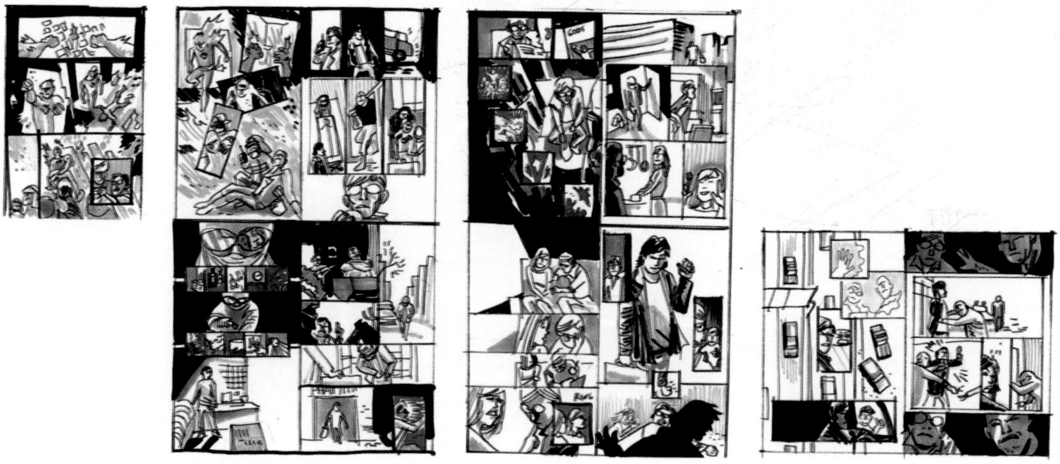

Pages 12-22

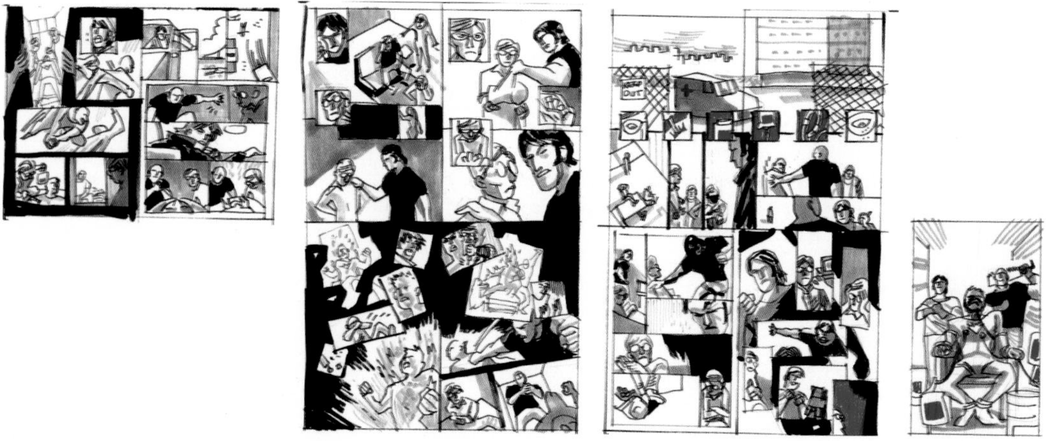

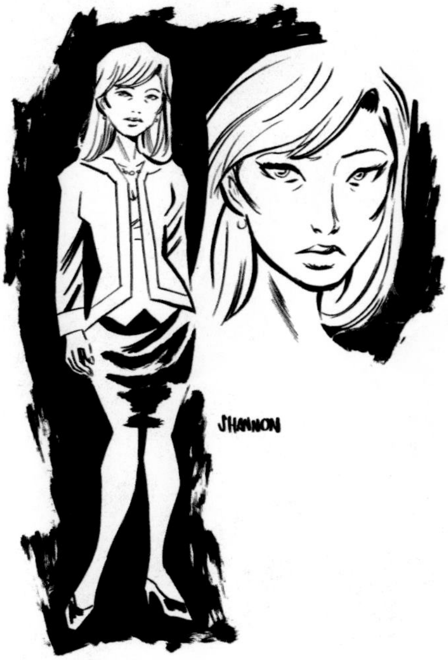
SHANNON
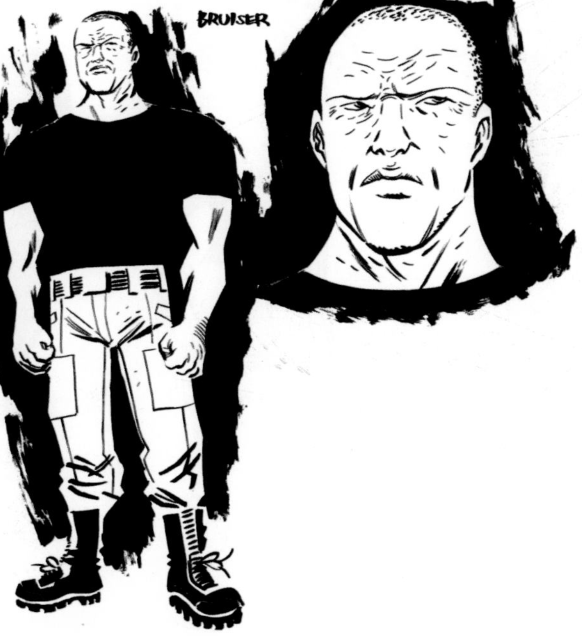
BRUISER

Issue Two Layouts, Pages 1-11

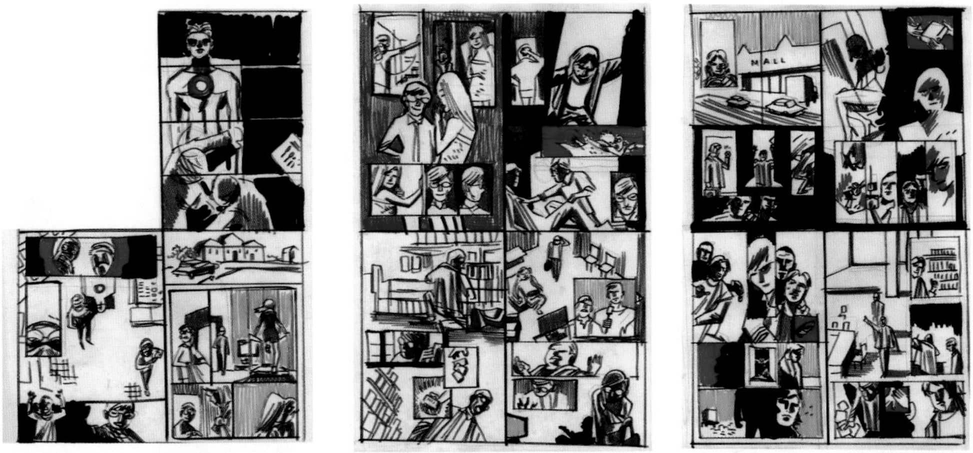

Pages 12-22

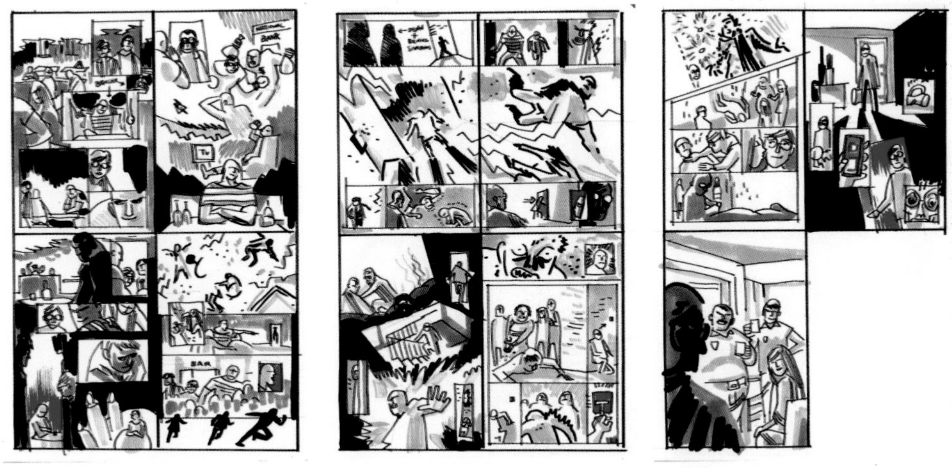

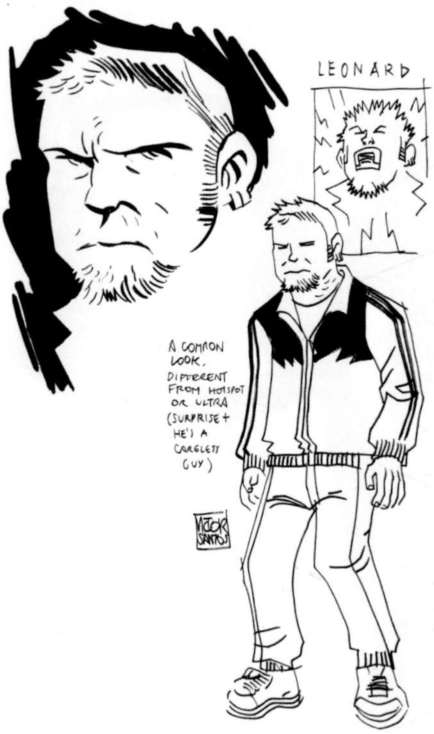
LEONARD
A COMMON LOOK, DIFFERENT FROM HOTSPOT OR ULTRA (SURPRISE+ HE'S A CARELESS GUY)

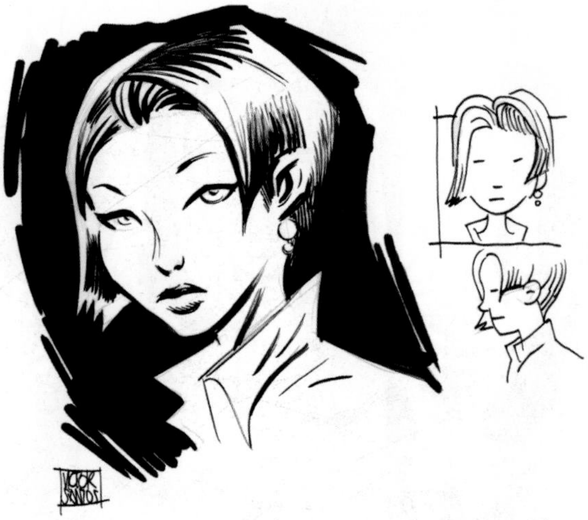

Issue Three Layouts, Pages 1-11

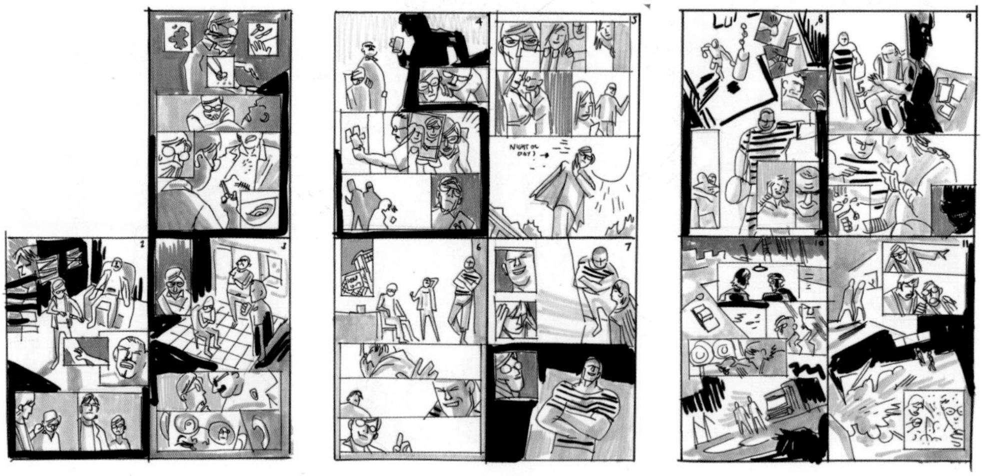
NIGHT OR DAY?

Pages 12-22

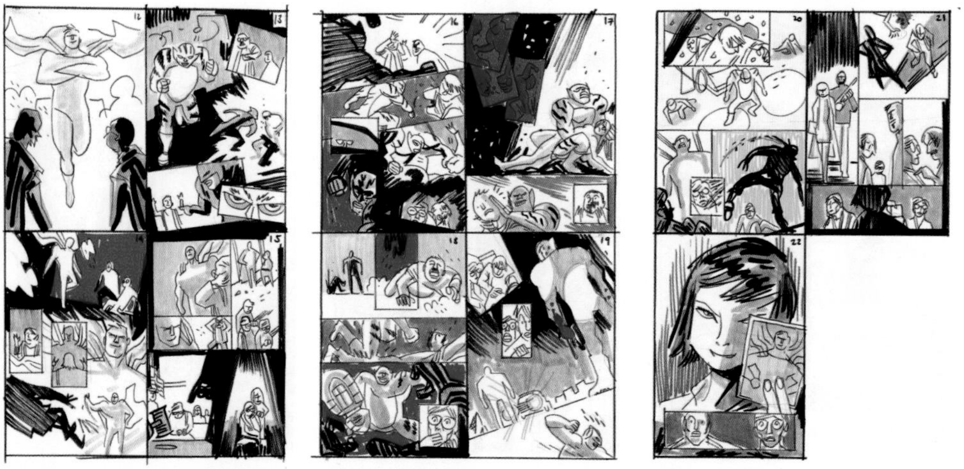

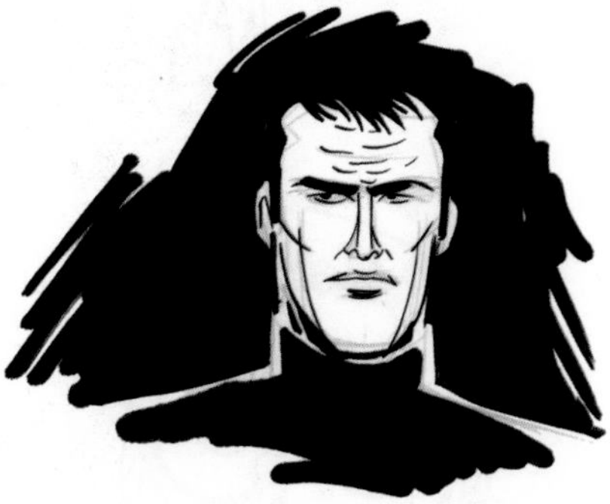

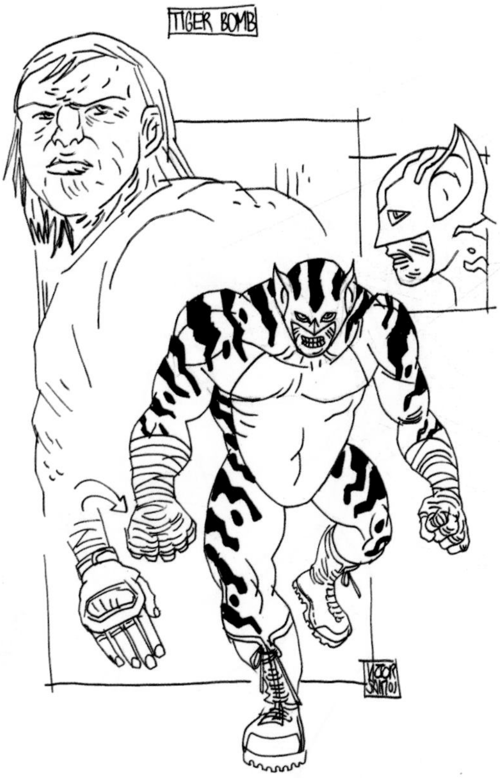
TIGER BOMB

Issue Four Layouts, Pages 1-11

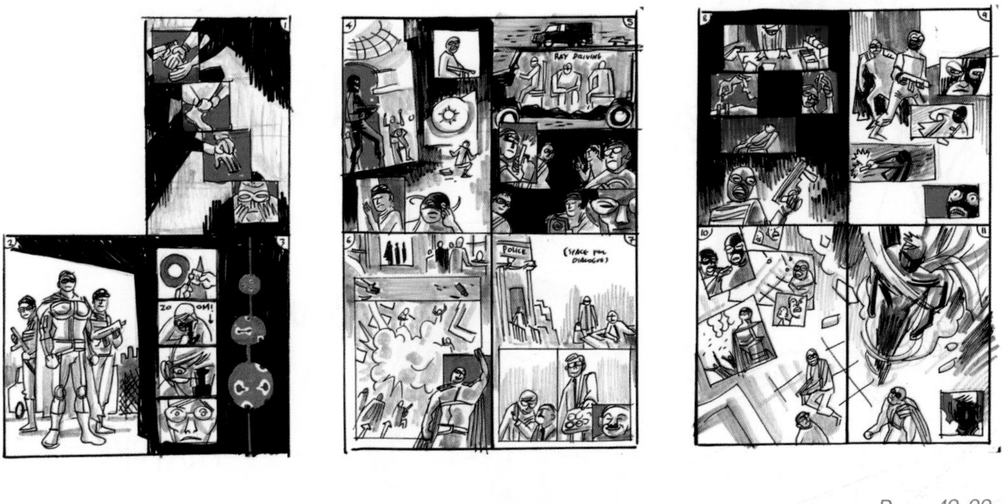
RAY DRIVING
POLICE

Pages 12-22

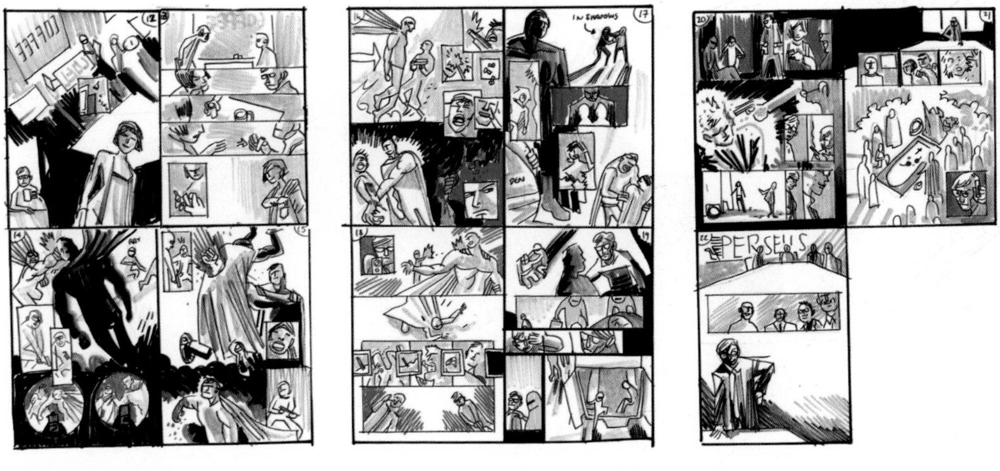
IN SHADOWS
PERSEUS

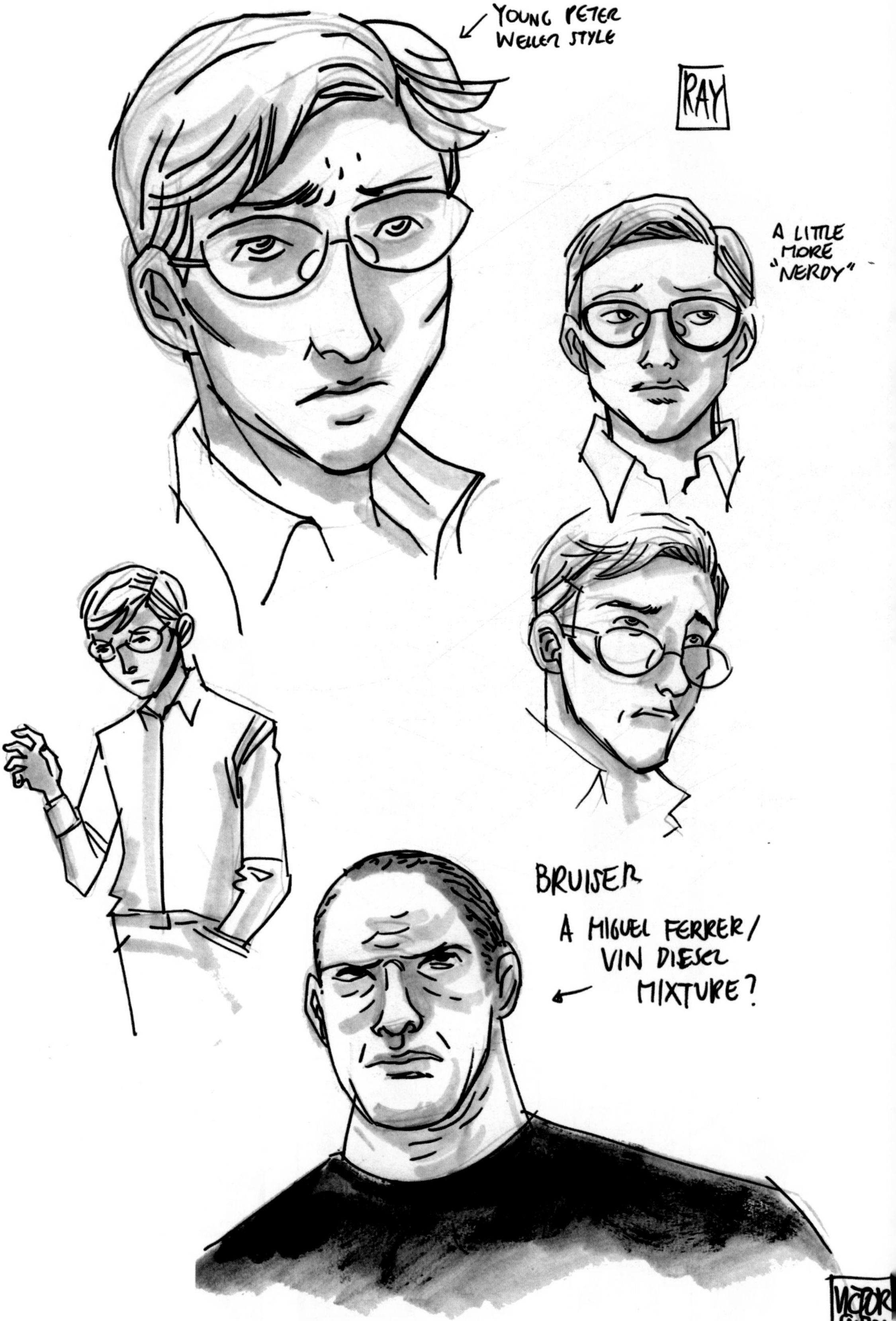
YOUNG PETER WELLER STYLE
RAY
A LITTLE MORE "NERDY"
BRUISER
A MIGUEL FERRER/ VIN DIESEL MIXTURE?
VICTOR SANTOS

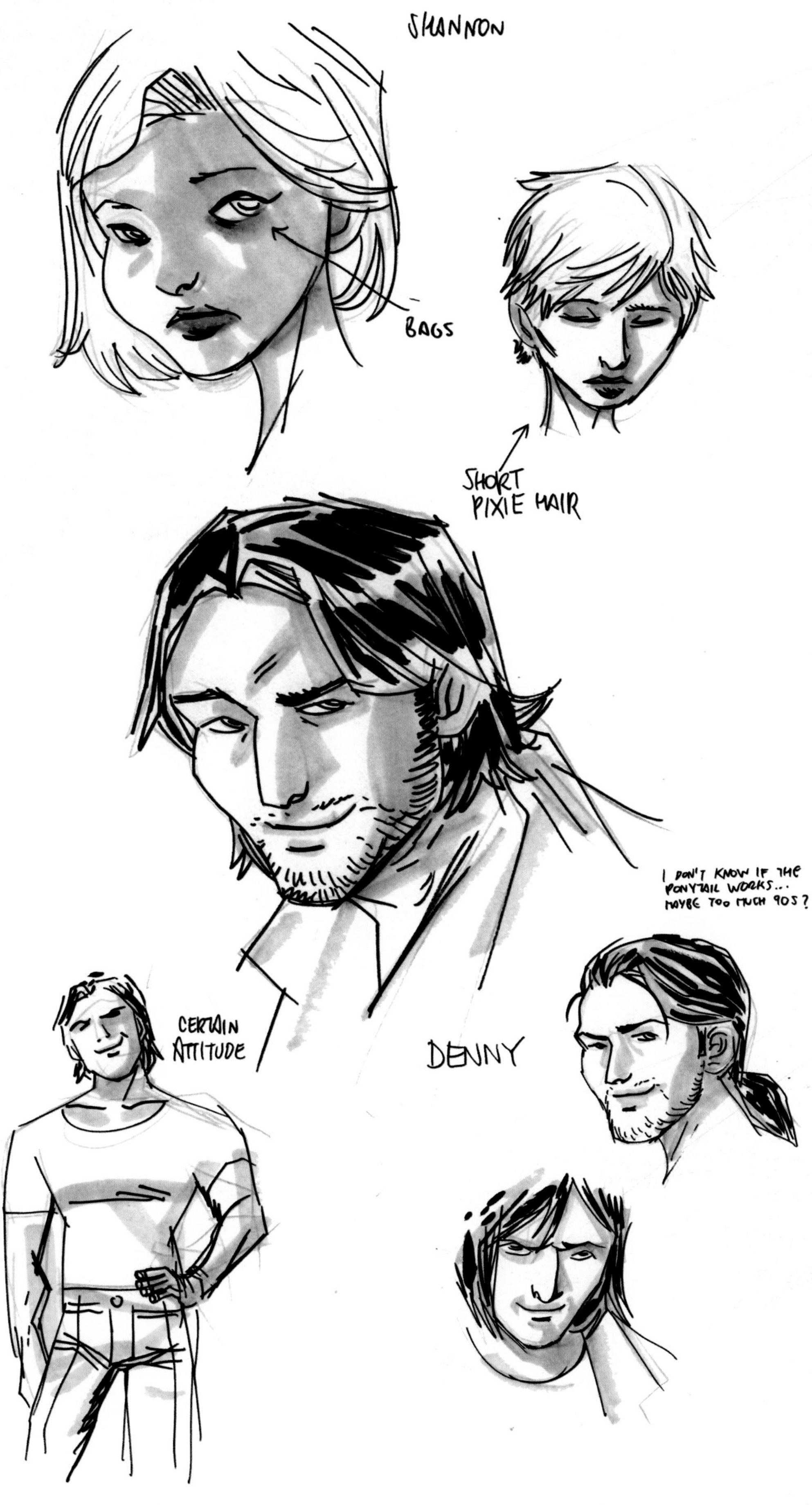
SHANNON
BAGS
SHORT PIXIE HAIR
I DON'T KNOW IF THE PONYTAIL WORKS... MAYBE TOO MUCH 90S?
CERTAIN ATTITUDE
DENNY